The
DOG
LOVER'S
GUIDE TO
TRAVEL

The
DOG
LOVER'S
GUIDE TO
TRAVEL

*Best Destinations, Hotels, Events,
and Advice to Please Your Pet—and You*

Kelly E. Carter

NATIONAL GEOGRAPHIC

WASHINGTON, D.C.

CONTENTS

Southwest & Southern Rockies

West & Hawaii

Canada

Who Let the Dogs Out?

Make no bones about it: You pamper your pet. Bailey sleeps with you or in a comfy bed near yours, accompanies you when you run errands around town, eats organic and natural foods, may wear canine couture, has scheduled play dates with other coddled canines, socializes at doggie day care, and sniffs new pals at your local Yappy Hour. Instead of calling yourself a dog owner, you're a pet parent, or guardian, to your furry friend, which goes on family vacations, girlfriend getaways, mancations, and business trips.

The travel industry, realizing that you consider Fifi a full-fledged family member, has changed with the times. Hotels that don't accept hounds are passé, and many upscale hotels have taken dog friendly to new heights. Plush beds for pampered pooches, elegant food and water dishes for distinguished dogs, massages to relax frazzled Fifi, doggie room-service menus to relieve puppy jet lag, canine concierges, gourmet treats, and turndown service are among the amenities lavished on four-legged guests. Perks for pawsengers include frequent-flier miles for Fido and airports with pet lounges and spruced-up animal relief areas with cute names.

Traveling with a dog isn't the hindrance it once was, either. A proliferation of off-leash areas at parks and beaches for Rover to romp, pet-friendly attractions such as boat cruises, gardens, and museums, and an increasing number of pooch-friendly pawtios at restaurants (some of which even offer a doggie dining menu) mean Fido can have a stimulating holiday, and you don't have to relegate yourself to the fast-food drive-thru. The latest trend of combining bars or beer gardens with dog parks gives new meaning to wine-and-wag events. Open-paw policies at many stores and businesses make it easy to tote your tyke. Even some sports teams have jumped on the puppy wagon. Many Major League Baseball teams host at least one dog-friendly game a season, usually calling them "Bark in the Park" or "Dog Days of Summer," to benefit a local shelter or rescue organization.

According to the latest figures available from the American Pet Products Association, pets—as American as baseball and apple pie—live in 68 percent of U.S. households, or 82.5 million homes. Maybe you didn't buy the "it" designer handbag of the season or a new set of golf clubs, but

Service Animals

The information in this book pertains to pets, not service animals, which the Americans with Disabilities Act (ADA) defines as dogs that are individually trained to do work or perform tasks for people with disabilities. Service animals are working animals, not pets. The work or task a dog has been trained to provide must be directly related to the person's disability. Dogs whose sole function is to provide comfort or emotional support do not qualify as service animals under the ADA.

Service animals are exempt from airline and hotel fees and can accompany their handler most anywhere, including restaurants and buildings where pets are prohibited. Emotional support animals are not subject to airline pet fees on U.S. carriers either, but they are not permitted inside restaurants and buildings where pets aren't allowed. Therapy dogs, meaning those animals trained to provide comfort to people in hospitals, retirement homes, nursing homes, and such are considered pets and do not travel for free.

man's best friend probably didn't suffer during the recession. Spending on pets has continued to climb significantly every year. What was a $17-billion-a-year industry in 1994 has more than tripled. And of the $53.5 billion shelled out on pets in 2012, $78 million went toward travel.

Pets aren't allowed on Amtrak trains, Greyhound buses, or cruise lines (with the exception of Cunard's *Queen Mary 2*), but plenty of regional trains, buses, and boat lines welcome pawsengers.

With a little planning, traveling with a dog has never been easier or more enjoyable. Whether you're a new pet parent eager to take your fur baby on the road, a dog-travel sage who remembers when pups had to be smuggled into swank hotels to avoid roadside motels, or you just want to know what's going on in your local pet community, you'll find the latest pet-ssential travel information on the following pages, to help you create a tail-waggin' petcation worth barking about.

Is Rover Road Ready?

The first thing you need to determine is whether your pet should travel. If your dog barks incessantly, whines, begs, bites, jumps on people, or exhibits other off-putting behavior, an obedience course is a must before taking your pet on the road. It takes just a few encounters with ill-behaved dogs for hotels, restaurants, or stores to change their pet policy and ban bowwows. Being a responsible pet parent goes far beyond picking up poop. Raising a well-behaved pet is just as important.

In addition to temperament, Fifi's health and age also dictate whether she'll earn her wings. If your pooch is very young or very old, in poor physical condition, or pregnant, traveling isn't recommended. Also, if you've tried a few times and your favorite canine companion isn't fond of traveling, don't force it. Not every biped enjoys traveling, and man's best friend is no different. Considering how luxe dog-boarding facilities flaunt well-appointed suites these days, you won't be banished to the doghouse if you leave your posh pup behind. Just remember to bring Fifi a nice gift when you return home.

Choosing a Carrier

Outside of choosing your pal, selecting a travel carrier might be the toughest decision to make. Size and safety should be your first priorities, but you should also take into account the mode of transportation. If your pet is small enough to travel with you on the airplane, you need to be able to place the carrier completely under the seat in front of you. Aircrafts vary in size, and what works for American Airlines may not suffice for United. For instance, American's maximum size for in-cabin carriers is 19 inches long by 13 inches wide by 9 inches high but the rules allow soft-sided carriers, such as Sherpa bags, to be slightly larger because they are collapsible. United's maximum is 18 inches long by 11 inches wide by 11 inches high. Disregard the claims of a manufacturer that its carrier is approved by the International Air Transport Association (IATA), a trade association that comprises 84 percent of the global air traffic. IATA does not certify, approve, endorse, or sell any particular manufacturer, brand, make, or model of pet container. Sherpa features a Guaranteed on Board program that will refund the cost of your flight and your pet's airline travel fee if you are denied boarding because of the carrier when traveling on U.S. domestic flights, Canadian domestic flights, or flights between the United States and Canada.

If you plan to travel by car, place your pooch in the rear seat in a harness or carrier.

To add to the confusion, there is no uniform weight limit either. While some airlines consider the combined weight of the animal and carrier, others simply mandate that your pooch needs to be able to stand up, turn around, and lie down in the carrier, which must be ventilated on at least two sides and leak proof. Although you pay a pet fee, generally ranging from $75 to $125 one way for in-cabin pets, your carrier still counts as either your carry-on or personal item, depending on the airline's policy.

If your furry friend is too large to travel in-cabin, or your airline doesn't allow in-cabin pets (see Hawaii section, pages 12–13), you will need to transport your pal as checked baggage or cargo in a carrier that meets U.S. Department of Agriculture Animal and Plant Health Inspection Service (USDA-APHIS) standards. Many airlines require kennels with steel nuts and bolts instead of plastic fasteners and will supply releasable cable ties that should be attached to all four corners.

If you plan to travel by car, place your pooch in the rear seat in a harness or carrier that can be secured with the car seat belt. Sherpa now features an Auto Safe Strap on each of its carriers, but soft-sided carriers don't provide much protection in the event of a crash. Consider a sturdy but stylish carrier by Sleepypod, whose carriers made of ballistic nylon (think Tumi luggage) have all passed the frontal crash test at 30 miles per hour, the standard for child-safety seats in the States.

Get your furry friend acclimated to its kennel or carrier well in advance of travel. Put the container out in the open, leave the door open, and make it an enjoyable place by placing treats and toys in it. Use it when you go on fun outings such as to the dog park and dog bakeries, so your pooch will associate the kennel with pleasure, not just a trip to the vet for a shot.

Checking Your Pet

If your pet is of a certain size or you're flying on an airline that doesn't allow in-cabin pets to a particular destination, such as Hawaii, you will have to check your pet either as baggage; when the pet is traveling unaccompanied or is too large to qualify as baggage, it may travel as cargo. Although airlines safely transport thousands of animals annually in the climate-controlled hold, there is always the risk of death, injury, and escape. The Humane Society of the United States does not recommend transporting animals in this manner unless absolutely necessary.

Make sure you do your research. The Department of Transportation requires U.S. airlines that carry passengers on scheduled flights to file reports concerning incidents involving the loss, injury, or death of animals during air transportation. DOT publishes

these reports monthly and also forwards the reports to the U.S. Department of Agriculture, which enforces the Animal Welfare Act. The redacted copies of the reports are available at dot.gov/airconsumer/air-travel-consumer-reports.

Find out the airline's procedure for transporting live animals. Request that your pet be loaded last and unloaded first. Some airlines, such as United with its PetSafe program, do this automatically, and make sure the kennel door is facing forward. United also operates three kennel facilities at its hubs at Chicago's O'Hare International Airport, Houston's George Bush Intercontinental Airport, and Newark's Liberty International Airport, allowing pets to be cared for, walked, fed, held in individual enclosures in temperature-controlled areas, and even bathed.

Tips for Flying Buster in the Cargo Hold

• Book nonstop flights and avoid connecting flights to minimize the amount of time your pet spends on the tarmac and in the loading area.
• Make sure you allow ample time to drop off your pal at the cargo facility, which is frequently in another location.
• Pets traveling as checked baggage generally don't require a reservation and are usually accepted on a first-come, first-served basis.
• Don't feed your pooch less than four hours before departure, but do give it water. Also, place a bowl of frozen water in the kennel.
• Make sure the kennel has outside access to the water and food containers.
• On the outside of the kennel, place a note with your pooch's name along with your name, contact information, and flight itinerary.
• Make sure your dog is wearing a collar (and not a choke collar) with ID tags.
• Put a T-shirt you've slept in inside the kennel.
• Let the flight attendants and pilots know you have a pet traveling in the hold and ask them to confirm when your pooch has been loaded. Some airlines will do this automatically.

The Airline Skinny

• Expect to pay between $75 and $125 to bring your pet in the cabin with you and between $175 and $200 to check your pet as baggage. Cargo rates are generally higher and based on total weight.
• Book your pet's passage early. All airlines have restrictions on the number of pets in-cabin, generally between five and seven in coach and business class and two in first class.
• Puppies must be at least eight weeks old to fly.
• Most airlines will not accept brachycephalic or snub-nosed dog breeds, such as Pekingese, Shih Tzu Pugs, and Boxers, or their mixed breeds, as checked baggage.

• Some airlines will not accept pets as checked baggage during the holiday season, when passengers tend to check more luggage.

• Most airlines won't allow pets as checked baggage during extreme hot or cold weather.

• Health certificates generally are not required for in-cabin pets on domestic flights, but some airlines require them for pets checked as baggage and all do for pets transported as cargo. Certificates usually must be issued no more than ten days in advance. Some destination states may require health certificates.

• Choose your seat with your furry friend in mind. Use a website like seatguru.com, which will warn you if there is reduced legroom due to entertainment equipment, for example. Pets are not allowed in the bulkhead or exit rows. Service animals are also banned from exit rows but can travel in the bulkhead row.

• Some airlines, including United, Delta, and US Airways, won't allow in-cabin pets in premium cabins with lie-flat beds due to insufficient space for the carrier. Other airlines, such as American, will place the carrier elsewhere for takeoff and landing.

Traveling to Hawaii and Canada

Don't let Hawaii's notorious 120-day animal quarantine deter you from visiting this rabies-free state. If your pooch meets specific pre- and post-arrival requirements, it may qualify for the five-day-or-less quarantine program, which also has a provision for direct release at the airports in Hawaii after inspection. To take pets to Hawaii, you must begin the process at least four months before traveling. Fees to clear the quarantine are $400 for the first pet and $100 for the second pet arriving on the same flight. To learn more about the quarantine and the direct-release program, visit the state's Department of Agriculture website, hdoa.hawaii.gov/. The process can be complicated, but the Maui Humane Society (mauihumanesociety.org) can help you get your four-legged friend on its island.

Although you may be able to get around the quarantine, getting your pooch to Hawaii is not that easy either. Because of the quarantine, airlines aren't eager to transport pets to the 50th state. Alaska Airlines, which flies to Lihue (Kauai), Kona (Hawaii), Kahului (Maui), and Honolulu (Oahu) airports, is the only U.S. carrier that allows pets to travel in the cabin to Hawaii. On other airlines, even small dogs have to travel in the hold, and that isn't a given either because some carriers restrict it. Due to strong headwinds at various times of year, Alaska Airlines limits the number of pets accepted as checked baggage on flights to or from Hawaii. American won't accept pets at all on its nonstop flights to Maui, the Big Island, or Kauai, and instead requires all pets going to Hawaii to fly to Honolulu, where there is an animal quarantine facility.

Canada is a lot less complicated, as long as you're not trying to take a Pit Bull into the province of Ontario, which bans the breed. All that is required for U.S. citizens to take a dog three months of age or older into Canada is a rabies vaccination certificate signed by a licensed veterinarian. It must describe the pooch, provide proof of vaccination, and include documentation of the vaccine product name, lot number, and lot expiration date. A rabies tag isn't proof enough. You'll need the certificate when you return as well, so make sure it doesn't expire while you're visiting.

To take pets to Hawaii, you must begin the process at least four months before traveling.

For Canadians bringing your pooch to the U.S., you'll need proof of rabies vaccination no less than 30 days before arrival. When you cross any border, be mindful of the amount of dog food you have. Large quantities of opened dog food could be confiscated.

Animal Relief Areas at Airports

Since 2009, DOT has required animal relief areas, where Fido can take a potty break, at all U.S. airports. Originally implemented for service animals, these areas come in handy for traveling pets. Water (let Fifi drink at her own risk), pickup bags, and trash receptacles are generally provided. In recent years, airports have made these areas snazzy with faux fire hydrants, bone-shaped patches of grass, and white picket fences. Phoenix Sky Harbor International Airport calls its relief areas "pet parks" and gives each one a name, such as the Pet Patch, the Paw Pad, and the Bone Yard. White pawprints on pavement at San Francisco International Airport lead to its animal relief areas. But the top dog is Atlanta's Hartsfield-Jackson International Airport, which has a 1,000-square-foot, fenced-in, off-leash dog park (located in the Ground Transportation area of Domestic Terminal South outside of doors W1 and W2), with biodegradable bags along with flowers, grass, rocks, benches, and two original pieces of art.

Although these relief areas are extremely useful, nearly all are outside of security. However, more airports are adding them inside security. Some of the airports with relief areas in the "sterile" zone are Washington Dulles International Airport; Pittsburgh International Airport; San Diego International Airport, also known as Lindbergh Field; Seattle-Tacoma International Airport; Dallas/Fort Worth International Airport; and Minneapolis-Saint Paul International Airport. Many airports list the exact location of all their animal relief areas on their websites. Some airlines, including Alaska and American, list the locations for the airports they serve but only for the one closest to their terminal.

The Skinny on Hotels

There are dog-friendly hotels and dog-tolerant hotels. It's important to know the difference, so you can manage your expectations. Truly dog-friendly hotels charge either no pet fee or a minimal amount and provide services and amenities to pets of various sizes, while dog-tolerant hotels charge outrageous fees (as high as $250 per stay, even if the stay is just one night) for a deep cleaning that costs around $20, provide little to nothing in return, accept only purse-size pooches, and allow dogs only in the least desirable rooms.

Hotels might charge a nightly pet fee, a cleaning deposit (sometimes nonrefundable), a combo of the two, or nothing at all. Most hotels limit the number and size of dogs allowed per room. And more are designating which rooms Fido can stay in. These dog-friendly rooms are often on the ground floor, to make it easier to take Fifi outside and to appease guests who may not want to share an elevator with a Great Dane. To snag that high-floor, ocean-view room that is off limits to pets, you might be inclined to not declare your little pal if it's quiet and wouldn't dream of marking its territory, but don't do it. Always let a hotel know when you're traveling with a dog, so you don't risk being thrown out if your friend is discovered. In the state of North Carolina, it is illegal to bring a pet into a hotel room where not permitted.

Although these relief areas are extremely useful, nearly all are outside security checkpoints.

Just because a hotel's website doesn't state it is pet friendly, it doesn't mean it isn't. Four Seasons, Mandarin Oriental, and Peninsula are among the luxury brands that will shower your pet with amenities and attention, yet they do not advertise it online. Therefore, call ahead and inquire. Also, don't be surprised if a pet policy on a hotel website differs from information provided by a live person. Some hotel personnel say they would rather have a big dog that is quiet than a noisy small one and that their weight limit is not necessarily enforced. This can be confusing when you're trying to book a hotel with a medium or large dog. If a website states a weight limit of 25 pounds and a reservationist says you can bring your 50-pound Labradoodle, request the reservationist's promise in writing and bring the email with you when you check in.

When you check in, be prepared to sign a waiver, which you can often review online before booking or have emailed to you, agreeing to certain terms, such as not leaving your dog unattended in the room; arranging for housekeeping; not taking your pooch by the pool, in the spa, or where food is served; and being responsible for lost revenue should your dog be so out of control that other guests flee. Some hotels don't mind your leaving your dog alone if the front desk has your mobile number or if your pet is crated. And some hotels love pets so much they will gladly keep your pet at the front desk while you go out for dinner.

Make sure you read the policies in advance, so you have ample time to research and arrange for a pet-sitter or doggie day care. Hotels often can make recommendations, and websites like DogVacay.com and Rover.com make it easy for you to find a sitter in another locale. Day care and boarding facilities often require a temperament test and proof of immunizations.

Tips to Make Rover Road Ready

• Before embarking on a coast-to-coast trip with your pooch, book a short flight to see how your pal does on a plane.

• Make a local trial run and stay overnight at a nearby hotel, rather than having your pup's first travel experience be a two-week trip that will be miserable for both of you if Fifi isn't having fun. New environments make some dogs nervous, resulting in pooping in hotel rooms.

• Before taking your pooch into an upscale department store, take him to a pet store. When he's able to walk around the store without relieving himself, he's ready for prime time.

• Avoid tranquilizers and sedatives. Some airlines will not accept sedated dogs because the medicine throws off a pet's equilibrium, which can be dangerous when the kennel is moved. Plus, the altitude can cause respiratory and cardiovascular problems.

• Use an anti-anxiety product like Thundershirt, which offers a money-back guarantee, or a calming product with ingredients such as valerian, chamomile, or natural pheromones.

Checklist

- Dog license
- Collar with your current mobile number
- Two leashes
- Food
- Treats
- Collapsible bowls
- Water bottle with a lickable spout
- Passport showing current vaccinations
- Medicine, including extra should you extend your travels
- Sweater (for airplane)
- First-aid kit
- Blanket or sheets if you plan to have Fido on the bed or couch at a hotel
- Recent photographs with full description of your dog(s)
- Name and number of local veterinarian; ask your regular vet for a recommendation

Also consider:
- Personal flotation device if you plan to go on the water
- Paw wear for hiking and extreme heat or cold
- Doggles or other protective eyewear

What to Expect at the Airport and on the Airplane

• Most airports require pets to remain in carriers at all times, except when going through security.

• Do not put Fifi through the x-ray machine, only her carrier.

• TSA will likely have you carry your dog through the metal detector, although at some airports, you'll hand your dog to a TSA employee after the carrier has gone through the x-ray machine and then go through yourself.

• At the security checkpoint, a TSA agent will swipe the palms of your hands looking for traces of explosive chemicals, which some people have been known to put inside pets.

• Canned dog food is considered a liquid and therefore subjected to the 3-1-1 carry-on rule, limiting the volume to 3.4 ounces, even if the can is unopened and you claim it is baby food.

• On the airplane, be prepared to keep your pup's carrier closed during the entire flight, although some flight attendants will allow you to open the carrier enough to feed your dog and give it water. Never remove your pet from its carrier.

• If your dog does not have a strong bladder and you are flying a long distance, let your little pal lick ice cubes to stay hydrated instead of giving it a bowl of water.

• Even though oftentimes other passengers will have no idea they are seated next to a dog, out of respect for passengers with allergies, do let them know so they can inquire about changing seats.

Keeping Sadie Safe in the Car

• Do not let your dog sit in your lap while you drive. Use a harness and put your pooch in the backseat. In some states, such as New Jersey, it is illegal to operate a vehicle with an unrestrained dog.

• Use the car's seat belt to secure a carrier.

• Never leave your dog unattended in a car, not even for a few minutes, especially

on a hot day when interiors heat up quickly.

• Dogs love to feel the wind blowing in their faces, but don't let your dog stick its head out of the window. Debris can fly in its eyes, and the flapping of its ears can cause damage.

• Use Doggles or a similar product to protect your pooch's eyes when the windows are down.

• Stop every couple of hours so your dog can stretch too. Always leash your pooch before opening the car door.

9 Tips for Hiking With Your Hound

• Bring fresh water, a collapsible bowl or water bottle, first-aid kit, sunscreen, and paw wear, if terrain is rocky.

• If you use a doggie backpack, make sure it is less than a third of your dog's weight. Don't start at the maximum weight.

• Know your dog's physical limitations and don't force it to exceed them.

• Watch for signs of overexertion, such as excessive panting, drooling, weakness, or bright red gums. Also look out for hypothermia, frostnip, injury to paw pads, lameness, and exhaustion.

• Take occasional breaks.

• Use a leash to help dogs avoid dangers such as poison ivy and wildlife.

• Be mindful of the weather, and don't hike in the hottest part of the day.

• Apply flea and tick prevention at least two days in advance.

• Have the address and phone number of the nearest emergency vet handy.

Restaurant Patio Petiquette

• Call ahead to a restaurant to find out what the local ordinance is regarding dogs. Some cities consider the outdoor patio as being enclosed if there is a railing, and therefore require dogs to be on the outside of the fence.

• Do walk and feed your dog beforehand.

Tips for the Beach

• Bring fresh water, an umbrella, towel, and sunblock, which you should apply to your pup's ears and nose.

• Keep an eye out for dangerous items, such as fish hooks, glass, sharp rocks, and jellyfish.

• Canines can find cool seawater irresistible. However, minimize their intake to avoid dehydration, diarrhea, and vomiting.

• Limit the time they spend on the hot sand to protect their feet.

• Dog paddling is not always instinctive. Introduce your pooch slowly and use a leash if necessary.

• If your pup is new to swimming, reduce his time in the water to preserve his muscles.

• Out-of-shape hounds can easily tire or get injured running in the sand, so try to avoid this activity until he's in ultimutt shape.

• If a lifeguard is available, inquire about the water conditions and be wary of strong tides.

• Rinse saltwater from your dog's coat as quickly as possible to protect his coat.

- Don't tether your tyke to the table.
- Don't let your dog drink or eat from the glasses and plates used for humans.
- Do bring your own water, bowl, and treats.
- Don't put your dog on the chair or in your lap.
- Keep your dog out of the aisle.
- Use a short leash, not a retractable one.
- Bring a mat or blanket.
- Be aware of the temperature.

When it came to selecting the 75 destinations showcased in this book, both popularity and pawpularity played a role. Some places, such as Del Mar, California, have characterized themselves as dog friendly for decades. Others, such as Branson and Las Vegas, both of which draw oodles of visitors annually, still have some work to do but are headed in the right direction. U.S. National Parks, notorious for being unwelcoming to dogs (the Grand Canyon is the exception), especially in comparison to Canada, where canines are allowed almost everywhere, are included because it's important let you know that it is not out of the realm of possibility to visit with your pup, but that there are restrictions.

Regardless of where you go, understand that no matter how cute and cuddly your dog is, not everyone likes dogs. But you can win over most people with a well-behaved dog. Practice leaving no trace behind wherever you go, to help ensure that other dogs will continue to be welcomed just like yours.

Northeast

Bethel, Maine

First-time visitors to this quaint New England town in western Maine usually come for the Alpine and Nordic skiing, snowshoeing, and snowmobiling options. Then they return after hearing about the summer offerings of beautiful rivers with waterfalls, swimming holes, terrific hiking, fishing, and golf. (It was, after all, a happening summer resort between the Civil War and World War I.) In the fall, they're back again for the fantastic foliage. As is the trend with mountain villages, Bethel is gaining a reputation as a four-season playland. Although some businesses take a break in April and November, there is always plenty to do when visiting this charming, canine-crazy community with your four-legged friend. In addition to the pet-friendly hotels, many agencies offer pet-friendly homes for vacation rental. Doggie pickup bag dispensers are mounted on telephone poles throughout the village, making it easier for you to do the right thing.

🐾 PLAY

Bethel is a hiker's heaven, with the **White Mountain National Forest, Grafton Notch State Park,** and many other public and conservation lands with trail systems in and around the town. Popular trails at Grafton Notch State Park, which allows leashed dogs, include the **Table Rock Trail** (take the blue-blazed trail instead of the orange-blazed trail, considered inappropriate for pets) and the **Appalachian Trail** to the summit of **Old Speck.**

In town, when the dog days of summer hit, cool off with your favorite canine companion in the **Letter S,** a local swimming spot that is part of the Sunday River, located several miles past the **Sunday River covered bridge** and down a dirt road. There's a small, rocky beach, perfect for a picnic with your pal.

Take your pup canoeing on the **Androscoggin River** or the local small ponds. Dogs are welcome at public areas surrounding the area lakes. In parks, Fifi can be on a leash or under voice command. Pet parents are working doggedly to find a central location to open the town's first dog park.

Enjoy the fall foliage, considered among the best in New England, with your furry friend during a scenic drive, stopping at the **Artist's Covered Bridge** in Newry and **Mother Walker Falls Gorge.** Or simply take paws to the **Bethel Common** in town.

Pet parents are working doggedly to find a central location to open the town's first dog park.

At the ski town of **Sunday River,** one of the largest and best ski resorts on the East Coast, and the family-friendly **Mount Abram ski area,** Bethel blazes in the winter. It's not uncommon to see four-legged friends on a cross-country and snowshoeing trail.

🐕 SIT

At Home Pet Grooming will make you and your pooch feel right at home. Professional certified groomer Janice Bjorkland, who is certified in pet CPR and first aid as well as Reiki, with a B.S. in animal science, has created a homey environment. Pups receive a private appointment slot; the only time you'll find multiple pets in the salon is if they come from the same family. There's even a sofa next to the bathing tub for you to watch your fur baby get a blueberry facial. **Barker Brook Kennels** also does grooming as well as boarding and doggie day care. At **Tucker's Dog House,** which offers boarding and day care, there are walks through woods and swimming field trips. **Bethel Animal Hospital** also has

Insider Tip

"Be sure your canine's immunizations are up to date. There's an abundance of wildlife in Bethel—moose, deer, foxes, rabbits, bears, bobcats, and porcupines! And because it's a rural town, the wildlife frequent backyards and resort grounds. Great for viewing, but they often aren't your dog's best friends."
— WENDE GRAY

boarding. If Bethel's beautiful scenery inspires you to book a pawparazzi session for your little pal, Craig Angevine of **Yeah Bud! Photography** specializes in pet photography.

HAUTE DOG

Although there are no pet stores in the immediate area, pet toys, treats, and food can be purchased at **Bethel Animal Hospital.**

CHOW TIME

Fifi can accompany you when dining al fresco at the **Millbrook Tavern & Grille,** overlooking the golf course at the dog-friendly **Bethel Inn Resort. DiCocoa's,** a café and bakery on Main Street that prides itself on making everything fresh from scratch in small batches, welcomes pooches on its patio in summertime. Pets can also join their people at the picnic tables outside the **Good Food Store and Catering Company,** at **The Foothills Grille & Catering Company,** and under the tall pines at **Smokin' Good BBQ.**

COME

Pets are welcome to shop with their humans at **The Philbrook Place,** a large Victorian house and barn on Main Street converted to several shops, including **Nabos Gift Shop,** where Martina, a black Labrador, often greets shoppers, **Elements Art Gallery,** and **Community Sports.**

UNIQUE ACTIVITY

Buy a Dog Trail Pass for your favorite canine companion at **Carter's X-C Ski Center** and take him cross-country skiing or snowshoeing on the trails the locals affectionately call the "poop loops." But please pick up. cartersxcski.com

Emergency Veterinarian
Bethel Animal Hospital—bethelanimalhospital .com; 207-824-2212 ■ Animal Emergency Clinic (Lewiston)—aec-midmaine.com; 207-777-1100

Stay
All Pups Welcome

■ *Sudbury Inn:* Pets welcome in the Carriage House. No number/size restrictions. Fee. thesudburyinn.com

■ *Bethel Inn Resort:* No number/size restrictions. Fee. bethelinn.com

■ *Chapman Inn:* No number/size restrictions. Fee. chapmaninn.com

■ *Bear Mountain Inn (South Waterford):* Two dogs max./no size restriction. Fee. bearmtninn.com

Boston, Massachusetts

I t's not just because Boston is known as America's Walking City that it's an ideal destination for dogs. But it helps. Here, your pampered pooch will have an abundance of dog parks and open spaces to romp during a petcation in Beantown. In addition, Fido has a wide choice of luxe dog-friendly hotels and can soak up the historical flavor by tagging along with you on pet-friendly tours, including one at Harvard University, the nation's oldest institution of higher learning. Even Boston's Logan International Airport shows how much it treasures pets with a "Passengers with Paws" Pet Safety First Aid Program. Here's hoping you never need it, but it's good to know it's there if you do.

PLAY

Perhaps no American city oozes history like Boston, site of the nation's first public park, the nearly 50-acre **Boston Common,** which dates back to 1634. The park's open parade grounds are *the* place for Beacon Hill's pet parents to gather at sunrise and sunset with their leashed pets. Now Boston Common has five designated unfenced locations (three near the Beacon Street side of the park and two in the vicinity of the Parkman Bandstand by Tremont Street) that rotate as off-leash dog parks, with two open at a time and switching every six months; open from 5 a.m. to 10 a.m. and 4 p.m. to 9 p.m.

At **Peter's Park** in Boston's vibrant South End, dogs can romp off leash at the 13,000-square-foot (including a separately enclosed 3,000 square feet for small dogs) **Joe Wex Dog Recreation Space,** Boston's first city-sanctioned off-leash dog park. Open 6 a.m. to 10 p.m. The **Ronan Park Dog Recreation Space,** on historic Meetinghouse Hill in the Dorchester neighborhood, is also off leash and open 7 a.m. to 10 p.m.

Leashed dogs are allowed on the **Minuteman Bikeway,** a 10.4-mile, multi-use path that passes through the historic area where the American Revolution began in April 1775 and a Rail-Trail Hall of Fame member. In Cambridge, take Rover for a 2.5-mile loop around the **Fresh Pond Reservoir,** but don't let him take a dip. South of Boston in Milton, you'll find the **Blue Hills Reservation,** a 7,000-acre dog-friendly (leash required) oasis that offers picturesque views of the entire metropolitan area from the summit.

Just north of Boston in Ipswich, **Crane Beach** allows leashed dogs to be walked on the beach October 1 to March 30 from 8 a.m. until sunset. Most important, there's a portion of the beach to the left of the westernmost boardwalk that has been designated as a leash-free zone for those with a Green Dog pass, which visitors can purchase at the beach gate that day.

🐕 SIT

Planning to catch a Red Sox game at Fenway Park? Drop your pooch off at **Fenway Bark** (no relation) in South Boston for doggie day care or boarding. **Bark Place,** in the South End, also provides doggie day care along with grooming (both professional and DIY) and a boutique.

🍖 HAUTE DOG

In the Back Bay, **Fish & Bone** sells apparel, toys, treats, modern pet essentials, and gifts for pets and the people who love them. Also in the Back Bay, **Pawsh Dog Boutique & Salon** sells apparel from T-shirts to winter coats, leashes, collars, beds, food, and toys.

🦴 CHOW TIME

When it's time to dine, head to South End, where most restaurants allow pups to join their people outdoors. **Coppa, Tremont 647, Blunch, Flour Bakery + Café,** and **Hamersley's Bistro** are a few of the popular spots. **South End Buttery** has portraits of dogs in the downstairs dining room, offers fresh dog biscuits from **Polka Dog Bakery** down the street, and donates cupcakes to local animal rescue causes. The Polka Dog Bakery, a must-stop for any mutt, sells locally sourced, made-in-the-USA, natural dog treats, and premium foods.

Pooches are a staple on the patio at the **Globe Bar & Café,** in the heart of Copley Square in Boston's historic Back Bay and perfect for pooch and people watching. Also in the Back Bay, count on your pal receiving a bowl of water at **Stephanie's On Newbury.** Overlook the marina with your salty dog at **Joe's American Bar and Grill** in the North End.

Know that if a restaurant's patio is fenced, it is considered indoors, so you'll have to keep your pal on the other side.

❀ COME

A trip to Beantown is incomplete without taking Max on the **Freedom Trail,** a 2.5-mile red-brick path past sixteen of the city's historical landmarks, including the Boston Massacre site and Paul Revere House. You can do the walk on your own or book through the Freedom Trail Foundation to enjoy a guide dressed in 18th-century attire. If Fifi is on a leash, she can join you on the 90-minute **Black Heritage Trail** outdoor tour at the Boston African

Stay All Pups Welcome

■ *Nine Zero Hotel, A Kimpton Hotel (Downtown):* Bed and bowls. Can arrange dog walking, dogsitting, grooming, or massage for supplementary cost. No number/size restrictions. ninezero.com

■ *The Onyx Hotel, A Kimpton Hotel (Downtown):* Provides bed, gourmet dog cookies, cleanup bags. Dog walking and dogsitting available for supplementary cost. No number/size restrictions. onyxhotel.com

■ *Fairmont Copley Plaza Hotel (Back Bay):* Dog biscuits at front desk. Food available upon request. Catie Copley, a black Lab, serves as hotel's canine

ambassador. Catie is available for scheduled walks and runs with guests. No number/size restrictions. Fee. fairmont.com/copleyplaza

■ *W Hotel Boston (Theater District):* P.A.W. (Pets Are Welcome) program provides custom pet bed, food and water bowl with floor mat, toy, turndown treat, cleanup bags, dog-walking service, pet-in-room door sign. Two pets/40 lb each max. Fee. whotels.com/boston

■ *Four Seasons Hotel Boston (Back Bay):* Bed and bowls upon request. Concierge can arrange dogsitting. One dog/15 lb max. fourseasons.com/boston/

■ *Ritz-Carlton Boston Commons (Beacon Hill):* Bed, blanket, clothing, bowls, treats, and woof door hangers provided. Can recommend dog walkers and groomers. Two dogs/60 lb each max. Fee. ritzcarlton.com/boston

■ *Liberty Hotel (Beacon Hill):* Custom pet bed and bowls placed in room for use during stay. Fee. No number/size restrictions. Fee. libertyhotel.com

■ *The Revere Hotel, Boston Common (Back Bay/South End):* Bed, bowls, treat. Two dogs/75 lb each max. reverehotel.com

American National Historic Site. Leashed pups are also welcome on **Boston Strolls'** off-the-beaten-path walking tours that cover the North End, Back Bay, and Beacon Hill, and on Cambridge Historical Tours' **Tour of Harvard,** led by costumed and comical guides.

If you're in need of retail therapy, check out the shops along quaint Charles Street, where many stores have water bowls and treats for your posh pet. Take a leisurely stroll south through the Theater District to the über-pet-friendly South End so your pooch can pose for a photo next to **Dancing with Spheres,** a 12-foot-tall bronze sculpture of animals at play inside the Animal Rescue League of Boston's dog play yard. It's located on Chandler Street between Arlington and Berkeley Streets and open to the public.

In Boston, it's not enough to have Yappy Hour. There's **Yappier Hour,** held Wednesdays during the spring and summer at the pet-friendly **Liberty Hotel** in Beacon Hill. On Thursdays from June through August, the **Hyatt Regency Cambridge** hosts "Dog Days of Summer" pup socials. **Fish & Bone** regularly throws quirky animal-friendly events at its Back Bay pet supply store. The Massachusetts Society for the Prevention of Cruelty to Animals puts on several annual events, including a **spring gala** and the **Walk for Animals,** still going strong after more than thirty years with approximately 2,500 humans and 1,500 canines participating in three locations (Boston, Hyannis, and Methuen) every September.

UNIQUE ACTIVITY

Enjoy three hours of fun with your well-adjusted and social salty dog on a **City Water Taxi,** which takes you and your favorite canine companion on a 25-minute boat ride, from **Long Wharf/Columbus Park** or **Scups Restaurant** in the Boston Harbor Shipyard & Marina in East Boston to **Boston Harbor Islands.** There your little pal can frolic freely and explore an uninhabited island. Cross-country skiing and snow-shoeing are also options. citywater taxi.com/IslandActivities.html

Emergency Veterinarian
Angell Animal Medical Center—mspca .org/vet-services; 617-522-7282

Insider Tip

"Boston is a great city to explore on two legs or four! Some of Catie's favorite routes in America's Walking City include a shady stroll past the Victorian architecture and brownstones on the Commonwealth Avenue Mall or a stroll through the Public Garden with a photo stop near the *Make Way for Ducklings* statue. There is a dog run on Boston Common where Catie will spend time with some of her neighborhood canine friends. (Dogs are permitted off leash in certain areas of the park.) Other favorite Boston dog parks include Peter's Park or Southwest Corridor Park—both walking distance from the hotel."

— JOE FALLON, *caretaker for Catie, canine ambassador at the Fairmont Copley Plaza*

Cape Cod, Martha's Vineyard, and Nantucket, Massachusetts

Whether you're hopping around with your favorite canine companion or staying put in one of Cape Cod's charming towns or picturesque islands, pet-friendly transportation options, hotels and restaurants that welcome four-legged guests, and even some beaches make it easy for you to enjoy these heavenly settings in southern Massachusetts. Sightings of furry friends in kayaks and bicycle baskets are nearly as frequent as glimpses of Black Dog T-shirts.

As beautiful as this area is in late spring, autumn, and early winter, the services aren't nearly as plentiful as they are in the summer, when the sun-splashed beaches and enviable dunes beckon visitors. **CapeFLYER,** a train from Boston to Cape Cod that operates on weekends from Memorial Day to Labor Day, allows dogs. But note that during off-peak hours, non-service dogs are allowed at the discretion of the operators, and during rush hours small pets must be carried in lap-size containers. Salty dogs can board any of the ferries, including those of the **Bay State Cruise Company,** which zoom from Boston to Provincetown in 90 minutes, **Hy-Line Cruises** (Hyannis to Martha's Vineyard and Nantucket and between the islands in summer), the **Steamship Authority**

(Woods Hole to Martha's Vineyard and Hyannis to Nantucket), and **Island Queen** (Falmouth Harbor to Martha's Vineyard). Regional airlines Cape Air and Island Airlines (Nantucket–Hyannis route) allow pawsengers, but book early because space is limited.

🎾 PLAY

When it comes to the beaches, it's apropos that leash laws are most lenient in Province-town, at the very tip of Massachusetts in Barn-stable County. Here, on the only off-leash beaches on the Cape, Fifi is free to frolic on town-owned beaches from Memorial Day to November 1 between 6 a.m. and 9 a.m. and 6 p.m. and 9 p.m. From November 2 to the day before Memorial Day, off-leash hours are 6 a.m. to 9 p.m. Pooches on leashes can prance at Ptown's **Race Point Beach** any time of year, as long as they avoid the lifeguard-protected areas.

For other parts of the Cape: Although no dogs are allowed on Eastham's town beaches from June 15 through Labor Day, they can hang out at **Dyer Prince Road/ Rock Harbor Beach Area** before 9 a.m. and after 5 p.m. Rover can also romp (don't for-get the leash) on **Cape Cod National Seashore's** ocean beaches year-round, except in lifeguard-protected swimming areas (passing through is fine) and posted shorebird nesting areas (passing through prohibited).

In Orleans, there's a point on **Nauset Beach,** from the parking lot south to trail 1, where dogs are banned from May 15 through Labor Day. But from south of trail 1 to the Chatham Inlet, all is well as long as your sidekick is on a leash of not longer than 30 feet and above the high-tide mark, from May 15 through Labor Day. In Wellfleet, from the third Saturday in June through Labor Day, dogs are allowed on a 6-foot lead, before 9 a.m. and after 5 p.m., on **Duck Harbor, Newcomb Hollow, Cahoon Hollow, White Crest,** and **Maguire Landing** beaches.

A resident of Martha's Vineyard calls **Lambert's Cove Beach** "doglarious—a Vine-yard Westminster." It is, however, one of the town beaches where in summer you'll need a local parking and/or beach permit (obtained at the Parks and Recreation shed at the West Tisbury School). Otherwise, stick to one of the public beaches, such as **Joseph Sylvia State Beach** (between Edgartown and Oak Bluffs), **Norton Point Beach** (end of Katama Road, Edgartown), and **Eastville Point Beach** (at the Lagoon Pond drawbridge in Vineyard Haven), all of which allow leashed tykes before 9 a.m. and after 5 p.m. daily, unless restricted because of nesting birds. On **South Beach** (Katama/Edgartown), pooches are allowed only after 5 p.m. daily.

Stroll along the magnificent beaches of **Nantucket** with your furry friend on leash before 9 a.m. or after 5 p.m. during the summer or anytime off-season. Regardless of the month, beaches that don't have lifeguards, such as **Brant Point** and **Frances Street,** just a five-minute walk from Main Street, welcome dogs on leashes anytime. Beware of the strong current at Brant Point, but it's a great place to take paws and watch the boats round the point at the lighthouse.

When it comes to dog parks, leave it to Ptown to have the ultimutt digs. **Pilgrim Bark Park,** at Shank Painter Road and Route 6, flaunts works by local artists who designed the benches (including a small-scale reproduction of the Pilgrims' *Mayflower* ship), poop-bag stations, and a humongous doghouse at the entrance to the 1-acre, off-leash park. A pet memorial and the painted fire hydrants resemble canine versions of Ptown's police officers, firefighters, and public workers.

On the Upper Cape, **Falmouth Dog Park,** open dawn to dusk, is also quite impressive, with artwork by local artists.

The Vineyard has a 70-acre "dog park" that is technically the functioning **Land Bank Tradewinds Airport** in Oak Bluffs, as well as a real dog park in **Vineyard Haven.**

Dog-friendly hiking trails are in abundance throughout the Cape and neighboring islands. **Cape Cod National Seashore** and **Long Point** in Ptown, **Sanford Farm** on Nantucket, and **Caroline Tuthill Preserve** on Martha's Vineyard are among the popular paths. The 22-mile **Cape Cod Rail Trail,** from Dennis to Wellfleet, is terrific for biking or just a leisurely walk. Nantucket's ten bike paths make cycling the preferred mode of transportation on the island.

Regardless of the month, beaches that don't have lifeguards ... welcome dogs on leashes anytime.

Deer ticks are common on the Cape and islands, so don't forget to apply tick prevention to your precious pal.

🐕 SIT

After all that playtime, clean up Max at **Hot Diggity Dog Wash and Boutique** in Dennisport, where you can do it yourself (even his blueberry facial) or hire the pros. **Klassy Kanine** in West Dennis provides professional dog grooming and doggie-care service, while **Howl-a-Day Inn** offers doggie day care and boarding. **Talk to the Paws,** in Mashpee, does grooming, day care, and boarding.

🦴 HAUTE DOG

In Oak Bluffs on Martha's Vineyard, **Good Dog Goods** sells everything from apparel to toys to grooming products and pet-themed home decor, advertising that all but three of its products are made in the USA. Hot Diggity in Mashpee and Dennisport draw posh pups, while **Uptown Dog Cape Cod Bakery and Boutique** in West Falmouth and **Cape Cod Dog** in Eastham outfit stylish hounds and provide the essentials, which include fresh-baked goods for Fido.

🐾 CHOW TIME

Many of the restaurants with outdoor seating in this region will gladly let your well-behaved pooch sit with you on the patio while you dine. In Provincetown, **Central House** at the Crown and Anchor and **Governor Bradford Restaurant** are among your 20-plus choices. While you're waiting to catch your ferry from Woods Hole to Martha's Vineyard, grab a lobster taco while your furry friend enjoys a bowl of water at the Woods Hole Inn's **Quicks Hole** restaurant.

On Martha's Vineyard in Oak Bluffs, **Nancy's Snack Bar** on the harbor, **Carousel Ice Cream,** and **Offshore Ale Co.** welcome pets. In Vineyard Haven, there's **Scottish Bakehouse** and the **Black Dog Bakery and Café.** On Nantucket, have a picnic with your pooch on the grassy area surrounding popular **Something Natural. LOLA 41** and **Dune** are other tasty options.

🏠 Stay All Pups Welcome

■ *Brass Key Guest House (Provincetown):* Dogs are welcome in cottages 111 and 112. Bowl and biscuits provided. One dog/no size restriction. Fee. brasskey.com

■ *Sage Inn & Lounge (Provincetown):* Bowls and boarding crates. One dog/35 lb max. Fee. sageinnptown.com

■ *Mansion House (Vineyard Haven):* Pet bed, dog-walking regulations for town, cleanup bags. No number/size restrictions. Fee. mvmansionhouse.com

■ *Harbor View Hotel (Edgartown):* VIP (Very Important Pup) amenity package with rope toy, natural treats, and cleanup bag; dog tag with hotel contact information can be purchased. No number/size restrictions. Fee. harborview.com

■ *The Cottages & Lofts at the Boat Basin (Nantucket):* Welcome basket of treats and toys, blissful bed, food and water bowls, personalized pet tags, dog-walking services, directory of vet clinics and pet stores, and nightly doggie

turndown. Dog-friendly beach bus takes you anywhere on the island. No number/size restrictions. Fee. thecottagesnantucket.com

■ *The Brass Lantern Inn (Nantucket):* Toy, treat, cozy "right-size" dog bed, food and water bowls, beach towel, list of pet-friendly restaurants, places to go with your dog, and names and numbers for pet supply stores and services. Pet-walking and pet-sitting services available in advance. Two pets/no size restriction. Fee. brasslanternnantucket.com

🐾 COME

Many businesses on the Cape don't mind if you bring your pooch. Banks dole out treats, and boutiques leave water bowls at their entrances. Some of the art galleries in Ptown welcome cultured canines. Dogs are welcome on the trolleys in Ptown and Edgartown, where Bowzer can help you browse for a book at **Edgartown Books,** and the buses on the Vineyard are pet-friendly. A slew of events will keep Daisy's dance card full. The Animal Rescue League of Boston's outpost in Brewster regularly holds special events and activities for people and their pets, including **Paws for Celebration,** a large dog walk and pet festival each June; a **Paws on Ice** skating event in the winter; a **Howl-o-ween Party** each October; and silent auctions and Yappy Hours throughout the summer. An annual **Walk for Dogs** on Memorial Day weekend benefits the Animal Shelter of Martha's Vineyard. There's a **Puppy Parade** on Main Street on Martha's Vineyard and a **Canine Boot Camp Weekend** at the pet-friendly Brass Lantern Inn on Nantucket. A pet parade down Ptown's Commercial Street, a dance, and a blessing of the animals are part of the annual **Pet Appreciation Week,** hosted every fall by the Carrie A. Seamen Animal Shelter.

> ### *Insider Tip*
>
> "Since Salty, my 78-pound Golden Doodle, loves to swim and roll in the sand, a must for my dog is that small square tin of Bag Balm. I learned that Bag Balm has been sold since 1899 and was originally intended to keep cows' 'private' areas from getting chapped in harsh winters. Saltwater and sunlight can irritate, but a bit of balm really helps. I have also used Skin So Soft."
> — SUSAN GOLDSTEIN

🐾 UNIQUE ACTIVITY

Have a whale of a time with your favorite canine companion on a **whale-watching cruise** by Dolphin Fleet of Provincetown, which bills itself the first whale-watching excursion in New England. whalewatch.com

Emergency Veterinarian

Cape Cod Veterinary Specialists—capecodvetspecialists.com; 508-759-5125 ▪ My Pet's Vet (Martha's Vineyard)—mypetsvetmv.vetsuite.com; 508-693-4040 ▪ Offshore Animal Hospital of Nantucket—offshoreanimalhospital.com; 508-228-1491

Cape May, New Jersey

Calling itself the "queen of seaside resorts," Cape May, with its nearly 600 preserved Victorian buildings, is a city so rich in history that it was declared a National Historic Landmark in 1976. Perched at the southernmost tip of New Jersey, where the Atlantic Ocean kisses the Delaware Bay, this peninsula was largely spared by 2012's Hurricane Sandy. The town of 3,600 people swells to some 40,000 in the summer, when tourists pack its award-winning beaches. Dogs can enjoy **Cape May City beaches** on leashes only from November to March. Pooches are allowed along the Delaware Bay year-round, on state-owned **Higbee Beach** from September 1 to April 30, and on **Sunset Beach** from September 15 to April 15. You'll find a **dog park with a gazebo,** water, and chairs on Lafayette near the corner of Broad and dog-friendly wineries. Dog-friendly restaurants include **Zoe's, Aleathea's Restaurant** at the Inn of Cape May, **Blue Pig Tavern, Ugly Mug,** and **Tisha's.** At the dog-friendly **Billmae Cottage,** owner Bob Steenrod makes homemade treats for four-legged guests for Yappy Hour. **Marquis de Lafayette Hotel** and **Palace Hotel** also accept four-legged guests.

The Hamptons, New York

There are destinations that cater to coddled canines and then there are the Hamptons, where posh pets preside. The pet-set crowd in this collection of villages and hamlets can have a private pet chef whip up a fabulous farm-to-bowl dish, hire a concierge to arrange a birthday pawty on the beach, book a beauty day at a spa, shop for doggie wedding dresses and pearls at a boutique—all necessary services and accoutrements for the VIPs (Very Important Pets) of the glitterati who flock to this summer playground on New York's Long Island. Each area is as distinct as a dog breed. If tony East Hampton, synonymous with artists, celebrities, and expensive shops and restaurants, is like a teacup Chihuahua, trendy with tremendous staying power, then Southampton, with its old money, socialites, celebs, golf and tennis clubs, and pricey boutiques, is the Standard Poodle, with the refined poodle clip, of course. Call Montauk, with its Bohemians, surfers, and outdoor lobster and seafood restaurants, the lovable Labrador retriever. Sag Harbor, Bridgehampton, and Wainscott also are popular destinations.

For getting to the Hamptons from New York City: **Hampton Ambassador,** Hampton Jitney's first-class, luxury coach company, allows pets in carriers, but note that if the coach is full, pooches must sit on their people's laps. Avoid traffic by taking the **Long Island Rail Road,** which offers Cannonball nonstop service from Penn Station to

Westhampton in 94 minutes and allows small pets in carriers. And for the well heeled, there's always helicopter service into East Hampton Airport from the East 34th Street Heliport or André Balazs' **StndAIR seaplane,** which welcomes pets up to 20 pounds and operates Thursday through Monday from May to September.

Insider Tip

"The real dog parks in East Hampton are the beaches. Wiborg is my favorite beach to take my dogs, Luke and Dixie, in the mornings and at night. The locals gather for coffee and social chat from 8 a.m. to 9 a.m. while their dogs play. Visitors are always welcome."
— MITCH KARSCH

PLAY

The Hamptons are as known for their wide beaches as they are for their scene. When it comes to dogs on the beach, each village has its own rules. All five beaches in the village of East Hampton (**Georgica Beach, Main Beach, Wiborg Beach, Egypt Beach,** and **Two Mile Hollow Beach**) are open weekends and holidays only starting Memorial Day until the last Friday in June. Beaches are open daily, seven days a week, from the last Saturday in June through Labor Day. Beaches are open weekends only from Labor Day to September 30. Dogs are not permitted on the beach between 9 a.m. and 6 p.m. daily from the second Sunday in May through September 30. Plastic bags for cleanup are conveniently provided at the entrance to each village beach.

Southampton village boasts eleven beautiful beaches along 7 miles, but Coopers Beach, considered one of America's top beaches, is the only one to not allow dogs at any time. Leashed dogs are always allowed at the other ten.

Fido can also get plenty of exercise inside **Springs Park,** on Three Mile Harbor Road in East Hampton, which is open from dawn to dusk and where leashes are not required. Half of the 42-acre park is a dog park. Also in East Hampton, the **Cedar Point Lighthouse Loop Trail** is a hike of 5.6 miles and allows dogs on leashes. A bone's throw from the village of Sag Harbor is the **Long Pond Greenbelt Trail,** which stretches 3.5 miles and allows leashed canines on the path that takes trekkers past marshes, ponds, and swamps.

SIT

Don't just book a grooming session at **The Classy Canine** when spoiled Sadie can enjoy an entire beauty day at the Southampton pet spa, which includes treatments like Dead Sea Mineral Mud Scrub and Red Clay & Gingko Oil Spot Treatment; go for its Royal Treatment package offering basic pampering plus three spa treatments. **Hampton Pet Club,** in the center of South Fork, offers doggie day care, boarding, and training, while **Beach Paws** in Wainscott will make your pup pretty. Pet parents can turn everything over to **Hampton Canine Concierge,** run by Dr. Cindy Bressler, a celeb veterinarian who arranges spa services, play dates, beach parties, acupuncture, private jet transportation, and anything else a pampered pooch in the Hamptons may require.

🐾 HAUTE DOG

In Southampton, **Little Lucy's Canine Couture Boutique** is where dapper dogs can be outfitted for everything from wedding dresses and tuxedos to bikinis and polo shirts for the Hamptons look. In Sag Harbor, stop by **Harbor Pets,** and in Amagansett make your one stop at **1 Stop Pet Shop.**

🦴 CHOW TIME

Hungry hounds only need to be well behaved and well groomed—but not guests— at c/o The Maidstone in East Hampton to order from the hotel's Woof Menu at **The Living Room** restaurant, where dishes are named after breeds and the beautiful people gather. Also in East Hampton, chefs will cook for four-legged guests at **The Mill House Inn,** and **Babette's** offers not just great people and pooch watching from its patio but a doggie menu and water—ice water on those dog days of summer. **Dockside Bar & Grill** in Sag Harbor's historic American Legion Building brings water bowls for thirsty tykes. Pet parents can ask the chef at **Foody's** in Water Mill to make something special for their furry friend.

Other popular pet-friendly restaurants include **Pierre's** in Bridgehampton, **Joni's** and **Gosman's Dock** in Montauk, **Hampton Chutney Co.** in Amagansett, **Sant Ambroeus** in Southampton, and **Nichol's of East Hampton.**

🏠 *Stay* All Pups Welcome

■ *c/o The Maidstone (East Hampton):* Welcome letter and tray with food and water bowls, water, gourmet biscuits. Pickup bags and information on pet-friendly resources. Woof menu available in restaurant and in room. No number restriction/size depends on room. Fee. careof hotels.com

■ *The Mill House Inn (East Hampton):* Dog beds, gourmet meals prepared by in-house chef. Dog walking can be arranged. Three dogs/no size restriction. Fee. millhouseinn.com

■ *Southampton Inn:* Bed. Treats upon arrival. Dog walking and dogsitting can be arranged. Two dogs/no size restriction. Fee. southamptoninn.com

■ *Ruschmeyer's (Montauk):* Two dogs/no size restriction. Fee. kingandgrove.com

■ *Topping Rose House (Bridgehampton):* Garden for walking. No number restriction/30 lb each max. Fee. toppingrosehouse.com

☸ COME

It's all about the social scene in the Hamptons. Any pet-setter worth their fur should bark their calendar for these annual shindigs: **Stroll to the Sea Dog Walk,** a leisurely 2-mile jaunt from Mulford Farm to Main Beach in East Hampton, then back for contests and luxe prizes to benefit the Animal Rescue Fund of the Hamptons, usually the Saturday of Columbus Day weekend; Wainscott Animal Rescue Fund's **Bow Wow Meow Ball** in August; Southampton's **Martinis for Mutts** fundraiser for Last Chance Animal Rescue in June; **Little Lucy's Halloween Pet Parade** and the summer **Pooch Socials and Adoptathons** put on by Little Lucy's Canine Couture Boutique; and also in June, **PetFest** at the Bridgehampton Historical Society Museum. **Foody's** in Water Mill can always be counted on to host charity-themed events throughout the season.

Refined Rovers wouldn't miss being seen at the **Bridgehampton Polo Club.** At **Wölffer Estate Vineyard** in Sagaponack, leashed dogs of a certain size are welcome to relax on the covered patio overlooking the vineyard, which puts on a slew of pet-friendly outdoor events.

> *Refined Rovers wouldn't miss being seen at the Bridgehampton Polo Club.*

ⓕⓘⓓⓞ UNIQUE ACTIVITY

For the ultimutt in pampering, hire **The Hampton Pet Chef,** Bonnie Emmerich, to whip up nutritional, palate-pleasing dog dishes or cater a furry fiesta, bark mitzvah, or other celebration with menu items such as fish tacos, curried coconut chicken, and frozen mutt-tinis. She'll also teach you pet parents how to cook at home for your pooch. hamptonpetchef.com

Emergency Veterinarian
Dr. Cindy Bressler—drcindybressler.com; 631-255-8556 ▪ East End Veterinary Emergency and Specialty Center (Riverhead)—pet-er.com; 631-369-4513

Lake Placid, New York

Best known for hosting the Winter Olympics in 1932 and 1980, Lake Placid can claim a gold medal in pet friendliness from both sporty canines and lapdogs. Although the quaint village is considered America's first winter resort, approximately 70 percent of its visitors flock to this scenic destination in upstate New York between May and October. The town of 3,000 swells to 10,000 in the summer, when an abundance of outdoor activities beckons visitors to the mountains and lakes of the Adirondacks, and businesses along Main Street leave out water dishes for dogs. Cape Air, the only commercial airline that serves Adirondack Regional Airport, 16 miles from Lake Placid, welcomes pawsengers, but book early as space is extremely limited. Three major airports—in Albany, New York; Burlington, Vermont; and Montreal, Quebec—are within a 2.5-hour drive.

PLAY

Dog parks are nonexistent in Lake Placid. Perhaps it is because the village is located inside **Adirondack State Park,** the largest protected area in the contiguous United States and the biggest state park in the country, encompassing approximately 6 million acres and one-third of the total area of New York State. More than 2,000 miles of dog-friendly hiking trails await active hounds near Lake Placid.

Pets and their people are often found on the **Peninsula Nature Trails,** a trio of trails consisting of Lake Shore, Ridge, and Boundary, where man and his best friend can take dips together in the lake in summer, or cross-country ski and snowshoe in winter. A climb up **Mount Van Hoevenberg** affords hikers and their little pals sensational views of the High Peaks. In the winter, there's also cross-country skiing on Mount Van Hoevenberg's dog-friendly loop; snowshoeing day passes for dogs (proof of rabies vaccination required) are available too. Enjoy a day skijoring, a demonstration sport at the 1928 Winter Olympics in St. Moritz using horses, where a dog or horse in harness or a motor vehicle pulls a human wearing cross-country skis with your pooch leading the way.

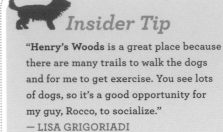

Insider Tip

"**Henry's Woods** is a great place because there are many trails to walk the dogs and for me to get exercise. You see lots of dogs, so it's a good opportunity for my guy, Rocco, to socialize."
— LISA GRIGORIADI

Or take Fido on a walk through history on the pet-friendly trail at the **John Brown Farm State Historic Site,** where the famed abolitionist is buried in front of his home. Open year-round during daylight hours.

In the middle of town, take the popular stroll along a red-brick path that loops 2.7 miles around scenic **Mirror Lake,** where doggie pickup bag stations and trash cans are plentiful. On the shore, the pet-friendly **Golden Arrow Resort** prohibits dogs on its sandy beach, but canines can enjoy the water from the grassy area. Rent a canoe or kayak from pet-friendly **Mirror Lake Boat Rental,** and don't forget to put a canine flotation device on Rover.

SIT

Lake Placid Animal Hospital offers not just veterinarian services but also **Pretty Paws Pet Grooming** and boarding facilities. Just outside of town, **High Peaks Animal Hospital** in Ray Brook also offers grooming and boarding, serving the Tri-Lakes area, including Lake Placid, Saranac Lake, Tupper Lake, and Keene. Some of the pet-friendly hotels, such as **Lake Placid Lodge,** will gladly watch four-legged guests while their guardians enjoy non–dog-friendly activities, such as visiting the Winter Olympic Museum, seeing a performance at the Lake Placid Center for the Arts, or catching a movie at the old-fashioned theater on Main Street.

⬤ CHOW TIME

Dogs can relax on the outside deck at **Lisa G's** and watch the Chubb River flow by. The mascot Rocco, a German Shepherd mix, roams freely at this local favorite that serves comfort food with a twist in a relaxed setting. The chef at **Generations** is known to whip up bison and potatoes or other dishes for dogs staying at the **Golden Arrow Lakeside Resort,** or those who happen to dine with their pet parents on the outdoor deck. Well-behaved dogs will feel right at home at **The Brown Dog Café & Wine Bar,** where drawings by legendary dog artist Stephen Huneck, canine-related plaques, and pooch photos adorn the walls. Pick up a scone or dessert at **Bluesberry Bakery,** which has a small outdoor, dog-friendly area, but head to the doggie bakery at **Jake Placid Doghouse** to reward an especially good boy or good girl.

A climb up Mount Van Hoevenberg affords hikers and their little pals sensational views of the High Peaks.

⬤ HAUTE DOG

In addition to the doggie bakery at **Jake Placid Doghouse,** the upscale pet boutique on Main Street offers a wide range of products, including fashionable apparel, gourmet treats, super-premium pet food, travel products, and gifts. Jake, a Wire-Haired Fox Terrier, is often in the house. A fireplace keeps canines toasty in the winter, and an outdoor deck overlooking Mirror Lake offers a picturesque view year-round.

Pick up animal-themed gifts for pet lovers at **Critters,** also on Main Street, where many of the eclectic variety of specialty shops leave water for perambulating pooches at their entrances in summer.

🏠 *Stay* All Pups Welcome

■ *Golden Arrow Lakeside Resort (Downtown Lake Placid):* Provides beds, toys, and treats. No number/size restrictions. Fee. golden-arrow.com

■ *The Point (Saranac Lake):* Bed, custom bowls, homemade treats, Bowser beer, and Frosty Paws (dog ice cream). No number/size restrictions. the pointresort.com

■ *Lake Placid Lodge:* Beds, treats from the hotel's farm-to-table kitchen, and maps of walking trails. The resident golden retriever, Maggie, is always eager for a playmate. Dogsitting and walking can be arranged with the front desk staff. No number/size restrictions. Fee. lakeplacid lodge.com

🐾 COME

Dogs take center stage every summer when the prestigious **Lake Placid** and **I Love New York Horse Shows** happen. A doggie costume contest, held for more than twenty years, has turned into the pooch event of the year, and during the two-week period, an overwhelming number of Welsh Corgis, one of the preferred dog breeds in the equine world, descend on the village.

🛡️ UNIQUE ACTIVITY

Pets and their people can attend summer camp together at **Canine Camp Getaway of New York** at the Roaring Brook Ranch in Lake George, about two hours from Lake Placid. Held twice annually, the weeklong camp allows dog lovers and their best friends to bond while enjoying activities together such as hiking, swimming, Frisbee, Yappy Hour, and "Barks & Crafts." The camp also offers classes in Canine CPR and dog nutrition. caninecampgetaway.com

Emergency Veterinarian
Lake Placid Animal Hospital—lakeplacidanimalhospital.com; 518-523-7319

New York City, New York

O f the 8.3 million stories in New York City, 1.5 million could involve a dog, since that's the estimated pooch population of the five boroughs. With so many canines in the city, it's impawsible for four-legged travelers not to have a fur-bulous time. Hotels don't just allow pets, some can arrange for a pet psychic too. The services are endless in Manhattan, known for getting anything delivered at any time. There's even a food truck for Fifi. Bocce's Bakery Biscuit Bike brings all-natural dog treats to pups on the go. As long as small canines are in carriers, they can ride the subway and buses. Taxi drivers aren't obligated to pick up pawsengers. But this is New York, where you can call Pet Chauffeur or Canine Cab Company to carry your precious pal to its play date.

PLAY

New York City boasts more than 1,700 parks, playgrounds, and recreation facilities across the five boroughs, none more famous than **Central Park,** a must for any mutt. Fifi can frolic freely in designated parts of the 843-acre park before 9 a.m. and after 9 p.m. The rest of the time, a leash is required. A restraint is always needed in the park's 136-acre woodland areas and in nine designated spots, including Strawberry Fields and Shakespeare Garden. Eleven places, including the playground and Sheep Meadow, always prohibit pooches. Fifteen **doggie drinking fountains** (with plans for more) are sprinkled throughout the park, so don't let your little pal drink or play in other fountains or any other bodies of water. Local pet parents and their furry friends tend to gather at one of the 23 designated dog-friendly areas, which include **Wollman Rink, Great Hill, East Meadow,** and **Harlem Meer.**

In the other parks, pets are also allowed to run off leash in certain designated areas from park opening until 9 a.m. and from 9 p.m. until closing. Note that pets are prohibited at the High Line, the elevated public park that opened on the West Side in 2009. Some of the parks have dog runs—large, fenced-in areas where no leashes are required. Popular ones include **Carl Schurz Park** (Upper East Side), where there's a promenade along the East River, and **Tompkins Square** (East Village), with three bone-shaped doggie pools.

For a change of scenery, head to a New York City beach. Leashed pooches are allowed on the sand and boardwalk at **Rockaway, Coney Island, Brighton, Manhattan, Midland,** and **South Beaches** from October 1 until May 1, and on the boardwalk/promenade at **Orchard, Coney Island, Brighton, Manhattan, Midland,** and **South Beaches** year-round.

Get in touch with nature on an easy hike with your favorite canine companion in Midwood, Brooklyn's oldest remaining forest.

Get in touch with nature on an easy hike with your favorite canine companion in **Midwood,** Brooklyn's oldest remaining forest, inside **Prospect Park.** There are even two places for Rover to dog-paddle in Prospect Park. **Long Meadow Dog Beach at the Pools,** known as Dog Beach, allows dogs off leash if under voice command during established off-leash times, but otherwise they must be leashed. Located near the Long Meadow ball fields, the beach is most easily accessed from the Ninth Street entrance to the park. Dogs are also allowed to swim in the lake adjacent to the **Peninsula** meadow during off-leash hours.

🐕 SIT

D Pet Hotel in Chelsea offers digs so swank, you'll want to check in too when you drop Fifi off for doggie day care, while you spend a day at the museums or enjoy a Broadway show. In addition to the stylish suites, there are three separate indoor dog parks for daytime or overnight guests, a boutique, chauffeur service, and grooming that includes hand stripping. Master groomers are on hand at **Canis Minor TriBeCa** and **Canis Minor Gramercy Park,** which also sell organic and holistic foods, designer dog clothing, collars, leashes, beds, carriers, and home accessories.

You and your furry friend can take an indoor swim together at **Water 4 Dogs,** a state-of-the-art rehabilitation center for canines in TriBeCa, which offers private swim sessions for pets and their people, as well as hydrotherapy, acupuncture, massage, and other types of therapy for dogs.

HAUTE DOG

Wearing a fur coat isn't enough for four-legged friends in New York. Canine couture is a must. For modish apparel, visit any of **Canine Styles'** four locations (Uptown East, Upper East Side, Downtown, Upper West Side), which also carry beds, carriers, leashes, and collars. **Zoomies** in the West Village will also please a furry fashionista with its chic offerings. **Beasty Feast,** with two locations in the West Village, is known for its natural foods and accessories, plus offers grooming at its Hudson Street store.

CHOW TIME

Just about any restaurant with an outdoor space will let your furry friend join you. On the Upper East Side, fill your belly and your heart at **Fetch Bar & Grill,** featuring a "Fetch a Friend" adoption wall of tail waggers available at **Animal Haven,** a no-kill shelter, as well as walls of customers' dog photos. A block away is **Barking Dog New York City,** which has doggie watering fountains outside and is crowded with canines during brunch. On the Upper West Side, enjoy sunset views from **Boat Basin Café** in Riverside Park or grab an outdoor table at **Fred's,** named after a female black Lab, where photos of customers' dogs adorn the walls. In the Flatiron District, order a Pooch-ini (ShackBurger dog biscuits, made by all-natural dog biscuit company Bocce's Bakery, peanut butter sauce, and vanilla custard) from the "woof" section of the menu at Danny Meyer's **Shake Shack** inside Madison Square Park, where **Jemmy's Dog Run** is a fave. In Central Park, **Le Pain Quotidien** (in the Mineral Springs Pavilion at 69th Street) has a dog-friendly patio. **Pastis** is a dog-friendly favorite in the Meatpacking District.

Dogs will devour the decadent foie gras dog biscuits sold at **Bouchon Bakery,** with locations inside Time Warner and Rockefeller Centers.

COME

Your furry friend can join you on a Central Park **horse and carriage tour,** a classic way to see the park, or on a **pedicab tour.** Stores such as **Bloomingdale's, Bergdorf Goodman, Barneys,** and **Saks Fifth Avenue** don't mind if you bring your

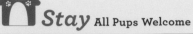 *Stay* All Pups Welcome

■ *70 Park Avenue, A Kimpton Hotel (Murray Hill):* Provides bed, bowls, disposable pickup bags. No number/size restrictions. 70parkave.com

■ *The Muse, A Kimpton Hotel (Theater District):* Provides bed, bowls, disposable pickup bags, leash. VIP (Very Important Pet) amenity delivered to your room upon arrival. Petsitting, grooming, walking, pet massage, and pet acupuncture services can be arranged through concierge. No number/size restrictions. No fee. themusehotel.com

■ *Ink 48, A Kimpton Hotel (Midtown West):* Provides bed, bowls, disposable pickup bags. No number/size restrictions. ink48.com

■ *Eventi, A Kimpton Hotel (Chelsea):* Provides bed, bowls, disposable pickup bags, dog leash. Petsitting, pet grooming, pet walking, pet massage, and pet acupuncture services can be arranged through concierge. No number/size restrictions. eventihotel.com

■ *W Hotels (Midtown East, Times Square,* Union Square, and Lower Manhattan):* P.A.W. (Pets Are Welcome) program provides pet toy, pet treat, W Hotels pet tag, custom W pet bed, food and water bowls with floor mat, pet-in-room door sign. Concierge can arrange dogsitting, dog walking, grooming, birthday cake, and veterinarian. One dog/40 lb max. Fee. whotelsnewyork.com

■ *The Surrey (Upper East Side):* Custom Surrey dog bed, gourmet biscuit menu from Bocce's Bakery, welcome note. No number/size restrictions. Fee. thesurrey.com

■ *Trump SoHo and Trump International Hotel & Tower (Upper West Side):* Trump Pets provides bed, in-room dining menu, bowls, fresh bottled water, toys, map of the city highlighting dog parks. Dog walking can be arranged. No number restriction/25 lb each max. Fee. trumphotelcollection.com

■ *The Ritz-Carlton, New York Central Park and The Ritz-Carlton, New York Battery Park:* Plush bone-shaped pillow, Ritz-Carlton-themed dog bowls, home-baked dog treats, personalized dog food menu. Loaner Burberry raincoat at Central Park location. No number restriction/60 lb each max. Fee. ritzcarlton.com/newyork

■ *Loews Regency Hotel (Upper East Side):* Loews Loves Pets program provides bowls, mat, treat, in-room dining menu. Two pets/no size restriction. Fee. loewshotels.com/Regency-Hotel/specials

■ *The Benjamin (Midtown East):* Dream Dog program provides specially designed, size-appropriate bed, bowls, loaner bathrobe, and information about local pet resources. No number/size restrictions. thebenjamin.com

■ *Flatiron Hotel:* Sleepypod & Friends Welcome Kit and Doggie Menu with pet travel essentials and local pet resources. Priority seating for dogs at Toshi's Living Room and Toshi's Penthouse. One dog/50 lb max. Fee. flatironhotel.com

well-behaved posh pal in either. A pawsome time for top dogs to be in New York is in February during the **Westminster Kennel Club Dog Show,** America's second-oldest continuously held sporting event. Buy a ticket for your tyke to compete in the Best in Show Costume Contest at the **New York Pet Fashion Show,** which kicks off the festivities. Other annual events worth barking your calendar for are the annual **Tompkins Square Halloween Dog Parade,**

Insider Tip

"If you are in the Macy's area, check out **Barking Dog** at 150 East 34th Street. They have dog bowls in three sizes outside year-round, plus the outdoor area is for people with pets. If you are into celeb-watching, **Madison Square Park dog run** is the place to go."
— NAOMI BURTON-ISAACS, *pet parent to Asta, a five-year-old Bichon-Poodle mix*

the country's largest Halloween dog parade; **AnimalFair.com's Howloween Pet Costume Benefit;** and the **DogCatemy Mutt-i-grees Rescue Awards Gala,** put on every December by the North Shore Animal League, which bills itself as the world's largest no-kill animal rescue and adoption organization.

Central Park Paws, a program of the Central Park Conservancy, has year-round events, including monthly **Bagel Barks** held at different locations in the park during off-leash hours, and the **My Dog Loves Central Park Country Fair** each autumn.

UNIQUE ACTIVITY

Take your cultured canine to the **William Secord Gallery,** which specializes in fine 19th-century dog and other animal paintings. Located on Manhattan's Upper East Side, it claims to be the only gallery of its kind in North America. The gallery welcomes pooches of all sizes with fresh water and doggie biscuits. dogpainting.com

Emergency Veterinarian
BluePearl—newyork.bluepearlvet.com; 212-767-0099 ▪ Fifth Avenue Veterinary Specialists—vcaspecialty vets.com/fifth-avenue; 212-924-3311

Poconos, Pennsylvania

T he heart-shaped "Sweetheart Tub" introduced at Cove Haven Resort in 1963 helped the Pocono Mountains earn their reputation as a honeymoon haven. Couples still flock here—but now often with a four-legged companion. Located within driving distance of many of the East Coast's major cities, this majestic region in northeastern Pennsylvania dazzles with gorgeous waterfalls, historical offerings, cultural activities, and an abundance of outdoor recreation. Its four counties (Carbon, Monroe, Pike, and Wayne) include 170 miles of winding rivers, 261 miles of hiking and biking trails, over 163 ski trails, and more than 35 golf courses.

PLAY

Summers are full of festivals, county fairs, concerts, and boating on **Lake Wallen-paupack,** one of Pennsylvania's largest lakes. Strap a personal flotation device on Brutus and let him enjoy the boating life too. In the fall, fabulous foliage makes for pretty drives that even pooches can appreciate. In the winter, blazing fireplaces warm humans and their furry friends after they return from the pet-friendly cross-country and snowshoeing trails, such as the ones at dog-friendly **The Inn at Pocono Manor.** Others within the park system include **Hickory Run State Park, Delaware**

State Forest, Delaware Water Gap National Recreation Area, and Promised Land State Park.

All nine state and two national parks allow leashed dogs on the numerous hiking trails. Perhaps the most well-known path is the **Appalachian Trail,** spanning 2,184 miles and fourteen states from Maine to Georgia, including a section of the **Delaware Water Gap National Recreation Area** in the Pocono Mountains. Offering equally stunning views is the **Lehigh Gorge Trail,** a 26-mile path along the scenic Lehigh River adorned with waterfalls. In addition, the region boasts several dog parks, with two of the most popular being **Judy Putek Dog Park** and **Skywood Park.**

HAUTE DOG

Stop by **PetSmart** in Stroudsburg to pick up dog essentials for the Poconos, including booties for deep snow, winter coats, life jackets, and fluorescent vests. **Pet Supplies Plus,** also in Stroudsburg, sells basic dog products as well as natural pet foods, treats, and supplements.

SIT

After a morning of exercise, dog-tired canines can enjoy services at **Milford Pet Spa,** where soothing music plays, and **Rachel Ann's Country Clips Pet Grooming** in Pocono Summit, where pawdicures and blueberry facials are paw for the course. Grooming is also available at PetSmart.

Doggie day care, for those times when humans and their pets must be apart, is available in Stroudsburg at **Mountain Mutts,** which also offers grooming, and **Pocono Bed and Biscuits.** Milford's **Hotel Fauchère,** which dates back to the 1800s, offers complimentary petsitting when guests dine in either of the hotel's two restaurants.

CHOW TIME

Grab an outdoor table along the flowing Sawkill Creek at **Waterwheel Café,** where many locals and visitors bring their dogs. Also popular is **Cocoon Coffee House and Catering Company,** in the historic Hawley silk mill and close to Lake Wallenpaupack.

Stay
All Pups Welcome

■ *Hotel Fauchère (Milford):* Pet amenities. One dog/no size restriction. hotelfauchere.com

■ *The Inn at Pocono Manor:* Pet amenities and a welcome letter with essential pet-related information, including local veterinarian services, provided. Designated area to walk dogs. Two dogs/no size restriction. Fee. poconomanor.com

■ *Chateau Resort & Conference Center (Tannersville):* Welcome amenities provided. Two dogs/no size restriction. Fee. chateauresort.com

If Duke appreciates having his own food, take him to **Mountain Mutts Gourmet Bakery,** where peanut butter biscuits, doggie ice cream cups, banana chip bonbons, and other tantalizing dog treats are on the menu. There's also a party room available to rent on Sundays for canines celebrating a bark mitzvah, birthday, doggie wedding, or other event. Also in Stroudsburg is **Annie's Pooch Pops,** home of the world-famous muttkins, beef-marrow bones wrapped in all-natural peanut butter biscuit and slow-roasted to perfection. The specialty shop also offers grain-free treats, Happy Dog Meals, and personalized treats.

🐾 COME

Well-behaved dogs can ride for free on the **Lehigh Gorge Scenic Railway,** which from Memorial Day to December takes pawsengers on a 16-mile trek from Jim Thorpe, a historical town formerly known as Mauch Chunk and dubbed the "Switzerland of America," into the beautiful **Lehigh Gorge State Park.** The **Water Gap Trolley,** which offers an hour-long narrated historic tour aboard authentic trolleys from March to November, also allows four-legged riders. Pooches are welcome at the weekly **Monroe Farmers' Market** from May to October and at **Pocono Candle Works,** where visitors can make their own candles. Pocono Raceway, host to two NASCAR Sprint Cup Series and an ARCA Racing Series, allows pets for its RV customers only. And from Sundays through Thursdays, pets are welcome on the deck of **The Lounge,** an adult nightspot in Bartonsville offering 52 varieties of martinis, food, and happy-hour specials.

Well-behaved dogs can ride for free on the Lehigh Gorge Scenic Railway.

🐾 UNIQUE ACTIVITY

Dogs can enjoy a trip down the Delaware River via canoe, kayak, or raft when they join their family at **Kittatinny Canoes.** kittatinny.com

Emergency Veterinarian
Pennsylvania Veterinary Medical Association—pavma.org; 717-220-1437/888-550-7862

Insider Tip

"The bike and hiking trail through the **Delaware Water Gap National Recreation Area** (between US 209 and the Delaware River, so quite scenic) is a great place to hike with your dog. Individuals who use these trails with their dogs must be sure to carry cleanup bags, keep their pet on a leash, and follow any other regulations required by the venue. Too many places have been closed to dogs due to owner negligence, and the new outdoor facilities that are opening are not allowing dogs."
— BUD COLE, *pet parent to Blue*

St. Johnsbury/Dog Mountain, Vermont

Serene, picturesque, and pure, with its mountains, lakes, and streams, St. Johnsbury, Vermont, has a lot going for it. But make no bones about it. The main reason for you to visit with your favorite canine companion is **Dog Mountain,** where you'll laugh, cry, and marvel at the haven for hounds created by the late artist Stephen Huneck and his late wife, Gwendolyn. Set on 150 acres on a private mountaintop with hiking trails and ponds, Dog Mountain is where canines can frolic freely year-round. There's an agility course, swimming in the summer, snowshoeing in the winter, and, regardless of the season, always **Dog Chapel** and the **Stephen Huneck Gallery,** where sales of his whimsical works (along with donations) help keep Dog Mountain going. A sign outside the chapel reads, "Welcome All Creeds All Breeds No Dogmas Allowed." The weather vane is a Labrador with wings. Inside, canine statues prop up the wooden pews, where you can sit and shed tears after seeing the walls covered with tens of thousands of multicolored squares with handwritten notes and photos of departed dogs posted by their bereaved humans. Dog Mountain is now run by staffers who vow to keep it open and free to the public. **Dog parties** take place twice a year. Dog Mountain is located about three hours north of Boston and 90 miles east of Burlington International Airport. Pet-friendly lodging is available in St. Johnsbury at the **Fairbanks Inn,** and in Lyndonville at the **Wildflower Inn.**

Southeast

Alexandria, Virginia

Geroge Washington, who lived in nearby Mount Vernon, was a pet parent whose fondness for dogs is well documented. His hounds could enjoy a pawsome life in Alexandria today. Twice a week they could drop in for Yappy Hour at Hotel Monaco. In all, 14 dog-friendly hotels wait to pamper them. There are also canine cruises, restaurants with pooch menus, businesses that provide free doggie treats, a slew of dog parks, and no shortage of historical attractions that welcome four-legged visitors. Should they need training, there's the prestigious Olde Towne School for Dogs, called the "Harvard for hounds, the Columbia for canines." The dogs can give a paw five to the school for helping make Alexandria, part of Washington, D.C.'s metro region, with one of the oldest and largest historic districts, the ultimutt destination.

PLAY

Its historic setting on the Potomac River provides the perfect backdrop for exploring this walkable city. On foot with a furry friend, an intriguing shop or architecturally impressive home awaits around every corner. For those who prefer to pick up the pace, check out the popular **Mount Vernon Trail,** a nearly 18-mile, multi-use path that runs along the Potomac stretching from Theodore Roosevelt Island to Mount Vernon.

Sociable pups have a bevy of play options, with Alexandria's 18 dog exercise areas and fenced dog parks that don't require leashes. The dog parks—**Simpson Stadium Park** at Monroe Avenue, **Duke Street** east of the Charles E. Beatley, Jr. Library, **Montgomery Park** at the corner of Fairfax and First Streets, **Ben Brenman Park** by Backlick Creek, and **Dog Run Park** at Carlyle—and exercise areas are open sunup to sunset and require pooches to be at least four months old. Leashes are required when tykes enter and exit the dog parks, and when pooches are in areas of public parks not designated as dog exercise areas.

SIT

Olde Towne School for Dogs, established in 1975 by Carlos and Sandy Mejias, has trained more than 20,000 dogs. Because its trainers work with pups on busy King Street to help accustom them to city life, residents are used to seeing well-behaved pooches in public, making the neighborhood more welcoming. Olde Towne offers grooming as well. This is where President Barack Obama's Portuguese Water Dogs, Bo and Sunny, get spruced up. The grooming appointment book fills up well in advance, so clients are encouraged to schedule a year at a time. Therefore, expect to wait for a cancellation. Other options in Alexandria are **A Dog's Day Out,** offering cage-free doggie day care, boarding, and grooming, plus a variety of "delivered" pet services, including dog walking, petsitting, pet taxi, and poop patrol; **Your Dog's Best Friends,** which provides day care, grooming, boarding, and training.

In nearby Arlington, there's **The Muddy Mutt,** which offers self-service and professional grooming, just steps from the Oxford Street entrance to **Shirlington Dog Park.**

HAUTE DOG

PetSmart, in Alexandria's Potomac Yard Center, received a slew of attention when President Obama and Bo waltzed in to pick up items for man's best friend. For a unique retail experience, head to **The Dog Park** in the heart of Old Town on King Street. Owner Anna Fitzgerald prides herself on stocking fanciful collars, delightful coats, and pet-themed artwork not found everywhere, while offering the essentials like all-natural foods and treats at competitive prices. Also, Olde Towne has an impressive retail space featuring a

Insider Tip

"In the winter, Hotel Monaco has a great lobby full of friendly dogs and owners! The restaurant Jackson 20 is extremely accommodating. Some of the servers will bring food into the lobby if they're not very busy. If they are busy, you can get drinks and food to go and bring it in yourself. Also, my favorite dog store in the area is **Dogma Bakery and Boutique,** which has a dog bakery. It's in Shirlington, 10 minutes from Old Town."
— STEFANIE DREIZEN, *pet parent to Holly*

vast selection of apparel, such as life vests for salty dogs and cooling vests to combat the dog days of summer. Other products include water bottles, toys, doggie backpacks and totes, plus premium food and supplements.

CHOW TIME

With more than 30 of Alexandria's restaurants featuring sidewalk or patio seating in warm weather, it's easy to find a pet-friendly restaurant, since most eateries that offer al fresco dining allow pets. There are always four-legged diners in the 60-seat backyard at **Ireland's Own Pub,** where a dog dining menu lists chopped chicken, lamb and beef stew, and chopped hamburger.

Seafood restaurants along King attract dog lovers, but be careful of the weekend foot traffic. Also popular in the historic district: **Chadwicks,** whose location on The Strand is ideal for pooches sensitive to crowds, and a good spot to dine when going on the Canine Cruise (see page 57). Le chien can relax on the large patio at **Bastille Restaurant & Wine Bar,** where brunch draws local pooches.

At the nearby Village at Shirlington, the **Carlyle Grand Café** offers homemade dog biscuits from its bakery next door, which also has a pet-friendly patio; dogs of all sizes are found at **Capitol City Brewing Company;** and **Cheesetique,** known for its great wine and cheese and friendly servers, has a patio popular with pets.

For good girls and good boys, pick up a pupcake made with wheat germ, peanut butter, oatmeal, and milk and topped with a crunchy dog bone at **Bittersweet Catering and Café** on King Street. **The Dog Park** offers handmade treats and sells holiday-themed

---

Stay All Pups Welcome

■ *Hotel Monaco, A Kimpton Hotel (Old Town):* Provides bed, food and water bowls, toys, disposable pickup bags, and information on parks and pet-friendly venues. Charlie, a Bichon, is Director of Pet Relations. Hosts popular Yappy Hour twice a week from April through October. No number/size restrictions. monaco-alexandria.com

■ *Lorien Hotel & Spa, A Kimpton Hotel (Old Town):* Offers bowls, bed, leash, and plastic bags. Pet-sitting, pet grooming, pet walking, and pet massage can be arranged through the concierge. No number/size restrictions. lorien hotelandspa.com

■ *Morrison House, A Kimpton Hotel (Old*

Town): Provides bed, bowls, toys, and leash. Concierge can arrange dog walking, petsitting, grooming, and other services. No number/size restrictions. morrisonhouse.com

■ *Westin Alexandria (Carlyle):* Provides Westin Heavenly dog bed and bowls. Two dogs/40 lb each max. westinalexandria.com

cookies. Local pooches know about the complimentary dog treats in a picturesque wooden dispenser at **The Enchanted Florist.**

🐾 COME

The estate of the Father of Our Country, the **Mount Vernon Museum, Estate & Gardens,** is open to tail waggers on leashes during visiting hours, and doggie water bowls are provided at the entrances. Although furry friends are not allowed in the historic buildings, they can stroll through the gardens and visit the 4-acre demonstration farm.

Pups are also welcome at the **Torpedo Factory Art Center,** built in 1918 for manufacturing torpedoes. It now houses 82 studios for more than 165 artists, some of whom bring along their favorite canine companion, as well as six galleries, the Art League School, and the Alexandria Archaeology Museum. Pick up a pet portrait or commission your own.

Take a canine on any of the **Potomac Riverboat Company's cruises** departing from the Alexandria marina.

Rent a custom-designed pet trailer and bike from **Bike and Roll Alexandria,** a block off King Street near the waterfront (open March through Thanksgiving) and take Daisy for a ride on the **Mount Vernon Trail** along the Potomac River.

Hotel Monaco's courtyard is something to bark about when **Yappy Hour** takes place on Tuesdays and Thursdays from April to October. Complimentary treats and fresh water are provided to pooches, and Jackson 20's bar menu is available to humans. During the holidays, Santa Paws visits Hotel Monaco.

Local pooches know about the complimentary dog treats in a picturesque wooden dispenser at The Enchanted Florist.

Beasts show their beads every year when **Mardi Growl** draws more than 300 boa-clad barkers to the U.S. Patent and Trademark Office for a fundraising gala put on by the Animal Welfare League of Alexandria, which also holds the **Alexandria Shelter Walk for Homeless Animals** each fall. In September **Olde Towne Dogge Walke** benefits an animal charity.

🐾 UNIQUE ACTIVITY

Cruise around the Alexandria Seaport with man's best friend on the Potomac Riverboat Company's **Canine Cruise,** a 40-minute sightseeing tour held on various Thursdays and Saturdays from June through October. Very popular, so book early. Dogs must be on a six-foot leash. No pet required to board. potomacriverboatco.com/canine-cruise.php

Emergency Veterinarian
VCA Alexandria Animal Hospital—vcahospitals.com/alexandria; 703-823-3601

Annapolis and the Chesapeake Bay, Maryland

Salty dogs will feel right at home in Annapolis, what many consider America's sailing capital. It's all paws on deck on **Cruises on the Bay by Watermark,** which welcomes canines on leashes attached to their human companions on all of its journeys, whether they be by a water taxi to dinner or aboard the *Harbor Queen,* a riverboat-style passenger vessel offering narrated cruises of the Annapolis Harbor. The **Haunted Ghost Tour** isn't for scaredy cats, but pups are welcome, as they are on many of the walking tours of downtown Annapolis, which boasts a 45-block historic district and more 18th-century brick homes than any other U.S. city. Pick up a nautical dog collar (and more) at **Paws Pet Boutique,** which throws regular pet events as well. Rover can romp at the off-leash dog park inside **Quiet Waters Park,** where there are also 6 miles of paved, pet-friendly trails. Pets are the norm at many restaurants with sidewalk seating. The **Federal House Bar & Grille** boasts a doggie menu, while **Harry Browne**'s Sunday brunch is pup-ular with pets and their people. **Loews Annapolis Hotel** offers an in-room pet-dining menu, and **The Westin Annapolis Hotel** invites your pooch to curl up on a custom Heavenly pet bed.

Atlanta, Georgia

Pups on Peachtree. Pooches in the Hooch. Canines are all around metro Atlanta, whose plentiful parks and green spaces are a haven for hounds. Your canine companion can be gone with the wind in Piedmont Dog Park, so popular that it attracts one in five visitors to Piedmont Park. The ATL prides itself on a hot evening social scene for pampered pets, ample al fresco dining options, a slew of doggie barkeries, and loads of dog-friendly hotels, making it a terrier-rific destination.

PLAY

The metro Atlanta area boasts approximately 20 off-leash dog parks, but there's only one **Piedmont Dog Park.** Hang with Atlanta's top dogs at the most visited free, off-leash dog park in the area. Spanning nearly 3 acres, the park features a separate small dog area for pups less than 30 pounds, benches, human restrooms, doggie waste bags, landscaping, and trails. Located at the Park Drive Bridge and open 6 a.m. to 11 p.m. daily. You can sniff around the rest of Piedmont Park with your pooch on leash. Four popular paths pass along **Lake Clara Meer,** which is off limits to humans and hounds.

More accessible is **Centennial Olympic Park** in downtown Atlanta, a legacy of the 1996 Summer Olympics. Leashes are required, and there are doggie waste bag stations sprinkled throughout the 21-acre park. Take your tyke for a hike in **Chattahoochee River National Recreation Area,** which requires a maximum 6-foot leash on the trails. Some people ignore the leash laws when their sidekick takes a dip in the river. Rent equipment from **High Country Outfitters** and go rafting or stand-up paddleboarding with Rover on the Chattahoochee.

Also a popular spot for Spot is **Kennesaw Mountain National Battle-field,** which boasts 18 miles of interpretive hiking trails to hike. Leashes no longer than six feet in length are required, and Mutt Mitts are available in the parking areas. Even privi-

> ### Insider Tip
>
> "Atlanta has lots of dog parks, including the newly revamped Piedmont Dog Park and the popular Oakhurst Dog Park, but Chewy, our Cocker Spaniel, and Abby, our Beagle/Border Collie mix, think that **Herbert Taylor Park** is the best in the city. Tucked into the Virginia Highland neighborhood, Herbert Taylor Park is frequented only by dog-loving locals and the occasional jogger. Well-behaved off-leash dogs (like Chewy and Abby) love running through the acres of forested trails and romping in the small river."
> — AKILA MCCONNELL

leged pets are not allowed in the visitor center, restroom facilities, shuttle bus, or water fountains. Other popular, pet-friendly hiking options are available at the **John Ripley Forbes Big Trees Forest Preserve,** a unique 30-acre Fulton County tree, plant, and wildlife sanctuary, and **Murphey Candler Park,** a 135-acre multi-use park in northern DeKalb County with multiple trails, including a lake loop and others in woodsy areas, through wetlands, and passing picnic pavilions.

SIT

When plans call for you to explore Atlanta's vast cultural attractions, drop your pooch off at **Greendog,** an eco-friendly urban farm in Castleberry Hill, or **Glamour Paws** in Virginia Highland, both which offer doggie day care, overnight boarding, and grooming. Glamour Paws' spa takes it up a notch with feather extensions, blueberry and sugar facials, and hair coloring. DIYers can head to **CityDog Market** in Brookhaven. **Barking Hound Village,** with five locations in Midtown and Buckhead, and **Atlanta Dog Spa** in West Midtown can also handle your doggie day care, boarding, and grooming needs. In Roswell, **K-9 Planet** offers similar services plus a barkery with fresh-baked dog treats and cakes.

HAUTE DOG

Glamour Paws' retail section includes apparel for coddled canines, including authentic collegiate, NFL, and MLB for the sports-lovin' dog, toys, treats, carriers, beds, and premium spa products. CityDog Market has natural food, healthy treats, and wholesome supplements. In addition to fresh-baked all-natural dog treats and cakes, **Dog City Bakery** in Marietta carries holistic dog foods and boutique items such as collars, leashes, toys, chews, and apparel. **Pooch N Paws** pet boutique and bakery in Suwanee carries a full line of pet accessories and stocks a large variety of natural and holistic dog food. Also, **Terra Dog Bakery,** in Norcross, specializes in creating handmade, organic dog treats that are free of gluten, wheat, soy, corn, and preservatives; they are breed specific to combat routine health issues associated with common breeds.

🐾 CHOW TIME

You'll never starve trying to find a dog-friendly restaurant in metro Atlanta. After Bruiser's play date at Piedmont Park, head to **Park Tavern,** overlooking the park. In Buckhead, **The Ritz-Carlton, Anis Café & Bistro, Bistro Niko,** and **Treehouse Restaurant and Pub,** which has a heated patio in the winter, allow al fresco diners to bring their four-legged companions. In the Old Fourth Ward, **4th and Swift** and **Noni's Bar & Deli** are among your options. Try **Der Biergarten** and **Midtown Tavern** in Downtown, **Dakota Blue** in Grant Park, and **Joe's** on Juniper in Midtown. **ParkGrounds** in Reynoldstown is a coffee shop and eatery with its own dog park. There's no outdoor seating at **Dough Bakery,** a human bakery near Inman Park, but you can pick up baked vegan dog treats when you treat yourself.

🐾 COME

One of the most beautiful places in Oakland is historic **Oakland Cemetery,** the final resting place of *Gone with the Wind* author Margaret Mitchell, golfer Bobby Jones, and Maynard Jackson, the first African-American mayor of Atlanta. The cemetery welcomes dogs on leashes and requires that you clean up after your pets and do not allow them on the monuments.

When you're strolling through neighborhoods like Virginia Highland or Decatur, you'll find water bowls by shops, and many stores will dole out treats to their furry customers. Shopping meccas **Phipps Plaza** and **Lenox Square** allow pets in strollers or held in arms (but not on leashes).

Hotels are happening spots for party animals. From spring to fall, the **W Hotel Midtown** hosts a regular **Mutts n' Martinis Yappy Hour** on its Living Room patio. **Canine Cocktail Hour** takes place every Tuesday throughout the summer at pet-friendly **Hotel Indigo. The Westin Hotel** in Buckhead hosts quarterly social pet fundraisers benefitting different local organizations. **Loews Hotel** puts on **Costumes on the Woof,** a doggie Halloween party, on the hotel terrace every October.

Atlanta Humane Society hosts an annual **Pet Parade** that draws thousands of dogs and their humans every May, as well as the annual fashion show **Doggies on the Catwalk,** billed as the "best doggone event of the season." About 600 pets and their people turn out for **Splish Splash Doggie Bash,** when pooches can swim in Piedmont Park's aquatic center the first weekend of October, before the pool is cleaned and closed for the season.

UNIQUE ACTIVITY

The grounds of the **Jimmy Carter Library & Museum** are an animal lover's delight, and your pooch can join you on a stroll around the 35 acres of ponds, rolling grounds, and wildlife that includes geese, ducks, hawks, and blue herons. jimmycarterlibrary.gov

Emergency Veterinarian
VCA Pets Are People Too Veterinary Hospital—vcahospitals.com/pets-are-people-too-atlanta;
404-875-7387

Stay All Pups Welcome

■ *Loews Atlanta Hotel (Midtown):* Loews Loves Pets program provides pet room-service menu, pet toys, bedding, leashes, collars, pet place mats, water bowls, treats, doggie poop bags, dog-walking routes, and pet walking and petsitting service. Two dogs/no size restriction. Fee. loewshotels.com/atlanta

■ *W Hotels of Atlanta (Downtown, Midtown, and Buckhead):* P.A.W. (Pets Are Welcome) program at all three properties provides custom pet bed, pet toy, in-house-made turndown treat, dog-walking service, food and water bowls, floor mat. Three dogs/40 lb each max. Fee. whotelsofatlanta.com

■ *Mandarin Oriental:* Plush pet beds and turndown service, with bottled water for the dog bowls. One pet/ 20 lb max. An English garden for canines. mandarinoriental.com/atlanta

■ *Hotel Indigo Atlanta Midtown:* Canine Cocktail Hour every Tuesday throughout the summer. Two dogs/no size restriction. Fee. ihg.com/hotelindigo/hotels/us/en/atlanta/atlfx/hoteldetail

■ *The Westin Buckhead Atlanta:* Signature Westin Heavenly dog bed, food and water bowls. No number restriction/over 40 lb requires approval. Fee. westinbuckheadatlanta.com

■ *Renaissance Atlanta Midtown Hotel (Midtown):* Water dish at front door, homemade dog biscuits at front desk, and ultra-plush dog bed in lobby. Complimentary personalized dog tag and dog treats, pet bowls upon request, and pet amenity delivered to your room. Petsitting, grooming, walking, and pet massage services can be arranged. Two dogs/no size restriction. Fee. marriott.com/hotels/travel/atlbd-renaissance-atlanta-midtown-hotel/

Baltimore, Maryland

B altimore's Inner Harbor attracts tourists like crazy, but to fully enjoy Maryland's largest city with your favorite canine companion, let your pooch sniff around the various unique and vibrant neighborhoods that combine to make this Charm City. Fell's Point, Federal Hill, Hampden, Canton, and the happening Harbor East are just a few of the quarters with dog-friendly offerings in this walkable metropolis.

PLAY

Your pooch can kick up its paws at South Baltimore's **Locust Point Dog Park,** in the southeast corner of Latrobe Park behind the basketball courts. There's a water slide but no separate areas for big and small dogs. Therefore, every day from 9 a.m. to 10 a.m. and 3 p.m. to 4 p.m. the park welcomes only small and senior dogs. **Canton Dog Park** (South Bouldin and Toone Streets), in East Baltimore, has two sections, shade, and pickup bags. **Patterson Park Dog Park** is inside Patterson Park, one of the oldest parks in Baltimore.

Paw Point Dog Park, inside Robert E. Lee Memorial Park, requires membership to its one-acre, off-leash, swim and play park, which is open from sunrise to sunset. Membership allows entrance for two licensed/vaccinated dogs. Out-of-staters can apply, but be sure to allow at least two weeks for processing.

Outside the Baltimore city limits, but worth the drive (about 20 miles from Baltimore's Inner Harbor) to see your pooch doggie paddle, is **Dog Beach** at John H. Downs Memorial Park in Pasadena. Choose from the abundance of dog-friendly hiking trails at several parks, including the aforementioned Robert E. Lee Park. On the National Register of Historic Places is **Druid Hill Park,** known for its rolling, tree-lined lawns complete with water features. Baltimore's public parks welcome pups on leashes no longer than six feet.

For a unique journey, take your tyke on **Gwynns Falls Trail,** an urban, multi-use, 15-mile trail that connects more than 30 neighborhoods in west and southwest Baltimore with parks, unique environmental elements, and historic landmarks. Dogs must be on a leash no longer than eight feet.

SIT

When a blueberry facial is in order, head to **Hair Off the Dog Grooming Salon & Spa** in Canton, which also has a retail section. Dare to be different at **Doggie Style** in Federal Hill, where stylist Jessica Zell does feather extensions and hair coloring. The **Downtown Dog Resort & Spa** handles your doggie day care and overnight boarding and grooming needs and features a jungle gym, toys, a doggie treadmill, an indoor hydrotherapy pool, and outdoor kiddie pools for pups to cool off. **Charm City Dogs** offers cageless day care and boarding, grooming, plus a dog cam so you can watch what Fifi is doing.

HAUTE DOG

Doggie Style in Federal Hill carries stylish apparel, leashes, and collars for city chic canines, as well as freshly baked cookies and grooming products. **Dogma,** with locations in Canton, Mount Washington, and Locust Point, carries specialty dog products and provides services, including self-serve bathing stations. For pet food and supplies, head to **Howl,** in Hampden, which prides itself on its nutrition

Stay
All Pups Welcome

■ *Hotel Monaco Baltimore, A Kimpton Hotel (Downtown):* Dog bed, food and water bowls, and treats provided. Offers dog walking, doggie day care, grooming, emergency veterinarian hotline. No number/size restrictions. monaco-baltimore.com

■ *Four Seasons Baltimore (Harbor East):* Dog bed, treats, and dog biscuits upon arrival. Two dogs/25 lb each max. fourseasons.com/baltimore

■ *Hilton Baltimore (Inner Harbor):* Bed and treats. Two dogs/75 lb each max. Fee. www3.hilton.com/en/hotels/maryland/hilton-baltimore-BWICCHH/index.html

■ *Royal Sonesta Harbor Court (Inner Harbor):* Full access to hotel grounds. Two dogs/40 lb combined max. Fee. sonesta.com/Baltimore

expertise and offers a self-service dog wash.

CHOW TIME

You don't have to sacrifice scenery when you bring your sidekick to a restaurant in Baltimore. In Harbor East, enjoy waterfront views on the seasonal patio at **Wit and Wisdom,** at **A Tavern by Michael Mina,** located inside the Four Seasons Hotel, and at **Cinghiale.** Also in the Inner Harbor, **James Joyce Irish Pub and Restaurant** welcomes dogs outside. Expect to see dogs and their people at brunches at **Miss Shirley's Café** (Inner Harbor and Roland Park) and **City Café** in Midtown Belvedere. In historic Fells Point, **Thames Street Oyster House** and **Kooper's Tavern** have pet-friendly patios. **Pitango Gelato** has been known to offer pups vanilla gelato, but for baked treats for dogs, stop by **Lamill Coffee** inside the Four Seasons.

> ### Insider Tip
>
> "A fun thing to do in Baltimore is walk or run with your dog along the Inner Harbor. Beau, my six-year-old Maltese, loves chasing the birds and smelling the water. Robert E. Lee Park, across from the Harbor, has an avid dog group also. After walking along the Inner Harbor, Bagby's is a delicious pizza place that allows your dog to sit out in the patio."
> — SOPHIE ELISSEEFF

COME

There's no better way to enjoy Baltimore than from the water. Your furry friend can come along with you on **Cruises on the Bay by Watermark** as well as **Seadog Cruises,** which operate April through October. Bark your calendar for these annual events: **Pets on Parade** hosted by the American Visionary Art Museum (Fourth of July); Maryland SPCA's **March for the Animals** at Druid Hill Park (spring); and **Howl-O-Ween** at the Can Company in Canton (October). **Howl** pet store in Hampden also has fun events from adoptions to informational seminars to dog psychics to ice cream socials.

UNIQUE ACTIVITY

Have a date night with your favorite canine companion at **Bengies Drive-In Theatre,** opened in 1956, which boasts one of the country's largest movie screens at 52 feet high and 120 feet wide, with a perfect picture, and shows double and triple features. Pets permitted on a leash no longer than six feet. bengies.com

Emergency Veterinarian
Falls Road Animal Hospital—fallsroad.com; 410-825-9100

Brunswick Islands, North Carolina

F or years, generations have watched spectacular sunrises and sunsets from North Carolina's Brunswick Islands, a chain of narrow barrier islands and several inland towns in the southern part. With Fido a full-fledged family member, he too can enjoy these islands, as different as their names. From dazzling Holden Beach to exclusive Bald Head Island to commercialized Oak Island, there's something for every dog.

🐾 PLAY

Canines can cavort on all six of Brunswick Island's beaches, but the rules vary. On **Bald Head Island,** reachable only by ferry or private vessel, a leash is necessary sunset to sunrise. At all other times, pets are permitted off leash but must remain under supervision. **Caswell Beach,** the least populated of the beaches, permits pups off leash but under handlers' direction from dawn until 9 a.m.; additionally, from the first of October through the end of April, dogs under control are allowed from 3 p.m. until dark on the beach. Bowwows are banned from **Holden Beach** from May 20 to September 10, except between 5 p.m. and 9 a.m. Your furry friend can frolic on **Oak Island**'s 10 miles of beaches year-round if on leash, and without a leash October 15 to March 15 from 6 a.m. until 9 a.m. Even privileged pets aren't permitted on **Ocean Isle Beach** between 9 a.m. and

6 p.m. from Memorial Day through Labor Day. From the Friday before Memorial Day through Labor Day, tail waggers aren't allowed on **Sunset Beach**'s gloriously wide sands between 8 a.m. and 6 p.m. After 6 p.m. and before 8 a.m. during that time period, dogs are allowed on leashes. After Labor Day and before the Friday prior to Memorial Day, dogs are permitted if leashed.

When beaches are off limits or restraints a nuisance, head your hound to the off-leash dog parks. **BARK Park** in Shallotte Park has separate sections for large and small dogs. On Oak Island, **Salty Dog Park** in Bill Smith Park boasts separate areas for large and small dogs, while a dog park within **Templeton Park** has one large area for dogs of all sizes. The 911-acre **Brunswick Nature Park,** in Winnabow, approximately 10 miles from Leland on N.C. 133, offers miles of hiking trails for dogs on leash. There's also a kayak/canoe launch site, should you want to spend an afternoon on the water with man's best friend.

SIT

If you plan to spend the day on the beach or golf course, drop your paw-footed pal off for **Doggie Day Camp** at **Doggone Healthy** in Calabash. Owned by veterinarian Dr. Ernie Ward, an expert on pet fitness, weight loss, and preventive medicine, Doggone Healthy is a grooming, behavior center, and pet store. **Magnolia's Bed & Biscuit Luxury Pet Resort & Daycare** in Leland offers doggie day care, and grooming. Grooming is also available at **Capeside Animal Hospital** and **Splish Splash Dog Wash** (self-service and professional) in Leland.

HAUTE DOG

Doggie life vests can be purchased at **Four Legs Good Pet Boutique** in Southport, which carries apparel, accessories, locally made doggie bakery goodies, and toys for the trendy dog. Pick up healthy food and treats, supplements, and toys at **Zeetlegoo's Pet & People Store** in Southport. **Wags & Whiskers** in Shallotte stocks a slew of products and supplies and provides grooming, boarding, and doggie day care.

CHOW TIME

The leggiest member of your group can join you for dining at **Calabash**

> ## Insider Tip
>
> "Oak Island has a reputation for having dog-friendly beaches, but our favorite spot is on the north side at the far west end, called **the Point**. Since there are no breaking waves, our dogs aren't intimidated and leap in the water and paddle away. At low tide, Foose, our Golden Retriever mix, and Captain Spriggs, our Jack Russell mix, can easily swim across the narrow channel with us and run around their own private island of sand, known as Sheep Island."
> — JOHNNA JALOT

Garden Tea Room, a Victorian-style tea house in downtown Calabash; **Archibald's Deli** in Holden Beach; **P.T.'s Olde Fashioned Grille** in Leland; and **The Pepperoni Grill** in Boiling Spring Lakes.

COME

Visit pristine **Bald Head Island,** where no cars are allowed, the site of the state's oldest remaining lighthouse, Old Baldy (circa 1817). Take the dog-friendly Bald Head Island Ferry across the Cape Fear River from Southport and rent a bike with a Croozer dog trailer from **Coastal Urge,** which also sells a full line of water toys. The **Sunset Beach Concert Series** allows well-behaved dogs to attend the shows.

Annual events include the Brunswick Forest Veterinary Hospital **Hound Hustle 10K and 5K,** which includes a one-mile **Trot with Spot,** in Leland in April; **Bark at the Beach,** a dog walk that is part of the annual **Festival by the Sea Parade** held in Holden Beach in October; and **Festival of Fur,** held in May in Sunset Beach.

UNIQUE ACTIVITY

You and your adventurous ally (up to 35 pounds) can explore the creeks, channels, and waterways of the Brunswick Islands together on **Summertide Adventure Tours'** pet-friendly **kayak tours**. Doggie life vest provided. summertidetours.com

Emergency Veterinarian
Seaside Animal Care—seasidevet.com; 910-579-5550 ▪ After hours: Animal Emergency Hospital of the Strand—animalemergencymyrtlebeach.com; 843-445-9797 ▪ Animal Emergency & Trauma Hospital of Wilmington (AETH)—ecvrwilmingtonnc.com; 910-791-7387(PETS)

Stay All Pups Welcome

▪ *The Winds Resort Beach Club (Ocean Isle Beach):* Two dogs/30 lb each max. Fee. thewinds.com

▪ *Brunswick Plantation & Golf Resort (Calabash):* No number/size restrictions. Fee. brunswickvillas.com

▪ *Coastal Vacation Resorts at Holden Beach:*
One dog/no size restriction. Fee. coastalvacation resorts.com

▪ *Best Western PLUS Westgate Inn & Suites (Leland):* Two dogs/40 lb each max. Fee. bestwestern leland.com

▪ *Holiday Inn Express Leland:* Dog bed, water
and food bowls, and special treats upon arrival. Two dogs/50 lb each max. Fee. hieleland.com

▪ *Comfort Suites (South-port):* Welcome bag includes a treat, chew stick, or toy. Two dogs /no size restriction. Fee. comfortsuites.com/ hotel/nc351

Carolina Beach, North Carolina

With a visit to Carolina Beach in southern North Carolina, your pooch can earn serious barking rights at your local dog park by learning to hang 20 at the Tony Silvagni Surf School. The professional's surfer school is helping lure more surfers and paddleboarders to this family-friendly coastal town at the northern end of Pleasure Island. In addition to riding the waves, your furry pal can romp off leash at **Freeman Park,** at the northern end of Carolina Beach, between October 1 and March 31, as long as he is under voice command and you are within a reasonable distance. Although you must keep Rover on leash from April 1 to September 30, he can still frolic in the waves. There are also off-leash dog parks at **Mike Chappell Park** in Carolina Beach and in nearby Kure Beach at the **Gurney Hood Dog Barking Lot** adjacent to Joe Eakes Park. Carolina Beach State Park boasts 6-plus miles of dog-friendly trails, and you'll find plenty of four-legged companions walking around the lake at **Carolina Beach Lake Park,** next to the pooch-friendly **Hang Ten Grill.**

Charleston, South Carolina

History and hospitality collide in Charleston, or Chucktown if you're on an intimate basis with the canine-loving city epitomizing the South. Cobblestone streets, secret gardens, and talk of ghosts give the place a romantic flair. Throw in Lowcountry cuisine and pet-friendly beaches, and you have a destination where you and your four-legged sidekick can have a howling time reliving the past.

🐾 PLAY

Charleston boasts five nearby beach towns, each with its own intricate rules about canines cavorting on the beach. Fifteen minutes from downtown Charleston is **Folly Beach,** a.k.a. "the Edge of America." Rover can't come on the beach from May 1 to September 30 between 10 a.m. and 6 p.m., and if he does, the fines are stiff. In the off-season, though, from October 1 through April 30, Rover can run, walk, fetch, and swim—but only under control. You may be inclined to let your pooch off leash because you see other canines frolicking freely on Folly, which is about 6 miles long, but don't. Special off-leash licenses went to 100 approved people, whose privileged pups can go leashless at various times from September through May. You'll find washing stations and doggie water fountains under the pier and by the public beach.

Pooches are permitted off leash at **Isle of Palms,** a family beach about 7 miles long, from 5 a.m. to 9 a.m. April 1 to Sept. 14 and 4 p.m. until 10 a.m. Sept. 15 to March 31. And remember to keep the leash in your hand and your sidekick under voice command. At other times, use a leash even in the water.

Kiawah Island, a 10,000-acre barrier island with 10 miles of uninterrupted beaches, lets furry friends frolic freely year-round in two "Dog Use Areas" on its beach, one located east of the Beach Club and the other west of Beachwalker Park. In between those two is another area that permits pups off leash November 1 to March 15, as long as you keep your sidekick under voice control and a leash in your possession. Keep him on leash March 16 to October 31. Anytime you're around the island's ponds, use a leash, because it's alligator territory. **Beachwalker Park,** one of the top beaches in the country, requires dogs to be on leash year-round and features a dog-wash station plus dog-friendly picnic and snack areas.

Anytime you're around [Kiawah Island's] ponds, use a leash, because it's alligator territory.

On **Sullivan Island,** which lies at the mouth of the Charleston Harbor, hounds must have a valid Sullivan's Island permit, available at Town Hall. From October 1 to April 30, off-leash hours are 5 a.m. to noon and on-leash hours noon to 5 a.m. From May 1 to September 30, off-leash times are 5 a.m. to 10 a.m. No pups allowed from 10 a.m. to 6 p.m., but leashed tykes are allowed from 6 p.m. to 5 a.m.

And then there's **Seabrook Island,** a private, oceanfront community with no hotels—only rental properties—or commercial development but wide beaches where dogs can romp in the waves. There's a designated beach area for dogs (left at end of North Beach Boardwalk) that permits pups off leash before 10 a.m. and after 5 p.m. between May 1 and October 31. They can be off leash at any time from November 1 to April 30. Outside of the designated areas, your furry friend has to be on a lead at all times from May 1 to October 31. Then from November 1 to April 30, leashes are required between 10 a.m. and 5 p.m., but otherwise dogs can kick up their paws without a lead.

Time of year doesn't matter at **Morris Island,** an uninhabited, 840-acre island at the entrance of Charleston Harbor. Canines on leash are always permitted. However, the island is accessible only by boat. Adventure Harbor Tours permits pups.

On the mainland, you'll want to check out these off-leash dog parks in Charleston: **James Island County Park,**

North Charleston Wannamaker County Park, and Mount Pleasant Palmetto Islands County Park. All have separate areas for big and small dogs. James Island features a large lake where your barker can flaunt his dog paddle skills; the park is also a terrific place to take your tyke for a hike on leash. Hiking is also plentiful on the nature trails and paved trails at the 943-acre Palmetto Islands County Park. Pets must be on leash.

Worth keeping your pooch on leash for is a visit to White Point Gardens, part of The Battery, a gorgeous place to take paws after exploring the historic district. Marion Square in Charleston and Shem Creek Park on Coleman Blvd. in Mount Pleasant (on the northwest side of the creek) are also worth sniffing around. In downtown Charleston, a fenced run at the northern end of Hazel Parker Playground is a neighborhood favorite. You are not allowed to walk your dog on the Ravenel (Cooper River) Bridge.

SIT

Dogs can clean up well at Coats and Tails Dog Grooming (Charleston), owned by certified master groomer Nancy Caldwell, and at Barks N' Bubbles in West Ashley. When tennis, golf, or spas are on your agenda, doggie day care is available. Pooch Palace Boarding & Daycare in Mount Pleasant offers just what the name says, plus grooming. My Three Dogs provides doggie day care, grooming, and boarding; certainly your pampered pup will appreciate the perfectly chilled pool during the dog days of summer and taking a relaxing hydro-surge bath before you pick him up.

HAUTE DOG

A must-stop for pet parents is Alpha Dog Omega Cat. This exclusive boutique in the historic shopping district is just as much for pets as the people who love them. All

---

Stay All Pups Welcome

■ *Wentworth Mansion (Downtown Charleston):* Milk-Bones, food and water bowls, plus packet of information on local pet-friendly places. No number/size restrictions. Fee. wentworthmansion.com

■ *John Rutledge House Inn (Downtown Charleston):* Welcome bag of treats at check-in, food and water bowls. Can recommend dog walkers. Pet concierge available. Two dogs/no size restriction. Fee. johnrutledgehouseinn.com

■ *Charleston Place (Downtown Charleston):* No number/size restrictions. Fee. charlestonplace.com

■ *The Resort Villas at Kiawah Island Golf Resort:* About 20 percent of the villas are pet friendly. No number/size restrictions. Note: The Sanctuary at Kiawah Island Golf Resort does not allow pets. Fee. kiawahresort.com

Is Well, with locations in West Ashley, James Island, and Mount Pleasant, takes a holistic approach to pet care and offers products and grooming. **Dolittle's** (West Ashley, Mount Pleasant, and Summerville) carries all-natural foods and has a self-service wash, while **Palmetto Paws** (Mount Pleasant) offers a wide selection of holistic and organic pet foods, supplements, accessories, and gifts, as well as a do-it-yourself bath and grooming area.

CHOW TIME

You and your tail wagger can sit on the front porch at **Poogan's Porch,** named after a dog that once resided in this restored Victorian that dates back to 1888. Also in downtown Charleston, the private patio at **Il Cortile del Re,** the courtyard at **Kudu Coffee and Craft Beer,** and **39 Rue de Jean** are pet-friendly. Take in the views with your sidekick on the pet-friendly patios at **Red's Ice House on Shem Creek** (Mount Pleasant), which also throws regular Yappy Hours, and **Red's Ice House Bohicket Marina** (Seabrook Island), where the sunset is amazing. On Folly Beach, **Lost Dog Café** and **Lil' Mama's** and are pet-friendly options.

COME

Being that this is the hospitable South, many of the shops along King Street in downtown welcome four-legged shoppers. The **Charleston Farmer's Market** in Marion Square, held Saturdays from April to December, draws nearly as many four-legged visitors as bipeds. Historic **Drayton Hall** not only welcomes well-behaved pets on leash, but a few of the Friends of Drayton Hall have pals with fur. Your pooch can't go on the house tour, but you two can do a self-guided nature walk. You can also take your pup on leash to **Magnolia Plantation & Gardens,** founded by the Draytons in 1676. Experience two views of Charleston with a combo **Old South Carriage Co.** ride and **SpiritLine Harbor Cruise.** After a one-hour narrated horse-drawn carriage tour over 30 blocks of historic Charleston, take a 90-minute narrated leisure tour around Charleston Harbor.

Convivial canines can mingle with others during Yappy Hour at **James Island County Park,** on select Thursday afternoons/evenings throughout the spring, summer,

> ### Insider Tip
>
> "The area west of Beachwalker Park on Kiawah Island is one of the more beautiful off-leash dog beaches on the East Coast. Because it's on a spit of the island not recommended for human swimming due to riptides, dogs here do not compete much with large picnicking families. The freedom and the joy experienced by my dogs, Casper, Bam-Bam, and Zorro, as they chase each other down the shoreline, stopping to marvel at a washed-up stingray and then playing in the foam, is indescribable. One major caveat: There is very limited public parking at Beachwalker Park. One must come early—even before the park opens."
> — DONNA POWELL, *charlestondoggytown.com*

and fall. Party animals won't want to miss **Pet Fest,** a two-day pet festival with dock div-ing, exhibitions, demonstrations, contests, and live music that takes place every spring in Palmetto Islands County Park. The Seabrook Island Dog Owner's Group puts on an annual **April Beach Walk** to benefit a local charity. Keep up with the local happenings on CharlestonDoggyTown.com.

UNIQUE ACTIVITY

Pack a lunch for you and Fido and take a one-of-a-kind day trip to **Charleston Tea Plan-tation,** a tea garden and true working tea farm. Spread over 127 acres on Wadmalaw Island, the picturesque plantation welcomes leashed dogs on the grounds. Take a trol-ley ride through fields filled with tea plants as far as the eye can see. The tea shop is off limits to four-legged visitors because food is served. charlestonteaplantation.com

Emergency Veterinarian
Charleston Veterinary Referral Center—charlestonvrc.com/emergency; 843-614-VETS (8387)

Decatur, Alabama

The classic southern charm and hospitality shown to visitors to Decatur, in northern Alabama on the Tennessee River, is extended to four-legged tourists as well. Cultured canines on leashes can stroll through exhibits at the **Carnegie Visual Arts Center.** Hounds into history can have a tail-waggin' time on the **Historic Walking Tour,** which includes one of the largest concentration of Victorian-era cottages and bungalows in Alabama within two of Decatur's five historic districts listed on the National Register of Historic Places. You and your leashed sidekick can go for a picturesque 3-mile trek at **Point Mallard Park,** along a trail that winds along the river. Afterward, grab lunch on the pet-friendly patio at **Albany Bistro** in the Historic Albany District. Although the water activities beckon guests to Decatur during the summer, winter is the peak time to visit the dog-friendly **Wheeler National Wildlife Refuge,** a 35,000-acre refuge with Alabama's only significant concentration of wintering Southern James Bay Canada geese and winter habitat for the state's largest duck population. The locals put their creative talents on display when they dress up their pets in festive costumes for the **Carnival Canines on Parade,** a Mardi Gras–style celebration the Saturday before Ash Wednesday, and the annual **Walk Your Paws** to benefit the local Animal Friends Humane Society. Pet-friendly lodging is available at the **Home-Towne Suites, Quality Inn,** and **La Quinta Inn & Suites.**

Fort Myers/Sanibel Beaches, Florida

You know your four-legged friend is in for a tail-waggin' time on the beaches of Fort Myers and Sanibel just by hearing names like Dog Beach, Pooch Park, K-9 Corral, and Barkingham Dog Park. Those are just a few of the places where canines can kick up their paws in this unspoiled southwest Florida island sanctuary, which includes Sanibel and Captiva Islands, Fort Myers Beach, Fort Myers, Bonita Springs, Estero, Cape Coral, Pine Island, Boca Grande and outer islands, North Fort Myers, and inland, Lehigh Acres, with more than one million acres of pristine beaches and award-winning state parks and wildlife preserves. Sanibel is famous for its seashells. The Sanibel Stoop, an island shell game, puts people in position not only to pick up shells, but to rub Rover's head as well.

🐾 PLAY

Lee County Parks & Recreation facilities, all open dawn to dusk, boast several designated areas where canines can cavort off and on leash. The prime locale is in Fort Myers at **Dog Beach**. As the only beach in Lee County where Fido can frolic freely, dogs can romp in the Gulf waters unleashed from 7 a.m. to sunset and then rinse off in the doggie shower station. In east Fort Myers, King and Queenie can play at **Barkingham Park,** a

1.5-acre, off-leash area inside Buckingham Community Park that has a separate area for shy or small dogs. Also at the park, hounds on leashes can stroll around a mitigation lake and through primitive back trails of pine and palmetto habitats. Other off-leash dog parks are **Woof-A-Hatchee,** inside Wa-Ke Hatchee Park in Fort Myers, and **Pooch Park,** inside Judd Park in North Fort Myers. At **John Yarbrough Linear Park** (formally Ten Mile Linear Park) in Fort Myers, there's a slender green space with paths where you can skate, run, walk, or bike with your pal on leash.

In Estero, the 2-acre **K-9 Corral** in the southeast corner of Estero Community Park features small and large dog areas with an abundance of shade. **Causeway Island Park** on Sanibel and Captiva islands offers 10 acres for tykes to play on leashes. Portions of **Caloosahatchee Creeks Preserve** and parts of **Prairie Pines Preserve,** both in North Fort Myers, also permit leashed dogs. As long as your furry friend is on a leash and under control, bring him or her to the beaches on Sanibel Island and the 7.5-mile beach in the town of Fort Myers Beach. Both **Centennial and Clement Parks,** in Fort Myers, allow dogs on leashes, as does **Wagging Tails Dog Park** in Cape Coral.

Most of the area's state parks welcome dogs on leashes, but your sidekick isn't allowed on beaches or playgrounds. Hiking trails are fair game. Take your tyke to **Cayo Costa State Park** and **Lovers Key State Park.** The **J. N. "Ding" Darling National Wildlife Preserve** on Sanibel, famous for bird-watching, allows dogs on leashes of no longer than six feet to prance on Wildlife Drive.

SIT

For professional grooming and doggie day care, head to **Glamour Paws** in Fort Myers, used by the Gulf Coast Humane Society. **All American Pet Resort** in Fort Myers, open 24 hours, provides day care, cage-free boarding, grooming, webcams, and televisions. **DipidyDawg,** a gourmet dog bakery, boutique, and groomer in Estero's Coconut Point offers its customers petsitting while they shop the mall or go to the movie theater next door.

HAUTE DOG

In addition to stylish apparel DipidyDawg also offers carriers; collars; harnesses; leashes; spa products; and nutritious, natural, holistic, and organic food. **Island**

Stay
All Pups Welcome

■ *Hyatt Regency Coconut Point Resort & Spa (Bonita Springs):* The Paws & Palms program provides bed, treats, food and water bowls, doggie room-service menu, and a special walking area. Two dogs/50 lb combined max. Fee. coconutpoint.hyatt.com

■ *The Gasparilla Inn & Club (Boca Grande):* The inn has a Gulf-front dog park with grass. No number/size restrictions. Fee. the-gasparilla-inn.com

■ *Royal Shell Vacations (Sanibel):* Upmarket and midmarket pet-friendly home and condo rentals. royalshell.com

Paws on Sanibel Island carries healthy food for pets, gourmet treats, a doggie bakery, and unique gifts for pet lovers. In Bonita Springs, **Pet Paradise,** in Bay Landing Shopping Center, stocks a good selection of food, vitamins, supplements, toys, and treats.

CHOW TIME

Dine stylishly with Fifi at your feet at **The Veranda,** in the historic section of Fort Myers. **Bistro 41** is one of the eateries in the Bell Tower Shops that allows pets. **Sweet Bean Coffee Cafe** and **McGregor Café** also welcome dogs in their outdoor areas. On Sanibel Island, there's **Over Easy Café,** a breakfast and lunch fave, **Cip's Place,** which loves furry friends, and **The Island Cow.** Right across from Over Easy Café in the Bailey's Center, you'll find **Zebra Frozen Yogurt,** which provides pups complimentary yogurt in dog cups, pickup bags, water bowls, and a shaded porch. In Bonita Springs, **Pinchers Crab Shack,** and **Big Hickory Fishing Nook Seafood Grill** at the north end of Bonita Beach have dog-friendly patios. In Estero, **Hemingway's Island Grille** and **Bice Grand Café** are among the eateries at Coconut Point to permit pets on their patios.

COME

Your four-legged friend is welcome at the majority of the 140-plus stores in Coconut Point, where water stations and plastic bag dispensers are sprinkled throughout the open-air mall. **Dog's Night Out** takes place the first Thursday of every month outside of **DipidyDawg Bakery and Boutique.** In Fort Myers, the **Bell Tower Shops** has regular pet events, including a Yappy Hour the second Friday of every month to benefit the Gulf Coast Humane Society.

UNIQUE ACTIVITY

Take your pooch for a doggie paddle in this area noted for its kayaking offerings. **Kayak Excursions** has dog-friendly kayak tours, generally departing from Dog Beach. You'll paddle along the mangroves and through the Estero Bay, with opportunities to view dolphins, manatees, a variety of birds, and other undersea life during this two-hour tour that includes a break. kayak-excursions.com

Emergency Veterinarian
Emergency Veterinary Clinic of Ft. Myers—
evcftmyers.com; 239-939-5542

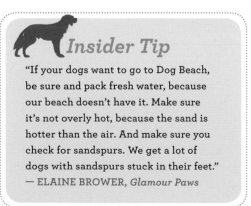

Insider Tip

"If your dogs want to go to Dog Beach, be sure and pack fresh water, because our beach doesn't have it. Make sure it's not overly hot, because the sand is hotter than the air. And make sure you check for sandspurs. We get a lot of dogs with sandspurs stuck in their feet."
— ELAINE BROWER, *Glamour Paws*

Hilton Head, South Carolina

D ogs who prefer checking the base of streetlamps for pee-mail messages will be out of luck on Hilton Head Island. Stars, not streetlights, illuminate the skies on an island that also bans flamboyantly painted buildings and neon to help maintain the natural setting for which this South Carolina retreat is known. A forest filled with palmettos, pines, and live oaks dripping in Spanish moss, this foot-shaped island treasures its rich history. As recognized for its red-and-white-striped Harbour Town Lighthouse in the Sea Pines Resort as it is for its world-class golf courses, Hilton Head also boasts beautiful beaches where man's best friend can dog paddle, pet-friendly restaurants, a canine-loving community, and an array of pet-friendly activities to keep Fido busy during a Lowcountry petcation.

PLAY

Pups can romp on Hilton Head's pristine beaches, among the finest in the country, but not year-round. As long as pooches are under voice control, the town allows dogs to frolic freely during the off-season and before 10 a.m. and after 5 p.m. during the summer. The official beach season runs April 1 through September 30. No pets are permitted between 10 a.m. and 5 p.m. from the Friday before Memorial Day through Labor

Day. Leash Lulu between 10 a.m. and 5 p.m. April 1 through Thursday before Memorial Day and Tuesday after Labor Day through September 30. At all other times, a leash or voice control is necessary. Note that whoever controls the pet is required to remove and dispose of its poop.

Only 12 miles long and 5 miles wide, Hilton Head manages to pack in more than 100 miles of multi-use trails, perfect for leashed dogs, which are also welcome in the town's parks. Pooches in need of more freedom can romp unencumbered at **Chaplin Park Dog Park,** inside Chaplin Community Park, just off William Hilton Parkway between Singleton Beach Road and Burkes Beach Road. Completely fenced and double gated, the town's only dog park is open sunrise to sunset and has separate areas for small and large dogs, benches, trees, mulch ground cover, drinking water, and pickup bags.

Biking along the hard-packed shoreline is a popular activity. Bike rental shops like Hilton Head Outfitters deliver to condos, villas, and hotels. Request a basket or kiddie cart for Fido.

SIT

If you're planning to spend a day golfing or frolicking on the beach on a hot summer day, utilize the doggie day care service at **Southpaw Pet Resort,** a luxury pet boarding and training facility with indoor and outdoor play areas, 20 private suites with individual backyards, and 10 day-care cottages with Kuranda beds and flatscreen televisions. Book posh pets early for a grooming session at the exclusive **Vanity Fur** in the Village at Wexford. On the south end

Stay All Pups Welcome

■ *Omni Oceanfront Resort Hilton Head Island (Palmetto Dunes):* **Provides bed, feeding dishes, treats, toys, a BowWow Welcome note, Pet Walk, a dog-friendly restaurant, and direct access to dog-friendly beach, where dogs are restricted from 9 a.m. to 5 p.m. No number restriction/50 lb each** max. Fee. omnihotels.com/hiltonhead

■ *Westin Hilton Head Island Resort & Spa (Port Royal):* **Provides a Westin Heavenly dog bed plus silver dog bowl. Restricts dogs from its beach from 9 a.m. to 5 p.m. Two dogs/20 lb each max. Fee. westin hiltonheadisland.com**

■ *Hilton Head Rentals & Golf:* **Pet-friendly homes and villas from one to six bedrooms. Plastic, bone-shaped poop bag holders and treats, plus a bowl of cold water provided upon arrival. No number/size restrictions. Fee. hiltonheadvacation .com/hilton-head-pet-friendly-rentals**

of the island, **All About Pets** also offers grooming. DIYers will prefer **Red Rover,** which also offers a full-service "spaw experience" and is the perfect stop after a day at the beach.

🐾 HAUTE DOG

Stop by **Tail-Waggers,** also in the Village at Wexford, to pick up unique pet products and fun pet-themed gifts, as well as pet food made with man-kind fixings, gourmet treats, toys, apparel, beds, leashes, and collars. But it's the doggie bakery, which sells cookies made with only natural ingredients, that makes pooches smile with their tails; Olive, a Basset Hound, greets customers. On the south side of the island, All About Pets also sells food, supplies, and toys. **Jake's Cargo** in South Beach Marina Village offers gifts for pets and the people who love them.

> **Insider Tip**
>
> "When the weather permits, I never miss Sunday brunch at the **British Open Pub** in Wexford Village. The outdoor tables all sport large umbrellas, and my Yorkipoo, Izzie, gets her own chair. Also, **Jarvis Creek Park** is a very nice park with a lake ideal for walking a pet and meeting others for playtime."
> — ANDREA R. PALMER

🐾 CHOW TIME

Furry friends dine in style at **Bistro 17,** a French café on the waterfront overlooking Shelter Cove Marina that offers a doggie dining menu and beautiful custom-made feeding bowls from Art Café in Coligny Plaza. **Skillets Café and Grill** in Coligny Plaza also has a doggie menu that boasts dishes made with human-grade ingredients from Lucky Dog Cuisine. At Skull Creek Boathouse's popular **Marker 13 Buoy Bar,** dogs can take in gorgeous waterfront sunset views from the outdoor deck, which is shielded from the elements.

Other popular dog-friendly restaurants include **Black Marlin Bayside Grill** in Palmetto Bay Marina, which offers plenty of outdoor seating to watch boats sail by, and **Palmetto Bay Sunrise Café,** known for its breakfast and for treating canines like local celebrities. And at the Omni Hilton Head Oceanfront Resort in Palmetto Dunes, pets and their people can enjoy breathtaking views of the Atlantic Ocean together at the **Buoy Bar** or lounge on the wraparound patio outside **Palmetto Market,** which serves breakfast, lunch, and dinner. Despite its name, the famed Salty Dog Café in South Beach Marina does not welcome its own.

🐾 COME

Take Fifi on a side trip to historic **Daufuskie Island,** just 1 nautical mile from Hilton Head and reachable only by ferry. As long as pups will sit in a golf cart, the mode of transportation on Daufuskie, they may ride to the enchanting 5-mile island for free on

Calibogue Cruises, which leaves from Hilton Head's Broad Creek Marina and docks at Freeport Marina.

Well-behaved pups on leashes are also welcome at **HarbourFest,** Shelter Cove Harbour's signature summer event. It takes place seven nights a week from mid-June through mid-August, features live entertainment, food, and arts and crafts from an array of vendors, and is free. Note that there are fireworks, which cause anxiety in some dogs.

Every May, the Hilton Head Humane Association hosts **Dog Walk on the Beach** at Coligny Beach. Frisbee dog entertainment, contests, give-aways, food, dancing, and entertainment by a local deejay make for a fun morning. In September, *Hilton Head Monthly* magazine puts on a **Pet Expo** with local vendors, a pet photographer, pet contests, pet adoption, food, drinks, and live music.

For pet-friendly shopping experiences, swing by **South Beach Marina** and **Harbour Town Yacht Basin,** the popular Sea Pines Resort destination where the island's landmark lighthouse sits proudly. Hang around to enjoy spectacular sunsets with your favorite canine companion.

Well-behaved pups on leashes are also welcome at HarbourFest, Shelter Cove Harbour's signature summer event.

UNIQUE ACTIVITY

Bring Spot along to spot Atlantic bottlenose dolphins on Vagabond Cruise's 90-minute, narrated **Ocean Dolphin Cruise,** which takes passengers through Calibogue Sound to the headwaters of the Atlantic Ocean. vagabondcruise.com

Emergency Veterinarian
Plantation Animal Hospital, LLC—plantationanimalhospital.vetsuite.com; 843-681-4586

Miami, Florida

Dogs don't need to see in full color to know they're in Miami. They'll know by the coifed canines in couture on Lincoln Road, where pooch watching rivals people watching. The fashionable Miami Beach promenade is just one of the many places you'll want to flaunt your fashionable, furry friend when you visit this pulsating paradise that caters to pets. Privileged pooches can enjoy a doggie brunch, South Beach's sizzling hotel pool scene, and beautiful beaches.

PLAY

On the weekends, cool canines hang at the designated doggie area at **Lifeguard Tower 3** at Haulover Beach Park, located directly across from Haulover Dog Park. (Access from parking lot #4, located on the east side of Collins Avenue on the south end of the park.) Pups can play on Saturdays and Sundays from 8 a.m. to 3 p.m. Fido can be off leash if he's in the water with you, but you must immediately leash after swimming. A canine wash-down station is available. If your pooch doesn't need to be with the in-crowd, visit lovely **North Shore Open Space Park** (Collins and 85th Street), which boasts a beachfront, off-leash dog park. Rover can romp on leash at **Hobie Beach** (also known as Windsurfer Beach), en route to Key Biscayne, just off the Rickenbacker Causeway.

The shallow water suits dogs that want to play in the surf. Pups are also allowed on the entire stretch of the **Rickenbacker Causeway Beach,** which extends the causeway's length from Downtown Miami to Key Biscayne. Leashes are required, but try telling that to the beachgoers.

With the reduced dog-friendly beach offerings here, a good number of pet parents risk a fine during the day by smuggling their pint-size pooches onto the beach under blankets, then after sundown walking them on the beach and along the Miami Beach Boardwalk, a no-no.

When it comes to dog parks, Fido has a slew of options, including parks with agility training equipment, jumps, and ramps. The popular ones include **Flamingo Bark Park** in South Beach, open 7 a.m. to 9 a.m. and featuring two doggie play areas, double-gated entrances, drinking stations for pooches and their people, biodegradable baggie stations, waste receptacles, and plenty of benches with shade; **Dog Chow Dog Park** in Coconut Grove's Kennedy Park, also with two sections, restrooms, shade, benches, and water; **Haulover Dog Park,** where there is a $2 user fee with a dog ($5 without one), drinking fountains for doggies and humans, and small and big dog areas within the 3.3-acre area; and Tropical Park's **Bark Park** (West Miami), near a small lake and featuring a cooling water spray station, tire jumps and other play equipment, and separate areas for small and large dogs.

Canines can also cavort in 13 "dog-friendly parks" in Miami-Dade County as long as they are on leash. Pickup bags and wastebaskets are available.

Oleta River State Park on Biscayne Bay in North Miami offers great hiking and jogging trails for you and your leashed pooch, while **South Dade Trail,** part of the Rails-to-Trails Conservancy, stretches 20 miles and is a popular mixed-use route that runs along the South Miami-Dade Busway between Florida City and Kendall Drive/ SE 88th Street, just north of the Dadeland South Metrorail station. Or simply let your privileged

> *When it comes to dog parks, Fido has a slew of options, including parks with agility training equipment, jumps, and ramps.*

Insider Tip

"My Rat Terrier JP goes everywhere with me, including out to dinner. His favorite spot is the **Burger & Beer Joint.** My boyfriend and I sit outside at a picnic table and split a Thunder Road burger, while JP devours a bowl of ground beef and rice under the table. B&B serves this free meal to all of their K-9 guests!"

— AMANDA BUSH

pooch prance down Lincoln Road like all the other diva dogs in South Beach.

SIT

Before you let Fifi strut down Lincoln Road, book an appointment at **Barks & Tales Dog Spa** (Edgewater), **Ace Grooming & Boarding, 4 Paws Only** (Shorecrest), or **Salon Pooch-ini** (Bay Harbor Islands). Barks & Tales, Ace, and **Wags-to-Wishes Doggie Day Care** (North Bay Village on Key Biscayne) also provide doggie day care should you want to spend an afternoon sunning on a non-dog beach.

HAUTE DOG

You can't get a barkarita at **The Dog Bar,** but you can find stylish apparel, including Florida essentials like sundresses and life jackets, a huge selection of leashes, harnesses, and collars, raw frozen food, treats, travel products, and professional grooming at this boutique with three outposts in Midtown Miami, Coral Gables, and South Beach. Your Fido doesn't have to be a foodie to appreciate the dog forks adorned with a Swarovski crystal and the doggie high chairs that clip onto your table for sale at the **Doggie Bag Café and Pet Boutique** (Little River). **Animal Crackers** (Downtown Miami) carries healthy food, treats, supplements, and toys. **Bleau Signature,** inside the Fontainebleau resort, sells branded doggie apparel, toys, and souvenirs.

CHOW TIME

A plethora of pets fills the outdoor patios of restaurants on Lincoln Road's pedestrian promenade. Bowsers of all breeds can be found lounging at **Meat Market Miami Beach, The Café @ Books & Books** on Lincoln Road, **Van Dyke Café,** and **Spris Restaurant.** At **Shake Shack,** order a Pooch-ini (ShackBurger dog biscuits made by all-natural dog biscuit company Bocce's Bakery, peanut butter sauce, and vanilla custard) for your pooch. **Michael's Genuine Food & Drink** (Design District) serves complimentary dog biscuits made by executive pastry chef Hedy Goldsmith. Pet-setters will enjoy a trip to **The Standard Spa** in South Beach, where furry friends are allowed but no children. Dine al fresco with your pooch at the Standard's **Bayside Grill** or, for the ultimutt splurge, purchase a pool day pass so you and your sidekick can take in the scene that epitomizes South Beach living.

In Coconut Grove, **Grove Isle Hotel & Spa** offers a complete doggie menu served poolside daily; **LoKal Burgers and Beer** has a doggie menu that includes after-dinner mints with its entrees and Bowser beer; **GreenStreet Café** is a brunch hot spot; **Peacock**

Garden Café has an exquisite setting; and Scotty's Landing offers casual waterfront dining. At Village of Merrick Park, an upscale lifestyle center in Coral Gables, **SAWA Restaurant and Lounge**'s doggie menu entices with fresh-off-the-grill meats as well as doggie tapas and entrees.

Stay All Pups Welcome

■ *EPIC Hotel, A Kimpton Hotel (Miami Downtown Waterfront):* VIP (Very Important Pet) amenity delivered to room; also available, bowls and bed for use during stay, leashes, and plastic bags. Petsitting, grooming, walking, and pet massage can be arranged through concierge. No number/size restrictions. epichotel.com

■ *Mandarin Oriental (Brickell Key, Downtown Miami):* MO Pets program provides a keepsake Mandarin Oriental collar tag, plush pet bed, bone-shaped place mat with food and water bowls, treats, bottled water, turndown service, in-room dining pet menu. Option of Doggie Boot Camp or day of beauty with a pet groomer in South Beach. Walking and petsitting services upon request. Two dogs/30 lb each max. Fee. MandarinOriental.com/miami

■ *Surfcomber Hotel, A Kimpton Hotel (South Beach):* Bed and food and water bowls for use during stay, and disposable pickup bags. Concierge can arrange for dog walking, petsitting, and grooming. No number/size restrictions. surfcomber.com

■ *W Hotel (South Beach):* P.A.W. (Pets Are Welcome) program provides a custom W pet bed and an exclusive pet treat. Dog-walking service available. Three dogs/40 lb each max. Fee. wsouthbeach.com

■ *Loews Miami Beach Hotel (South Beach):* Loews Loves Pets program provides pet tag as a gift, treat, bed, bowls, place mat, gourmet room service menu, leash, collar, dog-walking routes, and pickup bags. Dog walking and petsitting service available. On-site fenced-in dog park with benches, water bowls, and dog toys. Two dogs/no size restriction. Fee. loewshotels.com/Miami-beach-hotel

■ *Fontainebleau Miami Beach:* Dog tag, oceanside pet park. No number/size restrictions. Fee. fontainebleau.com

■ *Grove Isle Hotel & Spa (Coconut Grove):* Bed and bowl for use during stay, two Woof Water bottles, pet goody bag, Bark Bar room-service menu, 0.25-mile path around the island, grassy areas, and large rooms with patios. Two dogs/25 lb each max. Fee. groveisle.com

■ *Mayfair Hotel & Spa (Coconut Grove):* Bed, lounging mat, bottled water, bowl, Mayfair dog biscuits. Two dogs/25 lb each max. Fee. mayfairhotelandspa.com

■ *Turnberry Isle Miami (Aventura):* Bed, bowls, treats, Pooch Pouch in-room dining menu with special accommodations upon request. No number restriction/25 lb each max. Fee. turnberryislemiami.com

🐾 COME

Take your sidekick shopping with you at pet-friendly **Bal Harbour Shops** and the **Village of Merrick Park,** where at Neiman Marcus you can snag Charlotte Olympia shoes or handbags with poodles incorporated into the design. Hundreds of hot dogs turn out for the annual **South Beach Dachshund Winterfest,** held in January in Miami Beach. Also in January is **Pawpurrazzi,** Humane Society of Greater Miami's major annual gala, which draws 500 of Miami's most influential pet-loving philanthropists. February visitors can join more than 4,000 animal lovers for a 1-mile stroll around Bayfront Park in downtown Miami during Humane Society of Greater Miami's **Walk for the Animals,** which also includes music, food, activities, and games.

Hundreds of hot dogs turn out for the annual South Beach Dachshund Winterfest, held in January in Miami Beach.

🐾 UNIQUE ACTIVITY

Treat your favorite canine companion to brunch at **Doggie Bag Café & Pet Boutique** on Biscayne Boulevard, where an organic doggie menu is served on Saturdays and pawties are held on Sundays. There's also an outdoor area with a kiddie pool. Chef Laly Albalate also teaches a Cooking for Canines 101 class. doggiebagcafe.com

Emergency Veterinarian
The Pet Emergency Room—svrcflorida.com; 305-666-4142 ▪ Knowles Animal Clinics—knowlesanimal clinics.com; 305-649-1234

Myrtle Beach, South Carolina

Wor255ld-class golf courses, 60 miles of sandy beaches, a bevy of family-friendly activities, and entertainment options mixed in with southern hospitality combine to make Myrtle Beach the holiday destination of choice for 15 million annual visitors, a good number of whom bring their four-legged family members. Located in the northern part of South Carolina, the Grand Strand, as it's called, consists of 12 sun-drenched communities. Some travelers stick to one while others traverse US 17 Bus., enjoying the variety each town brings, from Little River, the oldest of the communities, to historic Pawleys Island in the south. Families flock to Surfside Beach, while those looking for the action descend on Myrtle Beach in the heart of the Grand Strand. Murrells Inlet beckons with spectacular sunsets along the MarshWalk. Whether in the central, north, or south portion, furry friends are welcome.

PLAY

It's impawtant to know that each municipality in Myrtle Beach has its own law regarding dogs at beaches. From May 1 through Labor Day, the city of Myrtle Beach and Horry County allow leashed tykes on the beach only before 10 a.m. and after 5 p.m. Pets can prance up and down Myrtle Beach's 1.2-mile **boardwalk**, which opened in 2010.

However, from May 1 through Labor Day, only morning strutting is allowed from 5 a.m. to 10 a.m. Whenever pups are in public, they must be on a leash of seven feet or shorter. Furry friends also must be leashed at all times in North Myrtle Beach, where no dogs are allowed on the beach from 9 a.m. to 5 p.m. from May 15 through September 15. Surfside Beach prohibits man's best friend at all times from May 15 through September 15. The most lenient is Georgetown County, which allows unleashed tail waggers on public beaches if they are under a human's voice command. **Pawleys Island beach,** in Georgetown County, requires bowwows on leashes from May to October.

Dogs can learn how to hang 20 at **Island Inspired Surf Shop** in Myrtle Beach, which offers morning and evening canine surfing lessons from March through October.

Land-lovin' pooches can romp freely at either of Myrtle Beach's two off-leash, fenced dog parks, both open sunup to sundown. **Barc Parc South,** off Mallard Lake Drive near Grand Park and the Market Common, spans 14 acres and includes a large lake, while **Barc Parc North,** on 62nd Avenue North Extension, covers more than 3 acres and offers separate areas for large and small pups. Pickup bags are supplied at both.

Dogs can learn how to hang 20 at Island Inspired Surf Shop . . . which offers morning and evening canine surfing lessons.

Fido will also feel at home at either of the two state parks, both of which offer hiking trails. **Huntington Beach State Park,** where visitors can enjoy some of the finest bird-watching on the East Coast, and **Myrtle Beach State Park,** with its maritime forest boasting live oak and southern magnolias, both allow dogs on a maximum six-foot leash.

For a different view, rent a bike with a basket or kiddie cart from **Woody's Beach Rentals** in Murrells Inlet, which delivers bikes to hotels, condos, and beach houses in the Surfside, Garden City, and Pawleys Island areas, and take Fifi on the 26-mile bike trail from Murrells Inlet to Litchfield Beach.

SIT

When the summer heat sizzles and pooches aren't welcome on the beach due to the crowds, doggie day care is available. Many of the businesses offer day care, overnight lodging, and grooming. Add training in behavior, obedience, and agility to the above offerings at **Dog's Way Inn** in Murrells Inlet. As the name implies, **K9 Cabana** in Myrtle Beach offers private cabanas and open boarding in its 6,800 square feet of indoor/outdoor space, along with grooming, training, and a bakery, plus a Cabana Cab to pick up pooches from homes or hotels. Pooches can also play and primp at **Diva Dogs Day Spa** in Conway, **Annie's Grooming Tails** in Surfside Beach, and **Spoof and Poofs Luxury Pet Salon** and **Sit & Stay Awhile,** both in Myrtle Beach, while **Market Common Grooming** offers a full-service spa.

🐕 HAUTE DOG

Many shops in the **Market Common,** an open-air shopping and dining village on the site of a former Air Force base, leave water bowls at the entrance for thirsty pups. **Orvis** even keeps a water dish inside its pet section; the store sells dog toys, natural foods, and treats made in the United States, its own line of beds and feeding dishes, and more. A short drive away, **Coastline Pet Supply** is the perfect place to pick up any supplies you may have left at home. There are also **Petco** locations in Surfside Beach and North Myrtle Beach.

🎾 CHOW TIME

With more restaurants per capita than many large cities, Myrtle Beach boasts 1,700-plus eateries, some of which welcome four-legged guests to accompany their guardians dining outdoors. Yet only the **Dead Dog Saloon** features a wall of photos of deceased pets submitted by patrons. Contrary to its name, the popular eatery on the **MarshWalk** in Murrells Inlet is a lively spot that draws hordes of locals and tourists for lunch and dinner and offers live music and dancing. Dogs can't wag their tail on the dance floor, but they can lounge just below on **Dudley's** tiki deck and soak up the scene of the MarshWalk, a .5-mile wooden boardwalk and pier that connects the seven restaurants of the MarshWalk District.

Ocean Front Bar & Grill, boasting the largest outdoor seating area on the Myrtle Beach boardwalk, also has a pet-friendly section that allows diners with dogs a direct view of the Atlantic. Other popular dog-friendly eateries are **Hanna Banana's Sunshine Cabana** in Murrells Inlet, **Damon's Grill** in North Myrtle Beach, and **Toffino's Italian Bakery and Deli** in Myrtle Beach.

For dessert, swing by **Baker's Dog,** a pet bakery and retail store in Bare-foot Landing, a favorite shopping spot in North Myrtle Beach. At Baker's Dog, treats are made from human-grade ingredients with no added salt, sugar, or preservatives, and wheat-free and corn-free nibbles are available for allergic pets. Plus, Baker's Dog allows shoppers to customize the bagged treat packages with a photo of their own pooch.

🐾 COME

The Grand Strand Humane Society in Myrtle Beach throws a couple of annual events that are the highlight of pet

🏠 **Stay**
All Pups Welcome

■ *Suites of the Market Common:* Rent a privately owned studio or one- or two-bedroom unit in this upscale urban work/live center that offers a multitude of shopping and dining options, plus a groomer. No number/size restrictions. Refundable fee. suitesofthemarketcommon.com

■ *Dunes Realty:* Its stable of vacation rentals includes more than 60 dog-friendly homes of various sizes. Two dogs/35 lb each max. Fee. dunes.com

parents' calendars. The **Foster's Bar & Café Golf Tournament** usually sells out every June as pet lovers raise money for the society. Also, more than 300 people gather for the **Walk for the Animals,** a family-friendly event held every October at Broadway at the Beach, showcasing animals dressed in their finest Halloween costumes that parade through Broadway to win a prize. Also in October, the annual Myrtle

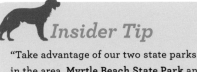

Insider Tip

"Take advantage of our two state parks in the area, **Myrtle Beach State Park** and **Huntington Beach State Park.** The setting is just beautiful, and you can take your dog out on the beach, watch the sunrise if you get there early, or enjoy the hiking trails to exercise your dog."
— KIMBERLY MILES

Beach Mini Marathon does a 1.5-mile **Doggie Dash** to benefit the Grand Strand Humane Society. It's worth regularly checking **A Dogs Way Inn's** website to find out about local events, festivals, and free activities you can bring pets to, including agility competitions.

UNIQUE ACTIVITY

Pooches and putting go together at dog-friendly **Hawaiian Rumble,** the most famous of Myrtle Beach's 50-plus miniature golf courses and home of the Masters National Pro Mini Golf Championship, where mini-golfers compete for a green jacket à la Augusta National. Canines are welcome on the course, considered among the best in the world, and the place where Dennis Hopper and Tom Berenger filmed a scene for the movie *Chasers*.

Emergency Veterinarian
Animal Emergency Hospital of the Strand—animalemergencymyrtlebeach.com; 843-445-9797

Naples/Marco Island/ Everglades, Florida

A delightful stay is in store for dogs traveling to Paradise Coast, as this area nestled in the southwestern tip of Florida's Gulf Coast is called. Chic canines will fit right into the luxurious shopping and refined dining scene in Naples. When you need to tone it down a few notches, there's Marco Island, the only developed land in Florida's Ten Thousand Islands. Beaches are a little bit challenging for bowsers but not impawsible.

PLAY

Pack a picnic lunch and spend a special afternoon with your sidekick on **Keewaydin Island,** a barrier island accessible only by boat located between Naples and Marco Island. Dogs must remain on leashes, but don't let that stop you from enjoying this nearly deserted, 8-mile, white sand beach. You can rent a boat from marinas in Naples or Marco Island, making the journey half the fun. Another option is Dog Beach (see the Fort Myers/Sanibel entry, page 76). It's in another county, but so close to Naples that hotels in North Naples recommend it to their guests, knowing how rare it is to find an off-leash dog beach in Florida—and what fun Fido has frolicking freely in the Gulf of Mexico.

With Bowser's beach access limited, head to **Central Bark,** as locals affectionately call the City of Naples Dog Park. But first make sure you bring your furry friend's vaccination records to register in person for a free City of Naples Dog Park numbered tag. This must be worn to use the 1.35-acre, off-leash park, which has a separate area for small dogs, a shade area called the Palmer House with benches, drinking fountains for people and pets, and a picnic area. Open dawn to dusk. No tag is needed for Rover to run at **Rover Run Dog Park** in Veterans Community Park in North Naples, open 8 a.m. to 10 p.m.

Canine Cove Dog Park, an off-leash area inside Frank E. Mackle Community Park, gives pets on Marco Island a place to socialize. Open 8 a.m. to dusk. Dogs are usually allowed on six-foot-maximum leashes throughout parks in Naples, such as **Collier-Seminole State Park** and **Delnor-Wiggins Pass State Park,** which boasts a spectacular, unspoiled beach that doesn't permit pets.

Hounds on leashes can meander along **CREW Marsh Trails,** where more than 10 miles of nature trails wind through fields of wildflowers, oak hammocks, marshes, and pine flatwoods. Or they can hike **Marsh Trail** in the Ten Thousand Islands National Wildlife Preserve, located halfway between Naples and Everglades City on the Tamiami Trail, best accessed by boat and offering remarkable bird-watching and photography. (Note: Alligators tend to sun themselves along this trail.)

SIT

Pampered pooches can enjoy a clay body mask, therapeutic herbal wrap, and pawdicure at the **Naples Dog Center,** where there are no cages or muzzles in the grooming salon and spa; it also boasts a health food store. **Shandra's Pet Salon** in Naples Park does hand

Stay All Pups Welcome

■ *Ritz-Carlton Golf Resort, Naples:* Welcome treats in the lobby, bed, food and water bowls, bottled water, plush toy, all-natural Ritz-Carlton bone treat, in-room pet dining menu, pet nanny service; map of the city highlighting dog-friendly parks and pet-friendly restaurants available at concierge; list of nearby veterinarians available upon request. Poolside Grill offers pet-friendly dining area. No number restriction/35 lb each max. Fee. ritzcarlton.com/resortsofnaples

■ *Naples Bay Resort:* U Nauti Dog package includes bed, food and water dishes, treats, sporty bandanna, plus list of nearby pet-friendly businesses, beaches, and parks. Refundable deposit. Two dogs/40 lb each max. naplesbayresort.com

■ *Hilton Naples:* Bed and bowl upon request. Designated dog-walking area. Three dogs/no size restriction. Fee. hiltonnaples.com

scissoring and fluff drying. **Custom Grooming** specializes in toy breeds. The **Wigglebutt Inn** in Naples provides boutique-style dog boarding and cageless day care, plus pickup and drop-off services. **Naples Safari Animal Hospital & Pet Resort** offers a Camp Safari Doggie Day Camp, while **Critter Café** on Marco Island offers doggie day care, grooming, a bakery, food, and supplies.

HAUTE DOG

Your furry fashionista will dig **Pucci & Catana,** which brings in canine couture collections from London, New York, Montreal, Paris, Brazil, and Peru to its chic Fifth Avenue South boutique along with doggie strollers, slings, carriers, and luxe accessories. At **Fergie's Closet Doggie Boutique** in the Shoppes at Naples Bay Resort, the mother-daughter team of Alexandria and Jackie Gross offer custom-made duds for dapper dogs from teacups to Danes, Doggles (doggie sunglasses), life jackets, choke-free harnesses, Naples bandannas, and more. Pick up healthy food and treats at **For Footed Friends** in Marquesa Plaza and **Goodness for Pets** in North Naples, which also carries accessories and stylish apparel.

Dining in Naples is like attending a doggie fashion show, with outdoor patios serving as the catwalk for pampered pooches.

CHOW TIME

Dining in Naples is like attending a doggie fashion show, with outdoor patios serving as the catwalk for pampered pooches. Now is the time for Fifi to flaunt the blinged-out collar you bought her for Christmas. Most of the restaurants, cafés, and coffee shops with outdoor seating at **The Village on Venetian Bay, Waterside Shops, Mercato,** and throughout the area welcome your well-behaved dog on leash.

Enjoy a large, pet-friendly patio and doggie theme at **Fred's Food, Fun & Spirits** in North Naples, named after the owners' deceased Chihuahua and featuring a wall of photos with customers and their dogs. There are always locals with their little ones at **Sunburst Café,** open for breakfast and lunch. Other pet-friendly patios in Naples include **Chez Boët French Home Cooking, Sea Salt,** and **The Dock at Crayton Cove.** On Marco Island, **CJ's on the Bay** is the happening spot for brunch.

Top Dog Kitchen sells freshly baked and dehydrated treats for pets. Stop by **Sassy Cakes,** a human bakery that sells specially baked, dog-safe pupcakes in two flavors—monkey buddy and carrot top buddy.

🐾 COME

Pick up dog treats from Top Dog Kitchen at the dog-friendly **Third Street South Farmer's Market,** held Saturday mornings. The outdoor veranda at **M Waterfront Grille** is the place to be on Saturdays, when Yappy Hour takes place from 1 to 4 p.m. Bark your calendar for these annual events: the Humane Society Naples' **Pet Lovers Gala** at Naples Botanical Garden (February or March); **Tea and Fashion Show** (November or December); **Run for the Paws 5K Walk/Run** (usually last Saturday in January); and **Strut Your Mutt** (usually the third Saturday in October). In January look for the **petfest and parade** that takes place on Third Street South.

🐾 UNIQUE ACTIVITY

You and your pooch can enjoy the **Naples Botanical Garden** when it hosts "Dogs in the Garden." Check for designated dog-walk hours. No need to worry about keeping your hound hydrated, as water bowls are strategically placed along the path of the 170-acre, world-class garden paradise. naplesgarden.org

Emergency Veterinarian
Animal Specialty Hospital of Florida—ashfl.com; 239-263-0480

Insider Tip

"I always recommend to our customers to take a pet-friendly boat charter while in the southwest Florida area. My three pups, Ozzy (a Chihuahua/Yorkie hybrid), Sharon (a Maltese/Yorkie hybrid), and their daughter Fergie, and I like to go out on **Captain Joey D Charters** when the weather is not too warm. We cruise down to Marco Island from the Naples Bay Marina, stopping at the doggie-friendly beach at Keewaydin Island for a little splashing and running around. The pups wear their Doggles and love to feel the wind blow in their faces during the ride. We always stop at **Mango's Dockside Bistro** on Marco Island, where there's even a doggie menu, before heading back."
— ALEXANDRIA GROSS, *Fergie's Closet Doggie Boutique*

Nashville, Tennessee

Just as country music's popularity has exploded, so has Nashville's. The days of sad songs about a man's wife leaving and his dog dying have been replaced by upbeat tunes where every dog has its day. And that's possible in Music City, where four-legged travelers can have a howling good time.

PLAY

Your favorite canine companion can kick up its paws at three off-leash dog parks in Nashville. There are plenty of pooch playmates on jaunts to **Centennial Dog Park,** in the West End, where separate areas for large and small hounds, a doggie water fountain, benches, and picnic tables are among the highlights. Open dawn to 8 p.m. Smaller than Centennial is **Shelby Dog Park,** inside East Nashville's Shelby Park and behind the Shelby Park Community Center. Much of the area is grass. Open dawn to dusk. The flat, open field at **Warner Dog Park,** inside Edwin Warner Park, is great for the Rover who wants to run. Open dawn to dusk.

Ten minutes from downtown Nashville, you and your leashed sidekick can escape into nature with a trip to **The Trails at Fontanel,** part of the 136-acre, immaculate compound once owned by Country Music Hall of Fame member Barbara Mandrell. The

2.5-mile shaded path with picnic tables that winds through the woods is well maintained but not paved, so expect mud following rain. Stop at **Café Fontanella & Wine Bar** (on the property) to pick up Italian fare to go (or dine on the pet-friendly patio), then head to the banks of Whites Creek, where you and your pooch can take a dip.

Other hiking options are Rails-to-Trails' 960-acre **Shelby Bottoms Greenway,** a multi-use trail that runs along the Cumberland River in East Nashville, and the **Warner Park Hiking Trails** inside Percy Warner Park. Canines on leashes are allowed at all Nashville parks. At **Radnor Lake Park,** pets are prohibited on the trails but can prance on the paved walk.

🐕 SIT

Your pampered pooch will be ready for Nashville's social scene after a trip to **Dippity Do Dog Pet Salon & Boutique** in Sugar Valley Market Place. When you're headed to a concert and need doggie day care or boarding, **The Dog Spot** provides both at its East Nashville facility, with indoor and outdoor play areas and webcams. It also offers grooming. **Camp Bow Wow** also has doggie day care and boarding.

🐾 HAUTE DOG

For the doggie diva, there's **come.sit.stay** in Belle Meade Plaza in West Nashville. Faux-fur-lined parkas, wool sweaters, and hoodies are among the stylish apparel at this boutique, which also offers handmade collars, leashes, toys, human-grade food, and accessories. **Baxter Bailey & Company,** located in The Shoppes on Fatherland in East Nashville, aims to please distinguished dogs and the people who care for them with an inventory that includes clothing, gourmet treats, home items, leads, and harnesses from their own brand and others. **Wags and Whiskers** (locations in East Nashville and 12 South) carries a wide variety of holistic food and offers self-service washing at its East Nashville store. **The Cat Shoppe and Dog Store** in Berry Hill sells toys, treats, food, and specialty items for your canine companion.

🦴 CHOW TIME

You and your pooch can enjoy treats together in Berry Hill. **See Spot Eat,** a dog bakery, sells healthy, fresh baked goodies. In the same building, you'll find **Pied Piper Creamery,**

> *Insider Tip*
>
> "Nashville is an extremely pet-friendly city. Whether it's getting lunch at Jackson's, walking around the shops in East Nashville, hitting the parks and greenways, or shopping for treats and supplies, I can do it all with Jackson, my loyal, eight-year-old Bernese Mountain Dog at my side getting lots of great attention."
> — CHRISTY WRIGHT

which serves homemade ice cream for humans. Grab an outdoor table and enjoy your sweets. Take a stroll with your sidekick in trendy Hillsboro Village, a collection of shops, boutiques, and restaurants within a 4-block radius. Stop at **Fidos,** named in honor of a pet shop that occupied the building for 50 years and is now a coffeehouse/restaurant. Other Hillsboro Village restaurants with pet-friendly patios include **Jackson's Bar & Bistro, The Dog,** and **Zumi Sushi Japanese Kitchen.** In the East End, there's **Drifters BBQ** and **Rumors East;** in Belmont **Bongo Java** and **PM; 12 South Taproom and Grill** in 12 South; and **Eastland Café** in East Nashville.

Some of the best local music can be heard at Musicians Corner in Centennial Park.

☸ COME

There's no need to leave Fifi behind when you want to enjoy Nashville's music scene. Some of the best local music can be heard at **Musicians Corner** in Centennial Park, which hosts free family-friendly music events on Saturday afternoons in May, June, September, and October. There's even a "dog of the day" award. Pooches are also welcome at **Live On The Green,** a free six-week concert series that takes place at Public Square Park near City Hall.

Every October, **Barktoberfest,** Middle Tennessee's biggest Howl-O-Ween festival for dogs and their people, takes place. Furry fashionistas in canine couture strut on the

🏠 Stay All Pups Welcome

■ *Loews Vanderbilt Hotel Nashville (West End):* Loews Loves Pets program provides pet tag, treats, bed, bowls, place mat, in-room pet dining menu, doggie poop bags, pet-walking and petsitting services, plus information on dog-walking routes and area pet services. No number/size restrictions. loewshotels.com/Vanderbilt-Hotel

■ *Hotel Indigo (Downtown/City Center):* Treats at front desk. No number/size restrictions. Fee. ihg.com/hotelindigo/hotels/us/en/nashville/bnaus/hoteldetail

■ *Hutton Hotel (West End):* Happy Tails Pet Program provides in-room menu of healthy, organic snacks, bedding, food and water bowls, complimentary Hutton treat, plus dedicated Critter Concierge with service recommendations for grooming, dog

walking, and signature pet spa treatment recommendations. No number/size restrictions. Fee. huttonhotel.com

■ *The Hermitage Hotel (Downtown):* Custom bed, treats, and nightly turn-down service. Dogsitting, walking, and dog massage available. In-room dining menus created specifically for pets. No number/size restrictions. Fee. thehermitagehotel.com

catwalk during the annual **Glitter & Glam,** a fashion show, auction, and wine tasting hosted by Agape Animal Rescue every July. The Nashville Humane Association puts on **Unleashed: Dinner with Your Dog** (January); **Cause for Paws Fashion Show and Luncheon** (May); **Dog Day Festival** (September); and **Music City Mutt Strutt** (September).

⬤ UNIQUE ACTIVITY

Your well-behaved and socialized pup can accompany you on the **Echoes of Nashville walking tour,** run by two public historians who take you on a historical stroll of the Music City. echoesofnashville.com

Finding A Veterinarian
Nashville Pet Emergency Clinic—nashvillepetemergency.com; 615-383-2600

New Orleans, Louisiana

C anines may not (or at least should not) fully appreciate the delectable cuisine and seductive mixology scene that permeates the Big Easy, but your party animal can still revel in a mutt-itude of dog-friendly activities available in New Orleans. From simply prancing through the historic French Quarter and admiring the unique architecture to enjoying a seaweed treatment and bubble bath at a spa in the Irish Channel neighborhood, there is plenty to keep Fifi busy. *Laissez le bon temps rouler pour les chiens.*

PLAY

Your pooch may find **NOLA City Bark,** the city's only official off-leash dog park, just as exciting as bipeds do. A permit for your pooch to play is required but well worth it. Temporary three-day ($10) and two-week ($15) passes are available. Lit until 9:30 p.m. Highlights of the 4.6-acre triangular park inside historic City Park include separate play areas for small and big dogs, doggie water fountains, dog pools, restrooms, dog-wash station, agility equipment, and a 0.25-mile walking trail. It is open from 5:30 a.m. to 9 p.m. every day except Tuesdays, when it opens at 1 p.m. Plans are under way to create more official off-leash parks.

Unofficial off-leash dog parks include **Cabrini Dog Park** in the French Quarter, **Markey Park** in Bywater, **Tchoupitoulas Dog Park,** and Uptown's **The Dog Levee,** which is dangerously close to railroad tracks and cyclists. Elsewhere, dogs must be on leashes. No pets are allowed in the Botanical Garden, Storyland, the amusement park, or stadiums. But you'll find nice trails inside the 60-acre **Couturie Forest.** Though it was heavily damaged by Katrina, you can still enjoy a relaxing respite there with Rover. Another option is to take the path around **Big Lake** on a path with your pooch. Open 5 a.m. to 10 p.m., **Audubon Park,** in uptown New Orleans, features a 1.8-mile paved, pet-friendly path that circles beautiful landscaping. A wonderful place to take paws is the **Riverview,** or the Fly, as locals call the Mississippi River portion of Audubon Park. Plenty of grass and picnic tables make this an idyllic location. Some pet parents use 20-foot leashes.

SIT

You'll be dog's best friend after a trip to **Belladoggie,** a resort spa for dogs in the Garden District that offers day care (activities include doggie television and an outdoor swimming pool), boarding, and treatments such as "be relieved: seaweed treatment for shoulder, back, and hip stress relief" and "be a sweetie pie: coconut, vanilla, and honey sugar scrub." **Canine Connection** (Uptown) also offers day care, boarding, and grooming.

HAUTE DOG

Furry fashionistas will be in heaven at **Petcetera,** on trendy Magazine Street. This boutique caters to those who like to dress their dogs. **NOLA Couture,** with locations on Magazine Street and in the French Quarter, sells dog collars that showcase special New Orleans–style prints. Belladoggie also has a retail section with the latest doggie fashions, and jewelry for pets and their people.

CHOW TIME

You'll find plenty of restaurants that welcome your bowwow when dining al fresco. In the French Quarter, **Café du Monde** is always a must. **Broussard's, Bayona, Café Amelie, Café Beignet,** and **El Gato Negro** are

Insider Tip

"Jaquemo, CoCo, and Mookie, all rescues, and I usually visit the dog park early in the morning. They play and I get my minimum eight laps (which equals two miles) around the walking path before the humid, hot temps have set in. After that we make our way to **Morning Call,** the dog-friendly coffee and beignet shop located right in City Park. They serve the most wonderful coffee on earth. I get to eat and they get to hang out and keep an eye on the people, squirrels, and ducks passing by and sometimes a friend or two from the dog park."
— MARY ANN CARDINALE

other options. In Uptown, **Café Freret** has an "A La Collar" menu with vet-approved dog treats. **La Crêpe Nanou** and **Reginelli's Pizzeria** also welcome dogs. In the Warehouse District, **Lucy's Retired Surfers Bar and Restaurant** offers a canine menu with items like Rover Easy and Canine Kahuna. In the Irish Channel, **Bulldog** brings water. In the Garden District, **Reginelli's Pizzeria** and **Byblos** are among your choices. In the Lower Garden District, bowwows belly up to the bar at **Bridge Lounge,** where photos of dogs adorn the walls and pups can expect treats.

❀ COME

Good Old Days Buggies welcomes your paw-footed pal for free on its French Quarter, Garden District, and cemetery tours, as long as no other guests object. Every fall the Louisiana SPCA puts on its **Howling Success Patron Party & Gala,** with a different theme yearly.

ⓕ UNIQUE ACTIVITY

Unleash your creativity and whip up matching costumes for you and your dawg to wear in **Barkus,** the annual Mardi Gras parade for canines, held two Sundays before Fat Tuesday. You'll stroll through the French Quarter and toss out beads to anyone in the crowd who shows their treats. barkus.org

Emergency Veterinarian
Prytania Veterinary Hospital—prytaniavet.com; 504-899-2828 ▪ After hours: MedVet Emergency (Metairie)—medvetforpets.com; 504-835-8508

🏠 *Stay* All Pups **Welcome**

▪ *Loews New Orleans Hotel (Downtown):* Loews Loves Pets program provides pet tag, bowls, treats, information on pet-friendly hotel services, gourmet room-service pet menu. Two dogs/ no size restrictions. Fee. loewshotels.com/neworleans

▪ *W Hotel (Downtown):* P.A.W. (Pets Are Welcome) program provides dog walking, custom W bed, treat. No number restriction/40 lb each max. Fee. wneworleans.com

▪ *The Roosevelt New Orleans, A Waldorf Astoria Hotel (French Quarter):* Can arrange any special request, upon prior notice. One dog/20 lb max. Fee. the rooseveltneworleans.com

▪ *Ritz-Carlton, New Orleans (French Quarter):* Prior to arrival, you can order a Ritz-Carlton pet bed, dog tags, chew toys, bowls, designer collars. Two dogs/25 lb each max. Fee. ritzcarlton.com/ neworleans

▪ *The Hotel Monteleone (French Quarter):* Mat, water and food bowls, treats, brochure with local pet-friendly places. No number/size restrictions. Fee. hotelmonteleone.com

Savannah, Georgia

As one of the hottest destinations in the South, Savannah is both artsy and historic. This Georgia city blends the old and the new masterfully, creating a romantic—and pet-friendly—atmosphere enhanced by picturesque squares, horse-drawn carriages that welcome doggies, and Spanish moss that hangs gracefully from live oaks. Travelers flock here to admire the 18th- and 19th-century architecture in the historic district, declared a National Historic Landmark in 1966, explore Civil War sites, and enjoy the sounds of music festivals that bring out the hipsters. Some call Savannah the Hostess City; others refer to it as Haunted City. With all its offerings for four-legged visitors, it can be considered Hound City as well.

🐾 PLAY

Noted for being pedestrian friendly, Savannah is best experienced on foot with a leashed canine companion in hand. Take paws at any of the 22 treasured historical squares (down from 24), especially **Troup Square,** at Habersham and Charlton Streets, commonly called **Dog Bone Square** because of its decorative drinking fountain for dogs. There's also a pet-friendly fountain near the visitors center in **Ellis Square** and another in **Forsyth Park,** an urban oasis spreading 30 acres and the southernmost boundary of the historic district.

Forsyth Park allows dogs on leashes, as does verdant **Bonaventure Cemetery,** one of the nearby attractions with magnolias, live oaks, views of the Wilmington River, and splendid statues. It's open every day from 8 a.m. to 5 p.m., with guided tours available. Closer to the Riverfront is the 6-acre **Colonial Park Cemetery,** also popular with pets and open to pedestrians from 8 a.m. to 8 p.m. daily. A short drive from the historic district, hounds on leashes can hike through a maritime forest in **Skidaway Island State Park.** Deer, raccoon, fox, opossum, heron, and egret sightings are common, and don't be surprised to spot an alligator. During low tide, expect fiddler crabs on the boardwalk that leads to an observation tower. Open from 7 a.m. to 10 p.m.

There's no wildlife in Savannah's three dog parks, just pups having a wild time. **Beasley Dog Park,** on East Broad Street in downtown Savannah, **Daffin Dog Park** in Daffin Park, and **Savannah Dog Park,** a private dog park in the Starland District, all welcome furry visitors. Furry friends, however, are not welcome on Tybee Island's beaches, 18 miles east of Savannah. But they can go on the water. **Tybee Jet Ski & Watersports** provides life jackets for bowwows accompanying their humans in kayaks or on Jet Skis. A beach alternative is **Little Tybee Island,** which, despite its name, is twice the size of Tybee. Take a favorite canine companion on a custom shuttle from Bull River Marina to Little Tybee for a day romp on the beach.

Active hounds can also soak up the past along the 6-mile **McQueen's Island Historic Trail,** part of the Rails-to-Trail network, where a railroad once carried passengers from Savannah to Tybee Island. Although eroding, an effort is under way to restore the nature path. While in the area, don't miss a visit to **Fort Pulaski National Monument,** where a wealth of hiking, biking, and walking trails await.

Stay All Pups Welcome

■ *Thunderbird Inn (Downtown):* Hipster hotel just outside of the historic district provides bed with duvet, bowls, food, treats, pickup bags, organic doggie shampoo and spritz, and red "Thunderbird Inn Loves Me" dog tag. There is an enclosed dog run at the hotel. Information on pet-friendly restaurants available. No number/size restrictions. Fee. thethunderbirdinn.com

■ *Foley House Inn (Historic District):* Provides treats and a list of pet-friendly restaurants upon arrival. Will walk dogs upon request. Two dogs/no size restriction. Fee. foleyinn.com

■ *Westin Savannah Harbor Golf Resort & Spa (River District):* Westin Heavenly dog bed, stainless steel water and food bowls on a Heavenly dog mat, doggie treats. Two dogs/80 lb each max. Fee. westinsavannah.com

SIT

Schedule a massage and blueberry facial for posh pets at **Diva Dogs Pet Grooming Salon,** outside of the historic district near Guckenheimer Park. Grooming is also available at **Catnip-n-Biscuits,** in the Victory Heights neighborhood, known for its doggie day care, upscale boarding suites with Kuranda beds, and indoor and outdoor play yards.

HAUTE DOG

From little black dresses and tiaras to party collars and jewelry, **Canine Palace,** a block east of Forsyth Park, carries apparel and accessories fit for princesses and princes, as well as licensed University of Georgia bulldog gear, leashes, harnesses, premium dog food, and beds. **The Grateful Hound** in Downtown Savannah offers stylish sweaters and rain-coats, high-quality foods and treats, leashes, environmentally friendly toys, dog-themed T-shirts and hats for humans, plus canine-inspired art gifts, books, and items for the home.

CHOW TIME

Dining is taken seriously in the Savannah area, which boasts more than restaurants and prides itself on its "coastal cuisine." Most of the eateries with outdoor seating welcome coddled canines. (Sorry, but Paula Deen's popular The Lady & Sons restaurant has indoor seating only.) **The Olde Pink House,** in Reynolds Square and one of the city's most popu-lar restaurants, offers dining in Savannah's only 18th-century mansion and brings thirsty tail waggers a bowl of cold water. Also in style with pet parents: **The Public Kitchen & Bar,** in the heart of Savannah's historic district; **Firefly Café** on Troup Square; **Six Pence Pub** near Chippewa Square; **Vinnie Van Go Go's** for pizza; **J. Christopher's** on E. Liberty for breakfast; and **Forsyth Park Café,** in the heart of one of Savannah's best-loved public spaces. **Leopold's Ice Cream,** which dates back to 1919, makes free doggie sundaes and tops them with an Ollie B. biscuit that leaves pooches begging for more. Head to **Oli-ver Bentleys, Ltd.,** on York Street, to pick up a tin of the gluten-free biscuits made with human-grade ingredients, free of wheat, corn, and soy, with no salt or sugar added. The tins are hand stamped with a paw print.

COME

Nothing puts visitors in the mood of old Savannah like hearing the clip-clop of horses while touring the historic district in a horse-drawn carriage. Pet-friendly companies include **Madison Tour Company, Carriage Tours of Savannah,** and **Plantation Carriage Company** (but check for size restrictions). Take Fifi for a stroll along Savannah's nine-block **Riverfront**

Area, where well-behaved pups are welcome in many of the stores and street performers entertain along the ballast-stone walls on River Street. **Old Savannah Tours,** whose offerings include a riverboat excursion and trolley tour, welcomes pets less than 25 pounds and requires they sit on their humans' laps.

Not only are socialized pooches always welcome to join their humans on **Savannah Pedicabs,** but pups can be left with the driver if their human wants to explore **Telfair Museums, Savannah College of Art and Design (SCAD) Museum of Art,** or any place that doesn't admit man's best friend. Make a reservation to get the best dog-friendly driver available.

Insider Tip

"When going for a stroll in the historic area of Savannah, know your poop shoots and watering holes. There are certain squares in the historic district that have poop receptacles submerged in the ground. They look like little submarine lids and you step on them with your foot. They are specifically to help keep the city in pristine condition and smelling nice. Also, look for the doggie fountains in **Ellis** and **Troup Squares.** Most people see the human fountains, but if you look down, there's another spout. Those are great places to stop and water."
— ERIC ZIMMERMAN, *pet parent to Ollie B.*

The eclectic **A. T. Hun Art Gallery,** in the historic City Market, not only features pet-themed art but welcomes cultured canines inside.

Annual events include **Doggie Carnival,** a fund-raiser benefitting the Humane Society for Greater Savannah that takes place every May in Forsyth Park; **Wag-O-Ween,** around Halloween, when pooches in costumes go trick-or-treating to approximately 40 businesses in the historic district; and the **Savannah Wiener Dog Race,** part of Oktoberfest on the river and held the first weekend in October. The Humane Society also puts on a number of fun events throughout the year such as a **Pup Crawl.** Four-legged friends are known to take part in the annual St. Patrick's Day Parade and celebration, one of the largest in the country.

UNIQUE ACTIVITY

Learn about Savannah's canine history on a walking tour through Savannah's historic district with Ollie B., the mascot at Oliver Bentleys. The King Charles Spaniel leads visitors on the Oliver Bentleys Historic Dog Walk Tour, designed and tailored specifically for traveling tykes and their humans. oliverbentleys.com/tour

Emergency Veterinarian
Savannah Veterinary Emergency Clinic—savannahemergencyvet.com; 912-355-6113

Virginia Beach, Virginia

Virginia Beach can boast that it has both the most and least visited state parks in the Commonwealth, which sums up the offerings in this resort city located in the Hampton Roads metropolitan area of Virginia. Whether your canine craves vibrancy, tranquility, or seclusion, Virginia Beach offers it all along 35 miles of Chesapeake Bay coastline, the Resort Area, and Sandbridge.

PLAY

Nothing personifies Virginia Beach more than its 3-mile-long boardwalk that runs from Second to 39th Streets. Pooches can prance down the boardwalk on leashes from the Tuesday after Labor Day until the Friday before Memorial Day. Rover can romp on the beach in the Resort Area (from Croatan Beach to the south up to the North End beaches) during the spring, fall, and winter months, but not from Memorial Day to Labor Day. However, in high season pooches can kick up their paws at the north end of Virginia Beach, above 42nd Street, and the south end, in the Sandbridge area, before 10 a.m. and after 6 p.m. All other times, hounds are allowed on the non-resort beaches. Regardless of time, pets must always be on leashes.

Both of Virginia Beach's dog parks, **Red Wing Dog Park** (in Red Wing Park in the Resort Area) and **Woodstock Dog Park** (in Woodstock Community Park in Kempsville), are fenced, 1-acre plots where canines can cavort off leash from 7:30 a.m. until sunset. Visitors have to pay the annual registration fee of $15 ($10 for a second pup) and show license and proof of rabies vaccination to receive a tag, which dogs must wear visibly on their collars and is good for both parks. Always use a leash when you take Fido to other city parks.

Hiking is available at **First Landing State Park,** the most visited state park in the Commonwealth. (For the record, False Cape State Park is the least visited.) Your leashed four-legged companion is welcome on all 19 of the trails and the beach. Be sure to carry proof of rabies vaccination.

During the dog days of summer, cool off your hot dog with a Doggie Dip at Skinny Dip Frozen Yogurt Bar.

🐕 SIT

Preppie Pooch, a day spa, groomer, and boutique, is where privileged pets can have a whirlpool hydrotherapy bath, blueberry facial, sweet brown sugar scrub, or Dead Sea mud wrap. Doggie day care and grooming are available at **Fur Frenzy Pet Spa** in the Regency Hilltop Shopping Center. **Two Brothers Self-Service Wash** handles the DIY crowd, but also provides full-service grooming in a kennel-free environment and sells food, treats, toys, and accessories.

🐶 HAUTE DOG

Diva dogs will drool over the designs at **Mrs. Bones Bowtique** in The Shops at Hilltop West, known for its custom collars (the smallest was 3.5 inches in circumference for a two-pound longhair Chihuahua and the largest 44 inches for a St. Bernard) and leashes made from more than 500 brocade, tapestry, velvet, tartan, and jacquard woven trims. The upmarket boutique also carries doggie collars and other stylish canine apparel, carriers, and beds that can be made in 300 different fabrics and shipped. At **Doggstuff,** a health food store for pets, you'll find natural, organic, and raw food.

🐾 CHOW TIME

The Town Center of Virginia Beach, a 17-block collection of retail, dining, entertainment, and living options, has turned into a hot spot, and your pooch can enjoy

Stay
All Pups Welcome

■ *Sheraton Virginia Beach Oceanfront Hotel (north end of Boardwalk):* Bed and bowls. Two dogs/40 lb each max. sheraton.com/virginiabeach

■ *Westin Virginia Beach Town Center:* Westin Heavenly dog bed, food and water bowls. No number restriction/40 lb each max. Cleaning fee may apply. westinvirginiabeach.com

the action too. Pet-friendly patios are available at **Sonoma Wine Bar and Bistro, Gordon Biersch, The Daily Grind,** and **Havana Nights.** Dining with your dog is available in the outdoor sections of **Abbey Road Pub & Restaurant,** which brings water to dogs; **Blue Petes Restaurant,** on the peaceful Back Bay, where there is also seating on a dock; and **Boneheads Beach Bistro.** During the dog days of summer, cool off your hot dog with a Doggie Dip at **Skinny Dip Frozen Yogurt Bar,** which has several locations in Virginia Beach; or **Bruster's Real Ice Cream,** where four-legged customers are treated to a sundae with a dog bone.

COME

Bring your sidekick to any outdoor event at Town Center, such as the **Town Fair,** held the third Saturday of each month from April through September, and the annual **Town Center Art & Wine Festival,** which takes place in May. Many of the retailers have water bowls outside and offer dog treats inside. Take paws at a shaded bench or umbrella-covered table in the **Fountain Plaza** (bordering Bank Street, Central Park Avenue, and Commerce Street), where a magnificent fountain, with the grand *Heron Trio* bronze sculpture, is on display.

UNIQUE ACTIVITY

Take your dog on a hike down the **Cape Henry Trail** through First Landing State Park. The park fronts the Chesapeake Bay, features 1.25 miles of bay beachfront and more than 19 miles of interpretive trails through protected salt marsh habitat, freshwater ponds, beach, dunes, forest, tidal marsh, and cypress swamp. A registered National Historic Landmark and National Natural Landmark, First Landing contains one of the most endangered habitat types in the world, the maritime forest. traillink.com/trail/cape-henry-trail.aspx

Emergency Veterinarian
BluePearl in Virginia—virginia.bluepearlvet.com; 757-499-5463

Washington, D.C.

Scheduling a play date with Bo and Sunny, the First Dogs, on the White House lawn may be a bit ambitious, but there is plenty more to keep your furry friend busy while in Washington, D.C., regardless of breed or party affiliation. Pawsible options include the plethora of dog parks, pet-friendly tourist attractions, and a photo op at the iron fence in front of 1600 Pennsylvania Avenue.

PLAY

Your pooch can get some great exercise and you can soak up history by strolling the 2-mile-long **National Mall.** Pets can visit the monuments, except for indoor and covered areas. Although pooches have to be kept on leashes, many still play Frisbee on the Mall, so make sure your pet's skills are up to par.

Bring a boxed lunch for you and Fifi to enjoy at the 1,700-plus-acre **Rock Creek Park,** where Fifi can revel on leash in thirty official picnic areas and on 32 miles of trails. A creek runs through it, but the water is unsafe for drinking or swimming.

Rover can romp freely at several dog parks in the District. **S Street Dog Park** (Dupont Circle) is small but nice. The **Lansburgh Dog Park** (Southwest) features an 8,000-square-foot area for large dogs and a 2,000-square-foot space for tinkerbells. The locals tend to forget about the leash law at **Montrose Park** (Georgetown), but no one seems to mind since the dogs are well behaved. There's also an off-leash dog run on the western side of **The Yards Park,** on the Capitol Riverfront, just south of Capitol Hill and to the east of Nationals Park. Pooches are allowed on leashes throughout the rest of the park, which boasts open grassy areas, a waterfall, a canal-like water feature, and a riverfront boardwalk.

Although pooches have to be kept on leashes, many still play Frisbee on the Mall, so make sure your pet's skills are up to par.

SIT

If you plan to spend a day tackling the Smithsonian or another attraction where four-legged visitors aren't welcome, drop your pooch off for cage-free doggie day care at **Planet Pet** (Adams Morgan), which also offers grooming, overnight boarding, and a pet store with all the essentials. Also offering doggie day care and boarding are **Wagtime Pet Spa & Boutique** (Northwest) and **Wagtime Too** (Southeast), both of which feature indoor and outdoor play areas, a spa, and boutique with apparel to please a furry fashionista. In addition to grooming, **Doggy Style** (Adams Morgan/Dupont Circle) has a bakery, puppy ice cream, and retail section with clothes, premium and raw foods, and essentials.

CHOW TIME

Hungry hounds can dine well at **Art & Soul** on Capitol Hill, where the Pooch Patio Menu lists Bowser Beer and a six-ounce grilled steak. **Brasserie Beck** (McPherson Square) and **Ris** (West End) are two other upscale restaurants that welcome dogs in their outdoor dining areas. In Georgetown, enjoy brunch at **Paper Moon.** The **Helix Lounge** at the pet-friendly Hotel Helix in Logan Circle also has a seasonal outdoor patio that is pet friendly.

COME

You and man's best friend can enjoy incredible views of Washington from the Potomac River while on **Capitol River Cruises'** 45-minute narrated tour that passes by the Washington Monument, Jefferson and Lincoln Memorials, and other sites. At the **Franklin Delano Roosevelt Memorial,** a 7.5-acre parklike setting where pups must be crated or on a leash of no more than six feet, look for the statue of FDR's beloved Terrier, Fala,

Southeast

 **Stay** All Pups Welcome

■ *Donovan House, A Kimpton Hotel (Downtown):* Bed, food and water bowls, water, treats, disposable pickup bags. No number/size restrictions. donovanhousehotel.com

■ *The George, A Kimpton Hotel (Capitol Hill):* Bed, food and water bowls, water, treats, disposable pickup bags, info on local veterinarians and petsitting services, map of great dog walks in the neighborhood. No number/size restrictions. hotel george.com

■ *Hotel Madera, A Kimpton Hotel (Dupont Circle):* Bed, food and water bowls, water, treats, disposable pickup bags. No number/size restrictions. hotelmadera.com

■ *Hotel Monaco, A Kimpton Hotel (Downtown):* Bed, food and water bowls, water, treats, disposable pickup bags. No number/size restrictions. monaco-dc.com

■ *Hotel Palomar, A Kimpton Hotel (Dupont Circle):* Bed, food and water bowls, water, treats, disposable pickup bags,

information card listing local veterinarians and petsitting services, map of great dog walks in the neighborhood. No number/size restrictions. hotel palomar-dc.com

■ *Fairmont (West End):* Healthy treats handmade by the hotel's executive chef, walking maps to nearby parks, a list of pet-friendly restaurants, cafés, and stores, and a special pet sign for your door. No number/size restrictions. fairmont .com/washington

■ *W Hotel (Downtown):* Pet welcome kit, toy, treat, W Hotels pet tag, cleanup bags, custom W pet bed, food and water bowl with floor mat, "Pet in Room" door sign, turn-down treat, dogsitting and walking, vet and grooming services, Wee Pads, pet First Aid kits. Four dogs/50 lb each max. Fee. wwashingtondc.com

■ *The Madison Loews Hotel (Downtown):* Loews Loves Pets program provides pet tag, bowls, pet room service menu, dog-walking routes, and area pet services. Dog beds,

leashes, and collars. Rawhide bones also available. Two dogs/No size restriction. Fee. loewshotels.com/Madison-Hotel

■ *The St. Regis Washington, D.C. (Downtown):* St. Regis pet bed and pet bowls. One dog/25 lb max. Fee. stregis washingtondc.com

■ *Mandarin Oriental (Downtown):* In-room doggie menu, lush beds, gourmet snack bones, bowls for water and food, plush toy in the shape of a panda. No number restriction/40 lb each max. Fee. mandarinoriental.com/washington/

■ *The Ritz-Carlton (Georgetown):* Special dog bowl, dog bed, water, a bag of dog treats, and a doggie cupcake. No number restriction/50 lb max. Fee. ritzcarlton.com/georgetown

■ *The Hay-Adams (Downtown):* Provides a welcome mat, two bowls, two bottles of water, and a dog bed if requested. Concierge can arrange dog walking and dogsitting. One dog/25 lb max. hayadams.com

the only presidential pet featured in a memorial in D.C. Your leashed pooch can walk the grounds at the **National Arboretum,** but not take care of business in the garden beds.

An annual **Doggie Day Swim,** where pups can take a plunge into pools, occurs in late summer at select DC pools. The big social events include **Fashion for Paws Runway Show,** held every April to benefit the Washington Humane Society, and the **Bark Ball,** held every June, the only black-tie event for D.C.'s boldface names where they can bring their posh pals as their dates. Bowwows are also welcome at the annual **Sugar & Champagne Affair,** the Humane Society's fancy dessert and champagne reception held every winter to honor local crusaders against animal cruelty.

> ### *Insider Tip*
>
> "For my dogs, living in D.C. means they embrace all sorts of adventures and interactions with wildlife on our daily walks through Rock Creek Park right off Reservoir Road in Georgetown. Each morning we head out for a two-mile walk on the trails, where my dogs race after each other in the woods, swim in the creeks, and frolic along the way with other four-legged friends. Having this connection and ability to let dogs be dogs while living in the city is what makes Washington, D.C., so great for dogs!"
> — TARA DE NICOLAS

UNIQUE ACTIVITY

On Saturdays coddled canines can join their humans for afternoon tea in the **Loggia Lounge at the Fairmont Georgetown,** overlooking the serene courtyard garden. While you nibble on crumpets, quiche, smoked salmon, and scones, Fifi can feast on housemade turkey and rolled oat pâté on toast, vegetable and whole-grain meatballs, carrot and peanut butter cupcakes, and organic rice milk. fairmont.com/washington

Emergency Veterinarian
Friendship Hospital for Animals—friendshiphospital.com; 202-363-7126

Midwest

Branson, Missouri

Neon and nature never mix as well as they do in Branson, where flashing lights and more theater seats than New York's Broadway coexist with three pristine lakes and the natural beauty of the Ozark Mountains. Situated almost in the middle of the country, this southern Missouri city known as the Las Vegas of the Ozarks attracts nearly eight million visitors annually and is becoming more dog friendly.

🐾 PLAY

Branson plans to unleash its first off-leash dog park in 2014. The **Elmo and Rosalea Marrs Memorial Dog Park,** inside local fave **Stockstill Park,** is a nearly 1.5-acre park open sunrise to sunset with separate areas for large and small dogs, agility equipment, a walking trail, and seating. Pups must be registered with the Branson Parks and Recreation Department prior to entry, and membership is required. Visitors can purchase a one- or three-day pass. Contact the Branson RecPlex (bransonparksandrecreation .com). Stockstill also boasts a popular .5-mile, paved walking trail next to Roark Creek. Fido needs to be on leash, the same as when visiting any of the city's 15 other parks. Also a hit is **North Beach Park,** on the banks of Lake Taneycomo, with a paved, 0.75-mile walking path along the lake that connects to the Branson Landing boardwalk. With benches along the trail, it's a lovely place to take paws.

Let your leashed hound sniff along the picturesque **Dewey Short–Table Rock Lakeshore Trail,** which winds 2.2 miles along Table Rock Lake from the Dewey Short Visitor Center, near Table Rock Dam, past the Showboat Branson Belle Landing to the Table Rock State Park Marina.

Take the rugged Rover to **Lakeside Forest Wilderness Area,** a naturalist's oasis with 140 acres and two trails through forest, along bluffs,

> ## Insider Tip
>
> "I like to take Piper, my Havanese, to the Table Rock Dam area. It's a great place to walk your dogs because they can go down to the water without getting totally immersed. It's a good place to socialize them, while entertaining yourself by watching the sailboats and big boats. The fish hatchery is right there also."
> — JEANNIE WINGERT

and across glades. But keep your pet off the 315 stone steps that lead toward Lake Taneycomo. Another terrier-rific place to hike your tyke is the **Ruth and Paul Henning Conservation Area** on the west side of Branson, a gift from the creator of the *Beverly Hillbillies, Green Acres,* and *Petticoat Junction* television series.

Fishermen love Table Rock Lake because of its bass, but your pooch will enjoy **Table Rock State Park,** a few miles south of Branson, for other reasons. A paved ramp makes launching easy should you want to take Fido kayaking or canoeing, a favorite pastime on these lakes. In state parks, pets must be on leashes of no longer than ten feet.

SIT

If you're headed to Silver Dollar City amusement park, a golf course, or just want to enjoy Branson's entertainment scene, doggie day care is available in Shell Knob at **Paw Prints Day Care for Dogs,** which offers indoor and outdoor play areas, transportation to and from day care, bathing, and grooming. **Branson Pet Resort,** about 3 miles east of old downtown Branson on Mo. Hwy. T, offers day and overnight boarding, training, and a retail section with the essentials. Tourists stop in just to see Mu-lan, a Shih Tzu who has been trained to take credit cards and cash and give customers a receipt. **Paw Pet Spa** can handle your grooming needs. **Petco** also has a grooming center in addition to its full retail offerings.

CHOW TIME

Be prepared to have a railing, gate, or divider between you and your bowwow if you bring him to a Branson restaurant with outdoor seating, since the Taney County Health Department follows a 1999 Food and Drug Administration Food Code that doesn't allow pets where people eat. In Branson's Landing, on Lake Taneycomo in downtown Branson, **Joe's Crab Shack** brings water to your poor, partitioned-off pooch. **Cantina Laredo** and **Black Oak Grill** are two other eateries where a railing will separate you and your best friend. You can make it up to your sidekick by picking up doggie treats at the no-dogs-allowed café and **Fall Creek Bakery.**

🐾 COME

Although **Branson Landing,** an urban setting in the Ozarks with waterfront shopping, dining, and entertainment options, does not "encourage" pets in its complex, four-legged visitors are allowed on leashes. And the promenade is a great place to walk pooches. There are grassy areas at each end, doggie waste stations throughout, and some businesses leave water dishes at their entrances. In the middle of the development, a spectacular water and fire show created by the producers of the Bellagio fountains in Las Vegas dazzles spectators.

Every Labor Day, dogs are the entertainment at the annual **Doggie Dive-In Swim,** where canines get to show off their doggie paddle skills and go off the diving board at the Branson AquaPlex, before the pool closes for the season.

🐾 UNIQUE ACTIVITY

Photogenic pups can step back in time to the Old West of 1880 at **Buster's Old Time Photos.** Pets and their people can dress up in western, Victorian, southern belle, gambling hall, or gangster attire to take home a photo souvenir worth keeping. bustersoldtimephotos.com

Emergency Veterinarian
Branson Veterinary Hospital—bransonveterinary hospital.com; 417-337-9777

Stay
All Pups Welcome

■ *Chateau on the Lake Resort, Spa, & Convention Center:* Two dogs/20 lb each max. Fee. chateauonthelake.com

■ *Hilton Promenade at Branson Landing:* Bed, bowls. Two dogs/no size restriction. Fee. hilton.com

■ *Hotel Grand Victorian:* Dog treat upon arrival. One dog/25 lb max. Fee. hotelgrandvictorian.com

■ *Stone Castle Hotel & Conference Center:* Dog walking based on availability. Two dogs/20 lb each max. Fee. bransonstonecastle.com

Chicago, Illinois

Chicago has become so pet friendly that dogs can romp off leash year round at Wiggly Field. OK, so the dog park is a play on Chi-town's iconic baseball field, Wrigley Field. But that tells you the status dogs have reached in this Midwest metropolis, which is experiencing a tourism boom. You'll be blown away by the Windy City's abundance of pooch-friendly hotels and attractions, dog beaches, and upscale restaurants for chic canines and the people who care for them.

PLAY

Your pup will need a permit to play in any of Chicago's 20-plus "dog-friendly areas," designated off-leash sections within the city's parks or beaches referred to as DFAs. The permit and tag is available for $5.00 (good January 1 through December 31) at participating Chicagoland veterinary offices (go to chicagoparkdistrict.com/facilities/dog-friendly-areas/participating-veterinarians/). If you're planning to visit with your tyke, contact one of the offices or have your local vet purchase the tag on your behalf from the Chicago Park District, which can be reached at 312-742-4687.

With a tag your furry friend can frolic off leash at the big and busy 2.76-acre **Montrose Dog Beach,** at the north end of Montrose Beach (Wilson Avenue and Lake Shore

Drive) in Uptown. More appealing to some because they're smaller are **Belmont Harbor Dog Beach** (Lakeview), located along the lakefront path, and **Foster Dog Beach** (Edgewater), located on the north tip of the beach and featuring a ramp and double-gated entrance.

Each dog park has its own personality. Posh pets will fit in at **The Park at Lakeshore East. Wiggly Field** appeals because it is a freestanding dog park and not a sliver of a larger park. The ultimutt is at **Lincoln Park** (Montrose Harbor), where 3.83 acres of grass at the north end of the park are reserved for dogs.

Insider Tip

"The Hyde Park neighborhood, located on the South Side, is one of the dog friendliest places around. My Shih-poo, Perry, and I love to take walks to explore the neighborhood. Whether strolling the lakefront or proudly strutting down Hyde Park Boulevard past President Obama's home, this community is a pooch paradise. We end our explorations with a visit to **Parker's,** a natural dog and cat market. (The treats are human edible, but Perry never wants to share.)"
— OVEDA BROWN

But the pride and joy of Chicagoans is the 18-mile **Lakefront Trail,** which runs from Hollywood Avenue on the north end to 71st Street on the South Side, and is flanked by parks and Lake Michigan. Bike, run, jog, or walk Fifi down this popular path past Lincoln Park, Soldier Field, Grant Park, and Navy Pier, but be prepared for the crowds when the weather is nice.

SIT

When the need calls for doggie day care or boarding, **Pooch Hotel** has locations in Lincoln Park and West Loop that are staffed 24/7 so you can pick up and drop off anytime. Blueberry facials are among the treatments at **Streeterville Pet Spa & Boutique,** located a few blocks from Magnificent Mile. **Paradise 4 Paws** provides transportation, doggie day care, spa and grooming, and massage therapy, plus a fitness and wellness program at this 20,000-plus-square-foot facility near O'Hare and Midway airports. Pooches can enjoy a cage-free spa experience at **D Spa & Pet Boutique** in Roscoe Village. **Soggy Paws,** with three locations (Uptown, South Loop, and Logan Square), offers self-service wash stations and also full-service grooming.

HAUTE DOG

Furry fashionistas can also experience the Magnificent Mile shopping thrill at **Tails in the City,** which counts Oprah Winfrey, Carrie Underwood, and Jennifer Hudson among its clients and carries apparel ranging from tees to tuxedos, designer pet carriers, luxury dog beds, fancy collars and leashes, toys, and grooming products. The Swarovski crystal dog brush is a must on a windy day. In Lincoln Park, **Barker & Meowsky** ("a paw firm") has clothing and accessories for pampered pets. Nutrition-focused **For Dog's Sake** has high-quality food, treats, and supplements at its two locations.

CHOW TIME

After a romp at Montrose Dog Beach, the restaurant for you and your sidekick is **The Dock at Montrose Beach,** about .25 mile southeast. You'll find every breed from Danes to Chihuahuas on the 3,300-square-foot deck, which provides water for canines. Pampered pets receive a bowl of water when visiting the pretty terrace at **Pierrot Gourmet,** a European-style café at **The Peninsula Chicago.** Coddled canines are welcome at **RL Restaurant,** Ralph Lauren's first restaurant, adjacent to the largest Polo store in the world. Hip hounds can lap from water dishes and nibble on bacon snacks while they gaze at

Stay All Pups Welcome

■ *Kimpton Hotels:* **Hotel Allegro** (North Loop), **Hotel Burnham** (Loop/ Theater District), **Hotel Monaco** (The Loop), and **Hotel Palomar Chicago** (River North). Amenities include treats, bowls, and bed. No number/size restrictions. kimpton hotels.com

■ *The Peninsula Chicago (Magnificent Mile):* Amenities include bed, bowls, treats, and bottled water. In-room pet dining menu and dog walking available. The Spa offers a Rover Relaxation massage. No number restriction/20 lb each max. No fee unless deep cleaning necessary. peninsula .com/chicago

■ *Hotel Lincoln (Lincoln Park):* Amenities include bed, bowls, Hotel Lincoln waste bags and dispenser, treats at front desk, and a personalized name tag. Also available, information on local dog-friendly parks, dog walking for minimal fee, and arrangements for grooming and spa services. Two dogs/ no size restriction. Fee (portion donated to no-kill animal shelter). jdvhotels.com

■ *The James (Magnificent Mile):* Amenities include bed and bowls. Collars, leashes, and toys are available for sale. Also, in-room pet dining menu and 15 percent discount at the Tails in the City boutique. No number/ size restrictions. Fee. james hotels.com/chicago

■ *W Hotels:* W Chicago Lakeshore and W Chicago City Center (Loop) feature P.A.W. (Pets Are Welcome) program including "Dog in Room" door sign, toys, W pet bed, turndown treat, bowls, and mat. Two dogs/40 lb each max. Fee. whotels.com

■ *Trump International Hotel & Tower Chicago (Near North Side):* The Trump Pets program provides gourmet treats, bed, in-room dining menu, bowls and bottled water, toys, and a map of the city highlighting dog-friendly parks. Dog walking can be arranged. Two dogs (with exceptions)/30 lb each max. trumphotelcollection .com/chicago

Lake Michigan from the expansive outdoor space at **WAVE Restaurant Chicago,** at the Lakeshore W. In the West Loop, **bellyQ** refreshes dog bowls hourly with chilled water and offers treats. From its corner of Erie and La Salle Streets, the furbulous dog-friendly patio at **Tavernita** affords a prime view of the action in the heart of the bustling River North neighborhood, and the tapas-style eatery occasionally hosts special events for pooches.

Watch boats float by on the Chicago River while at **Cyrano's Café & Wine Bar** (The Loop), open from early May through October. Sister restaurant **Cyrano's Farm Kitchen,** in the River North District, allows pets al fresco too. And keep an eye out for **Fido to Go,** a doggie food truck with gluten-free treats, specially formulated Fi-Yo doggie frozen yogurts, and Midwest-sourced natural treats and chews.

🐾 COME

Enjoy a pet-friendly shopping experience at **The Shops at North Bridge,** which boasts Pet Comfort Stations supplying tasty treats, fresh water, and pickup bags on levels 1 and 2 of the Mag Mile mall. Your sidekick can join you in the outdoor common areas at the scenic and historic Navy Pier, which calls itself Chicago's "lakefront playground," with a bevy of dining, shopping, entertainment, and other attractions. Some merchants will allow your four-legged friend in their outdoor space, but ask first. From Navy Pier, you and Fido can embark on a **Lakefront Speedboat Tour by Seadog,** which allows leashed and friendly pups on all its tours for free and operates year-round.

Every year, top dogs prance down the red carpet at the annual PAWS (Pets Are Worth Saving) **Chicago Fur Ball,** a black-tie gala held in November at the Drake Hotel. Bow-wows in beachwear turn out in force at PAWS' yearly **Beach Party** in July. The Chicago Botanic Garden allows dogs in for two hours so that the cleverly costumed canines can take part in the **Spooky Pooch Parade** to celebrate Halloween.

Your sidekick can join you in the outdoor common areas at the scenic and historic Navy Pier.

🐾 UNIQUE ACTIVITY

Paws aboard the **Mercury Canine Cruise,** Chicago's only cruise for dogs. Every Sunday from July through September, well-behaved and leashed canines (and their humans) can enjoy a 90-minute lake and river tour with lively commentary about dog-friendly Chicago, followed by a post-cruise canine-friendly shopping excursion. On-board amenities include large bowls of fresh water and a newspaper-lined restroom. chicagocaninecruise.com

Emergency Veterinarian
Chicago Veterinary Emergency & Specialty Center—chicagoveterinaryemergency.com; 773-281-7110

Cook County/North Shore, Minnesota

Tucked between Lake Superior and the Boundary Waters Canoe Area Wilderness, and with the ancient Sawtooth Mountains rippling up the middle, Cook County, Minnesota, comprises the communities of Lutsen-Tofte, Grand Marais, Gunflint Trail, and Grand Portage, with 386 miles of picturesque hiking trails and tens of thousands of acres of unspoiled wilderness on the North Shore of Lake Superior, on Minnesota's northeastern tip. Tackle the **Superior Hiking Trail** with Fido on leash, or take a canoe trip into the **Boundary Waters,** a bike ride on the **GitchiGami State Trail,** a hike through **Grand Portage State Park** to gaze at Minnesota's tallest waterfall, or simply for a drive along **North Shore Scenic Drive** (Highway 61), an All-American Road. After you two have worked up an appetite, bring your four-legged friend with you when you dine on the deck or patio at **Coho Café & Bakery** (Lutsen-Tofte), **Gunflint Lodge** (Gunflint Trail), and in Grand Marais at **Angry Trout Café, Harbor House Grille,** and **Sydney's Frozen Custard & Wood-Fired Pizza.** The majority of the accommodations in Cook County welcome four-legged guests. Going the extra tail is Gunflint Lodge, which several times a year offers **Dog Lover's Weekends** with seminars and training activities on dog massage, baking homemade dog treats, training, communication, and pet health, plus K-9 Olympics and dog socials.

Door County, Wisconsin

Dogs are as cherished as fish boils and cherry pies in Door County, a narrow strip of land that extends into Lake Michigan in Wisconsin's northeast corner. Bursting at the seams in the summer and a scenic destination in the less populated winter, the collection of quaint, harborside towns spread along this 75-mile-long by 18-mile-wide peninsula just 40 miles from Green Bay have earned it the nickname the Cape Cod of the West. The absence of chain hotels, shops, and restaurants adds charm, while the 300 miles of shoreline and five state parks provide you and your active bowwows ample opportunities to work up an appetite before reloading at one of the many dog-friendly restaurants.

PLAY

Door County boasts three dog parks, including two that are open 24 hours: Sturgeon Bay's **Shiloh Road Bark Park** and Egg Harbor's **Harbor Hounds,** a 2-acre plot with separate large and small dog fenced runs, plenty of trees, and a gently sloping hillside. **Sister Bay Dog Park,** a fenced 200-by-300-foot grassy area adjacent to the Sister Bay Sports Complex, is open for romping from dawn till dusk.

For the most part, your pup is welcome in Door County's five state parks—**Newport, Peninsula, Potawatomi, Rock Island,** and **Whitefish Dunes**—which offer swimming and hiking opportunities for pups, and in its nineteen county parks, all of which require leashes. Unless in the water, keep Fido on a leash no longer than eight feet when inside state parks. Furry friends can frolic in their own special section on the beach at Whitefish Dunes in spring, summer, and early fall. From late fall to April 1, Rover has the run of the entire beach in Sturgeon Bay. An easy and convenient place for Daisy to take a dip is the canoe/kayak launch area in **Tennison Bay,** at Peninsula State Park in Fish Creek. Leashed pups can romp on the beach at **Lakeside Park Beach** in Jacksonport, and along the shores of the bay at **Frank E. Murphy County Park,** south of Egg Harbor. Hiking is also available in county parks, and some community parks around Door County may also allow pooches.

> *Furry friends can frolic in their own special section on the beach at Whitefish Dunes in spring, summer, and early fall.*

🐕 SIT

Appletree Kennels can handle your Fifi's day care, boarding, bathing, and grooming needs at its 17-acre facility in Sturgeon Bay. **Door County Kennels** in Egg Harbor and **Idlewild Kennel** in Sturgeon Bay offer similar services. Self-service and full-service grooming are offered at **Stove Dog Bakery and Bath House** in downtown Sturgeon Bay.

🦴 HAUTE DOG

Stylish apparel, toys, and treats for distinguished dogs, as well as gifts for pet lovers, are available at **Pet Expressions,** with locations in Carlsville and Ephraim. **Trendy Tails** pet boutique in Fish Creek stocks collars, harnesses, and leashes plus gourmet natural treats, food, and toys. You'll find dog toys and gourmet treats in the backroom of the **Santa Fe Shop** on Main Street in Fish Creek. Homemade dog treats and food, including frozen and freeze dried, can be purchased at **Stove Dog Bakery and Bath House.**

🦴 CHOW TIME

Say bone appétit to your pup at **Harbor Fish Market & Grill** in Baileys Harbor, where a doggie menu includes beef hot

🏠 Stay
All Pups Welcome

■ *Country House Resort (Sister Bay):* In-room food and water dishes and dog beds. Dog basket at check-in that includes dog towels, furniture cover sheets, coupons, information from local dog-friendly businesses, and an all-natural welcome treat. Outside dog-wash area. Two dogs/80 lb each max. Fee. countryhouseresort.com

■ *The Shoreline Resort (Gills Rock):* Provides all-you-can eat Milk-Bones. Two small dogs. Fee. theshoreline resort.com

■ *White Birch Inn (Sturgeon Bay):* No number/size restrictions. Fee. white birchinn.com

dogs, ground beef patty, kibble, scrambled eggs, and dessert. Enjoy a cold one with your dawg at **Gibraltar Grill** in Fish Creek, which sells Bowser Beer, has a monthly Dog Pal contest, and spotlights visiting Dog Pals on its website. Also in Fish Creek, **Pelletier's Restaurant & Fish Boil** in Founder's Square welcomes pooches. Canines are also welcome on the pretty patio at **Mission Grille** in Sister Bay, **The Bistro Bar & Grille** in Egg Harbor's Liberty Square, and **Mink River Basin** in Ellison Bay. Stop by **Not Licked Yet** in Fish Creek, which gives "puppy custard" cones to furry customers.

COME

Take your salty dog on a narrated cruise on Sturgeon Bay with **Door County Fireboat Cruises.** For a Terrier-ific time, there's the annual **Door County Scottie Rally** every May, when nearly two hundred Scottish Terriers converge in Baileys Harbor and strut their Scottitude. The Door County Humane Society hosts events year-round, including the annual **Bark by the Bay Pet Walk,** with live music and vendors, in August.

FIDO UNIQUE ACTIVITY

You and your cultured canine can sit together under the stars and watch **American Folklore Theatre**'s professional actors and musicians perform at the Peninsula State Park Amphitheater in Fish Creek from late June to late August. folkloretheatre.com

Emergency Veterinarian
Animal Clinic of Sturgeon Bay—animalclinicofsturgeonbay.com; 920-743-2628 ▪ After Hours: Green Bay Animal Emergency Care Center—gbaec.com; 920-494-9400 ▪ Fox Valley Animal Referral Center—fvarc.com; 920-993-9193

Insider Tip

"We enjoy walking our Irish Setter, Willy, in the picturesque village of Fish Creek. Our favorite stop is the Gibraltar Grill, whose friendly staff greets Willy with a fresh bowl of water at his table. A favorite event at the Grill is watching the **Fourth of July** fireworks from the outdoor patio. In the fall, Fish Creek has a **Halloween pet parade** culminating in a pet costume party hosted by the Grill."
— GREG AND GLORIA WEYENBERG

Lake Erie Shores & Islands, Ohio

From families to party animals, bird-watchers to history buffs, nature lovers to thrill seekers, Ohio's Lake Erie Shores & Islands appeals to all. Some come to this coastal retreat between Toledo and Cleveland for the first-rate amusement park and water parks on the mainland, while others island-hop on the pet-friendly ferries to South Bass Island, where the nightlife in the village of Put-in-Bay lures, or the quieter Kelleys Island and Middle Bass Island. Whatever your pet-icular pleasure, you can have a fun-filled time with your furry friend by your side.

PLAY

Your tail wagger can **Bark Until Dark,** the name of the only dog park in Ottawa County. Located in Danbury Township, on the eastern point of the Marblehead Peninsula, the off-leash park has separate areas for large and small dogs and is open daily from 8 a.m. to dusk. Huron boasts the other off-leash dog park, **Erie MetroBark Park** (fee). Tucked inside Osborn MetroPark, the most popular park in the Erie MetroPark system, the dog park is located near the Maple Grove Center on Hull Road and open daily from 7 a.m. to dusk.

In Huron, Fifi can frolic on leash anytime at **Lakefront Park Beach,** at the end of Park and Center Streets, but at **Nickel Plate Beach** only between 6 p.m. and 10 a.m. from

Memorial Day to Labor Day. There are no restrictions, except to keep Rover on a leash, at Vermilion's **Main Street Beach,** next to the Inland Seas Maritime Museum at the north end of Main Street.

Pets aren't permitted on swimming beaches at state parks, but some beaches, such as **Catawba Island State Park Beach,** have a designated section for four-legged beach-goers. Keep your pups on leash until they are in the water. On Kelleys Island, the largest American island in Lake Erie at more than 4 square miles, Rocky can romp on a long stony beach anytime at **Kelleys Island State Park,** but never on the island's short sandy beach. Dogs can also cool off on a rocky beach on the east side of **Seaway Marina. Portside Marina**'s doggie swim ramp makes it easy for canines to get their paws wet. Locals congregate to watch the sunset on an inactive boat ramp on the west shore of **Put-in-Bay,** and some let their pooches take a dip there. Hiking is plentiful throughout the state parks, especially on Kelleys Island, where the **East Quarry Trail** is popular.

SIT

The Chelsea Dog in Perkins Township, Sandusky, offers doggie day care, grooming, and retail. But if you're headed to **Cedar Point Amusement Park** in Sandusky, there's no need to search for a pet sitter for your sidekick. America's second-oldest amusement park, dating back to 1870, offers a **Pet Chek** (you'll recognize it by Snoopy's big red dog-house) outside the park for day sitting. Located near the Bay Harbor Restaurant across from the bus lot, it is first come, first served and opens one hour before the park does.

HAUTE DOG

Life vests for dogs and essential pet products can be found at chain stores in Sandusky, **Pet Supplies Plus** and **Petco,** which also offers grooming.

CHOW TIME

When dining on Put-in-Bay, your pup can join you at **Books Seafood** on The Boardwalk's Main Deck, **The Backyard at Frosty Bar**, the patio at **Joe's Bar,** the back patio at **The Goat Soup and Whiskey,** and the patio of **Tony's Garage.** On Middle Bass, check out the patio at **J. F. Walleyes.** On

Stay
All Pups Welcome

■ *Sawmill Creek Resort (Huron):* One dog/30 lb max. Fee. sawmillcreek.com

■ *Wagner's 1844 Inn (Sandusky):* Homemade biscuits. Two dogs/ no size restriction. Fee. lrbcg.com/ wagnersinn/

■ *Bay Lodging Resort (Put-in-Bay):* One dog/20 lb max. Fee. baylodging.com

■ *The Pascoe House (Kelleys Island):* Bed, bowls, toys, pickup bags. Two or three dogs depending on size. Refundable security deposit. kelleys island.com/cottages-and-homes/ the-pascoe-house

Catawba Island, the **Beach Street Bar & Grille**'s pooch-friendly patio overlooks Gem Beach Marina. On Kelleys Island, pups on leashes are welcome at **The Caddy Shack, Dockers Waterfront Bar and Restaurant,** and the outdoor patio of **The Casino Restaurant & Bar,** which is great for watching sunsets and where there's live music on weekend afternoons during the summer.

COME

During the summer, pets can board the **Put-in-Bay Tour Train** with their people for a one-hour narrated tour of the island. Four-legged visitors are also welcome at **Perry's Cave Family Fun Center, Saunders Resort Golf Course,** and the exterior of **Perry's Victory & International Peace Memorial,** which commemorates the Battle of Lake Erie. On the plaza here in summer, National Park rangers offer interpretive talks. Bark your calendar for the **Put-in-Bay Pooch Parade,** which takes place every June. Also, the **Woollybear Festival** in Vermilion, Ohio's largest one-day festival, features an annual Woollybear costume contest for pets.

> ### Insider Tip
>
> "We have some wonderful walking areas for dogs in the county parks in Sandusky, such as an old quarry, **Castalia Quarry Reserve.** At **Eagle Point** you can walk back to the East Sandusky Bay. My favorite place to take Maxi, who is part Golden and part Shepherd, is **Edison Woods.** I go to some of the more primitive back trails where I can let him off leash, and he has a wonderful time. Maxi is a very gracious host when we have dogs at the inn."
> — BARB WAGNER, *Wagner's 1844 Inn*

UNIQUE ACTIVITY

Rent a kayak from **Kayak the Bay, Ltd.,** in Put-in-Bay's downtown harbor, and take your adventurous ally on an exploration to see the unique **Benson Ford Shiphouse,** get a close-up view of the limestone rocks along the island's shoreline, and thread **Needle's Eye,** a rock formation at Gibraltar Island. If you really want to show off for your pal, paddle to Middle Bass Island for lunch and more exploring. Guided sunset and eagle watch tours also available. kayakthebay.net

Emergency Veterinarian
Sandusky Animal Hospital—sanduskyanimalhosp.vet
suite.com; 567-256-3615

Mackinac Island, Michigan

Y ou'll never have to worry about your dog being hit by a car on Mackinac because automobiles are not allowed in this Victorian community on Lake Huron. Horses and bikes are the preferred modes of transportation. Reachable via three pet-friendly ferry companies (Arnold Mackinac Island Ferry, Shepler's Ferry, and Star Line Mackinac Island Ferry) from Mackinaw City and St. Ignace, as well as Great Lakes Air, all of which let pawsengers travel for free. The island is most alive from Memorial Day to Halloween. Plan to stay the night or even longer, as it goes from touristy to small town after sunset. Mission Point Resort and Harbor Place Studio Suites welcome dogs.

PLAY

Pups must be leashed within the city limits, but they can romp along the rocky freshwater coast anytime. No dog parks exist, but **Mackinac Island State Parks** covers 82 percent of the island. Of the 70-plus pet-friendly hiking trails, half are paved; the rest are dirt and shared with horses. Horses' "road apples" are overlooked, but please pick up after your pet.

SIT

Adding to the small-town charm of Mackinac Island are the local schoolchildren, who pet sit and dog walk during the season, as there are no professional services like doggie day care here. Ask the housekeeping staff once you arrive. In Harbor Springs, about a half-hour drive from the ferry docks, **Bay Pines Boarding & Grooming** offers doggie day care, boarding, and grooming at its facility, which includes indoor runs with heated floors, large outdoor runs, and two large fenced play yards. It's also connected to **Bay Pines Veterinary Clinic** in case of emergencies.

CHOW TIME

Oodles of restaurants have pet seating areas, whereas others will let you bring your pooch to the table on their verandahs or patios. Full-service pet-friendly restaurants include **Mary's Bistro, Bistro on the Greens** (at pet-friendly Mission Point Resort), and the **Jockey Club** at the Grand Strand (Grand Hotel). **Chillin' & Grillin' Waterfront Café** (on the Arnold Line ferry dock), **Mr. B's**, and **The Doghouse** (Windermere Hotel) are among your outdoor café options. Stop at **Cannonball Inn** at British Landing if you're biking around the island. Fudge is a staple on this island, and your furry friend can indulge too. **Ryba's Fudge Shops** sells pet-friendly, fudge-dipped dog treats.

COME

All of the shops and most of the attractions on the island are dog friendly. Fort Mackinac welcomes dogs, but if your pooch gets skittish by the sound of guns and cannon, check the demonstration schedule and take your little one to the west end of the fort at that time.

UNIQUE ACTIVITY

Your favorite canine companion can join you on a horse-drawn carriage circuit of the island with Mackinac Island Carriage Tours. Small dogs can sit on their human's lap for free. Dogs that need their own seat will be charged a child's fare. mict.com. Or be adventurous with your ally and DIY by booking a Drive Your Own Buggy tour from Jack's Livery Stable, which welcomes quiet, horse-friendly pooches. jackslivery.com

Emergency Veterinarian
Al Sibnick, Mackinac Island Carriage Tours barns—mict.com; 906-847-3307 ▪ Bay Pines Veterinary Clinic—baypinesvet .vetstreet.com; 231-347-4552

> ### Insider Tip
>
> "Neeko, my 14-year-old Alaskan Huskie, is a true 'Islander.' She was born on the island and has hiked every one of our wonderful trails. It's a great place to exercise her very curious mind. Our favorite time of the year is winter, when we can skijore [be pulled over snow or ice on skis by a dog] on the many groomed ski trails that the island has to offer."
> — MARY PATAY

Minneapolis/St. Paul, Minnesota

I f ever there was a need for the Gucci backpack for dogs that debuted to conflicting reviews several years ago, it is in Minneapolis. You can dress Fifi in pearls for a night on the town or strap a dog pack on her for a morning trek through the woods. Either way, she'll fit into the canine community in the City by Nature where lakes, parks, trails, and outdoor adventures entice naturalists and city slickers alike.

Add in St. Paul and you have twice the fun.

PLAY

This city of lakes boasts seven parks within the Minneapolis Park System for Fido to frolic freely, but an off-leash dog park permit is required for all. Travelers can buy a daily permit for $5 online at minneapolisparks.org, by mail, in person, or by phone at 612-230-6400. All seven parks are open during regular park hours, 6 a.m. to 10 p.m.

At 0.22 acre, the dog park in the north corner of **Loring Park** is the smallest of the seven but extremely popular. But the ultimutt is **Minnehaha,** a partially fenced, heavily forested, 7-acre haven for hounds, located at the south end of Minnehaha Park and adjacent to the Mississippi River. It's a bit of a hike to a sandy beach, but worth it for

Fido to take a dip. Be aware of the swift current and soft, muddy ground that guarantees he'll need a bath afterward.

Brutus needs to be leashed when you join the bikers, bladers, and walkers on the scenic **River Road Trail** that takes you past parks and gorgeous homes along the Mississippi River. Keep the leash on for a stroll around **Lake Calhoun** (Uptown), sprinkled with water pumps along the 3-mile trail, and picturesque **Lake Harriet** (Southwest), whose two beaches are off limits to even privileged pups. Both are part of the Chain of Lakes. For a country road atmosphere, hike along the **Luce Line State Trail.**

In St. Paul, Rover has plenty of room to romp in two off-leash dog parks. **Arlington/Arkwright Off-Leash Dog Area,** commonly referred to as OLDA and located on the corner of Arlington and Arkwright, spans approximately 4.5 acres and includes wooded trails. Seven-acre **High Bridge Dog Park,** a former coal power plant site, is located just south of Shepard Road, west of Upper Landing, north of the river, and just beneath the Smith Avenue High Bridge.

> *Brutus needs to be leashed when you join the bikers, bladers, and walkers on the scenic River Road Trail.*

🐕 SIT

If you need doggie day care while you tackle Bloomington's ginormous Mall of America, where only service animals are allowed, drop your furry friend off at **Metro Dogs Daycare and Boarding,** which offers late-night pickup and a webcam and app so you can watch your hound; **Fun City Dogs** (cage free, with webcams); or **Downtown Dogs.**

🏠 Stay All Pups Welcome

■ *The Grand Hotel, A Kimpton Hotel (Downtown):* Food and water bowls, bed, pickup bags. No number/size restrictions. grandhotelminneapolis.com

■ *W Minneapolis The Foshay (Downtown):* P.A.W. (Pets Are Welcome) program provides pet welcome letter, custom W pet bed, turndown treat, "Dog in Room" door sign, toys, food and water bowls, and floor mat. Concierge can arrange dogsitting, walking, grooming, and birthday cake; help find a veterinarian, and provide locations of the nearest dog park, dog runs, and specialty pet stores. Two dogs/no size restriction. Fee. wminneapolishotel.com

■ *Graves 601 Minneapolis (Downtown):* Bed, bowls, and treats. Two dogs/25 lb each max. graves601hotel.com

■ *Le Méridien Chambers Minneapolis (Downtown):* Bed and bowl. No number restriction/50 lb each max. Fee. lemeridienchambers.com

Pampered Pooch Playground in St. Louis Park and **The Woof Room** in Roseville are two more options. At **Ollu Dog Salon,** a dog wash and grooming salon in Southeast Minneapolis, you can do the bathing yourself or hire a pro. Grooming is also available Uptown at **Royal Pet Beauty Shop,** and in St. Louis Park at **LuLu & Luigi Pet Boutique and Grooming Pawlour** (more below) and **Bubbly Paws,** which also offers self-service.

HAUTE DOG

Created for pooches with panache and the people who love them, LuLu & Luigi Pet Boutique and Grooming Pawlour in St. Louis Park (there are also locations in Wayzata and White Bear Lake) carries stylish apparel and all the accoutrements chic canines covet. There's also a doggie bakery and grooming. Catering to less prissy pooches who won't sacrifice quality is **Bone Adventure,** offering pet gear, grooming, and healthy food and treats at its three locations (Northeast Minneapolis, Wayzata, and Edina).

CHOW TIME

Considering the short al fresco dining season, allowing your sidekick at sidewalk tables and on patios is appreciated immensely, and many restaurants provide water for their four-legged guests. At **Pizzeria Lola,** named after owner Ann Kim's dog, furry friends receive complimentary treats and can lap from a watering station for pooches. Furry diners at neighborhood fave **Lucia's** not only receive complimentary biscuits made from house-made chicken stock, but can belly up to a mosaic-tiled Dog Bar to hydrate. In Seward, canines are common on the patio at **Birchwood Café,** which occasionally has locally sourced, organic dog treats on the menu.

Pooches can also join you when you dine outside at **Café and Bar Lurcat** in Loring Park, and Uptown at **Barbette** and **Bryant Lake Bowl,** where, yes, bowling is available. Enjoy river views from the back patio at **Sea Change** (Downtown) and **Psycho Suzi's Motor Lounge's** spacious patio in Northeast Minneapolis. **Pumphouse Creamery** in South Minneapolis sells tiny cups of doggie ice cream (organic whole milk and peanut butter) and donates all proceeds to local rescue organizations. You can order an extra patty on your burger for your

Insider Tip

"Minneapolis is famous for its lakes, and they are an incredible backdrop for a walk! I love grabbing a bite at one of the open-air restaurants along the lakeshore: **Bread & Pickle** on Lake Harriet, **Tin Fish Restaurant** on Lake Calhoun, or the **Sandcastle** on Lake Nokomis. Maggie Moo, my Cavalier King Charles Spaniel, won't let me leave Bread & Pickle without a bag of their house-made dog treats!"
— ALI JARVIS, *sidewalkdog.com*

pooch at the **Galaxy Drive In** in St. Louis Park, which gives all dogs a free puppy-size vanilla ice cream cone, sells doggie bones, and has a grassy area and waste station for hounds.

In St. Paul, the refined Rover will feel at home on the patio at **W. A. Frost and Company. Salut Bar Americain** in Summit Hill and **Costello's Bar & Grill** in Cathedral Hill also welcome pets outside.

🐾 COME

Walking your dog through the **Downtown Minneapolis Skyway,** which offers 8 miles of climate-controlled comfort, can be hit and miss since some buildings allow pets to saunter through and some do not. Leashed dogs are allowed at the **Lyndale Park Rose Garden** and the **Minneapolis Sculpture Garden,** which highlights works from the Walker Art Center's collection. And **The Hitching Company** welcomes four-legged riders on its horse-drawn carriage tours.

Bark your June calendar for **Wine & Wag,** a benefit for Homeward Bound Rescue; **Pet A Palooza; Dog Day 5K** in nearby Waconia; and **Doggy Drag,** a doggie fashion show that is part of Pride weekend. In August, a two-day Pet Fest takes place as part of the **Minnesota Renaissance Festival,** which occurs over six consecutive weekends. In St. Paul, the annual **Fast and the Furry** race takes place in May, and in August **Paws on Grand** celebrates the dog days of summer on St. Paul's Grand Avenue with contests and more.

🐾 UNIQUE ACTIVITY

Your adventurous ally can join you on a paddle on the Mississippi River with **Above the Falls Sports,** which offers numerous kayaking tours, lessons, and rentals. abovethefallsports.com

Emergency Veterinarian
BluePearl—minnesota.bluepearlvet.com; 952-942-8272 ▪ Animal Emergency Clinic (St. Paul)—aercmn.com; 651-293-1800

Northwest

Bend, Oregon

E ven dogs would have to agree that Bend, beautifully nestled in the mountain-
ous high desert of central Oregon, lives up to its billing as "the recreation playground of the West." Home to international retailer Ruffwear, the Patagonia for
dogs, Bend is where four-legged travelers can partake in many of the same activities as
those on two legs—and that includes visiting breweries.

🐾 PLAY

Thank DogPAC.org, a nonprofit organization that helps create off-leash areas in the
Deschutes National Forest, Bureau of Land Management lands, and Bend City Parks,
for helping establish an environment that allows your hounds to have a furbulous time
in the outdoors, whether it be winter, summer, spring, or fall. Hiking? Check. Skijoring?
Check. Snowshoeing? Check. Cross-country skiing? Check. Swimming in the lakes and
rivers? Check. Paddle-boarding? Check. Kayaking? Check. Mountain biking? Check.

Hiking is a popular pastime for pets and their people in Bend, which boasts 51 miles
of urban trails in town, some that allow pooches off leash. Both the **Shevlin Park Loop** and
the **Deschutes River Trail** near Farewell Bend Park have winding paths along the river,
offering plenty of opportunities for Daisy to take a dip. In the winter, a Sno-Cat groomer

takes care of the trails at **Wanoga Sno-Park,** providing ideal dog-friendly trails for snow-shoeing, cross-country skiing, and other winter sports.

With so many options, visiting off-leash areas inside parks may seem mundane. But not in Bend. Topping the city's seven dog parks, **Pine Nursery Community Park,** known informally as the Bob Wenger dog park for the man who helped build this magnificent spot, spans 17 acres and features an open meadow, an agility course, trails marked with lava rocks, and drinking fountains. Bend requires dogs on leashes except while in the seven off-leash areas. Every park in the city has pooper-scooper bags in handy dispensers.

SIT

After all that fun in the outdoors, head to **Deschutes Dog Salon** or **Muddy Paws Bathhouse,** where you can DIY or hire a pro. Should you have to part with your pup, two-step your way to **Dancin' Woofs,** a popular doggie day care and training facility.

Hiking is a popular pastime for pets and their people in Bend, which boasts 51 miles of urban trails.

HAUTE DOG

Bend Pet Express, with a knowledgeable staff at both of its locations, focuses on premium natural pet foods and supplies, plus offers Wet Pet Express self-service dog wash and full grooming at its Windy Knolls store. You'll also find **Petco** and **PetSmart** in Bend.

CHOW TIME

Some of the many restaurants with outdoor patios that welcome your little pal to join you while dining are **Brother Jon's Public House, Anthony's Home Port, Chow,** and **Crux Fermentation Project,** which has an off-leash dog park adjacent to its pet-friendly

---

Stay All Pups Welcome

■ *The Oxford Hotel (Downtown):* Size-appropriate pet bed, bowls (one you keep as a gift), Joshua Tree Pet Salve sample, organic treats from hotel restaurant personalized with your dog's name, map of dog-walking trails and parks. Available upon request: loaner leashes, collars, dog-walking services, and doggie massages. No number/size restrictions.

Fee. oxfordhotelbend.com

■ *The Riverhouse Hotel and Convention Center:* Treats at check-in. No number/size restrictions. riverhouse.com

patio and pours Off-Leash NW Session Ale. It's one of a bevy of breweries that allows bowwows on its patio and outside dining areas. Others are the pub at **10 Barrel Brewing Company, Cascade Lakes Brewing Co., GoodLife Brewing,** and **McMenamins Old St. Francis School Brewery.** At **Boneyard Beer,** pick up a nonalcoholic, organic brew for dogs called Dawg Grog.

🐾 COME

Bark your calendar for the elegant **Tuxes & Tails,** an annual June fundraiser for the Humane Society of Central Oregon, which also puts on **Santa Paws** in late November; the city's annual **Fourth of July Pet Parade;** DogPAC's annual 5K **Ruff Run/Walk** held in August; and **Race for the River,** where you can swim, paddle, or float with your dog during a river race competition.

🐾 UNIQUE ACTIVITY

Enjoy a 2.25-hour canoe ride with your favorite canine companion on Wanderlust Tours' **High Cascade Lakes Canoe Tour.** Bring your own Ruffwear K-9 Float Coat for your pal. wanderlusttours.com

Emergency Veterinarian
Blue Sky Vet Clinic—blueskyvet.com; 541-383-3833 ▪ After hours: Animal Emergency Center—bendanimalemergency.com; 541-385-9110

Coeur d'Alene, Idaho

Visitors may mispronounce and misspell the name of this piece of paradise in northern Idaho, but that doesn't stop those who come with their favorite canine companion from having a pawsome time in this picturesque town on the northern shore of Lake Coeur d'Alene (pronounced *core-da-lane*). The French name loosely translates to "heart of the awl," and *les chiens* are the heart of this city. With 125 miles of shoreline and four ski resorts within an hour's drive of downtown, CDA draws year-round visitors, who come for the outdoor activities and well-known Christmas atmosphere.

PLAY

Pooches can have a grand time outdoors in this city that bills itself as "Your Lakeside Playground." Furry friends are not allowed at the Coeur d'Alene City Park/City Beach area or on the grassy areas of the municipal parks, though if leashed, Lou Lou is fine on the paths that intersect or encircle the park grounds. And there are plenty of other places for pups to kick up their paws. Two off-leash dog parks, the 1.8-acre **Central Bark,** adjacent to Northshire Park in the western part of town, and the half-acre **Cherry Hill Dog Park** in the city's eastern section, are open 6 a.m. to 10 p.m. A new dog park, with fenced areas for large and small dogs, a covered double-gated entryway to both areas, park benches, doggie water fountains, and agility equipment, is located inside the reconstructed **McEuen Park** on Front Street downtown.

Leashed pooches can prance along the **North Idaho Centennial Trail,** a multi-use, nonmotorized paved trail that begins in Spokane and runs alongside the Spokane River and then Lake Coeur d'Alene. The beach areas along Centennial Trail, **Higgens Point,** and the dike road next to **Honeysuckle Beach** in Hayden, a 15-minute drive up Fourth Street, are canine compatible as well. During the dog days of summer, you and your hot dog can cool off with a dip in the lake at Higgens Point, then take paws in the picnic area overlooking the lake.

As long as dogs are on leashes, they can enjoy any of the trails on **Tubbs Hill,** the pride of CDA. The 135-acre publicly owned forested peninsula is accessible by foot and offers picturesque scenery and tranquil lake views, all close to downtown. A 2.2-mile trail loops around the perimeter. Eleven miles east of the city, take your tyke for a hike at **Mineral Ridge National Recreation Trail,** where views of Wolf Lodge Bay Lake and Coeur d'Alene dazzle and eagle sightings in winter are common. Hiking hounds will also appreciate the 24-acre **Canfield Mountain** trails on E. Mountain Vista Drive.

Rent a kayak from **Kayak Coeur d'Alene,** or have a howling time stand-up paddleboarding with your pup, which **Coeur d'Alene Paddleboard Company** will teach you how to do. For the thrill-seeking tail wagger, **Coeur d'Alene Parasail and Watersports** allows dogs in life jackets to parasail in tandem with their humans. Or stroll with your sidekick along Coeur d'Alene Boardwalk, the world's longest floating boardwalk at 3,300 feet long and 12 feet wide, complete with picnic and rest area, at the pet-friendly Coeur d'Alene Resort.

🐾 SIT

When you're headed to Silverwood Theme Park, just north of the city, skiing, or the Coeur d'Alene Golf Course, you can drop your little friend off at **Coeur d'Alene Pet Resort** or **Northwest Pet Resort**. Both offer doggie day care, grooming, and boarding. **Star's Pet Grooming** also does what its name states.

🏠 Stay
All Pups Welcome

■ *The Coeur d'Alene Resort (Downtown):* Gourmet dog treats. No number/size restriction. Fee. cdaresort.com

■ *Holiday Inn Express Hotel & Suites:* Doggie goodies upon check-in. Arranges for off-site doggie day care. Guest services manager Dodger, a Weimaraner, is the town celeb; he goes on walks with guests and sleeps in their rooms. No number/size restrictions. Fee. cdahie.com

HAUTE DOG

If you've left anything at home or need a life jacket for your dog, head to **GoodDog,** whose large inventory includes apparel, gear, raw and premium foods, and the essentials. **Coeur d'Alene Dog Company** in Harbor Plaza also has food, treats, and collars, and there's a **Petco** in town, too.

CHOW TIME

Soak up the wonderful views of Tubbs Hill, Lake Coeur d'Alene, and McEuen Park while enjoying breakfast with your bowwow at **Bakery by the Lake** on Front Avenue. **Rogers Ice Cream & Burgers** is one of the several eateries on Sherman Avenue, the main drag, that doesn't mind if you bring Brutus.

COME

Banks dole out dog treats, business owners bring their pooches to work, and stores leave a bowl of refreshing water outside for passing pets. Shop with your sidekick at **Kootenai County Farmers' Market,** held downtown on Wednesday afternoons from May to October with organic dog treats for sale. At **Christmas at the Lake,** open year-round on Sherman Avenue, pick up gifts for your fellow pet lovers. Personalize a handmade dog ornament or treat your good dog to locally made dog cookies in the shape of the state of Idaho.

These annual events are something to bark about: In May, **Dog d'Alene,** a fund-raiser for local rescue groups, features vendors, demonstrations, contests, adoption, and **AJ's Tails & Trails,** a 5K run/walk you can do with your pooch. Summer brings **Tails at Twilight,** the Kootenai Humane Society's big fund-raiser. The **St. Patrick's Day Parade** in March and the **Holiday Lighting Ceremony Parade** in November wouldn't be complete without man's best friends.

UNIQUE ACTIVITY

Dogs under 20 pounds are welcome to join their humans on the **Lake Coeur d'Alene Loop Flight,** a 40-mile, 20-minute flight offered by Brooks Sea Plane.

Emergency Veterinarian
Lake City Pet Hospital—lakecitypethospital
.com; 208-664-5629

> ### Insider Tip
>
> "Having our Labradorables (Lab mixes), Mika and AJ, at our store in downtown Coeur d'Alene is a bonus for us. They always love to greet the customers who are visiting and need a dog fix because they miss their babies. Plus our dogs can go for walks downtown and we can hike with them on Tubbs Hill. Our new dog park is a block away and gives them another opportunity to enjoy downtown."
> — MARY AND GREGG PEAK, *Christmas at the Lake*

Missoula, Montana

Fly-fishing in Missoula, romanticized in Robert Redford's Academy Award–nominated film *A River Runs Through It,* takes on a special meaning when your favorite canine companion joins you. It's just one of the bonding activities you two can experience on a trip to Missoula, where there is one resident dog for every two humans. At the confluence of three rivers (Blackfoot, Bitterroot, and Clark Fork) and framed by seven wilderness areas, Missoula couples natural resources with its offerings as Big Sky Country's cultural center to attract the majority of its visitors in the summer. Even so, its fall foliage rivals New England's, and temperate spring weather makes for an ideal time to visit without the crowds.

PLAY

Missoula boasts 26 miles of dog-friendly biking and walking trails and a walkable downtown that includes the Clark Fork River. The popular gathering spot for the city's canines is **Jacobs Island Bark Park,** on Van Buren Street, just over the walking bridge and open 6 a.m. to 11 p.m. The off-leash dog park spans 6 acres, with a fence enclosing one side and the other three sides surrounded by the Clark Fork River, making it the perfect place to play fetch and for pups to cool off during the dog days of summer. With picnic tables and park benches, bipeds enjoy themselves as well. Missoula's other dog park, **Fort Missoula Canine Campus,** just west of the horseshoe pits in Fort Missoula Park and open during daylight hours, offers a great area for obedience and agility training in a .33-acre, fully fenced area.

The city parks welcome all dogs, whether on leashes or under voice restraint. The hiking possibilities are endless. **Mount Jumbo,** which overlooks Missoula, requires dogs on leashes for the first 300 yards of the trailhead, then on voice command. The same rule applies for **North Hills** and **Mount Sentinel,** a preferred trail in winter for those who don't have a Husky, because it faces south and is a little warmer. Your buddy can romp off leash, under voice control, in the 4,900-acre **Blue Mountain Recreation Area** in the Lolo National Forest, which boasts 41 miles of trails and views of the Missoula Valley and the Sapphire and Rattlesnake Mountains. **Pattee Canyon Recreation Area,** a favorite spot since the 1930s, features picnic grounds shaded by large ponderosa pines. Remember to pick up and pack out your pet's waste.

The popular gathering spot for the city's canines is Jacobs Island Bark Park, on Van Buren Street.

 ## SIT

When you and your buddy want to do different things—maybe you want to check out the art galleries, and he wants to hike—**Alpine Canine** will send a Buddy Bus to pick up (and later return) your pal and take him or her on a trek, as an alternative to doggie day care. Alpine Canine also has a fenced 72-plus-acre **Dog Recreation Ranch** with trails, shade breaks, and a small stream where Fido can take a dip.

Quick Paws, near downtown, provides doggie day care, overnight lodging, mountain hiking adventures, one-on-one walks, and professional dog grooming. **Equus & Paws, LLC** offers professional grooming and canine massage, while **Rods-N-Dogs** is where you can self-serve wash your car and dog.

HAUTE DOG

With three locations you can **Go Fetch!** no matter where you're staying in Missoula. Between the three pet stores you'll find a biscuit bakery, self-serve bathing tubs, professional grooming services, and a wide variety of high-quality foods, supplies, and accessories, plus agility equipment and a training center.

> ### Insider Tip
>
> "As a local who has a very high-energy Lab, what I enjoy is being able to get on a bike and ride from just about anywhere in town to a trailhead and being able to take my dog Sancho or pack of dogs (with friends) off leash and let them run around in open and safe places (no traps)."
> — TROY PAYTON

🦴 CHOW TIME

Your pup can join you on the outdoor patio of many of the cafés in downtown Missoula, including **Catalyst Café & Espresso Bar,** open for breakfast and lunch, and **Doc's Sandwich Shop.** Afterward, take him or her to **Bernice's Bakery** for a bingo (dog biscuit), or to **Big Dipper Ice Cream** for a free cone made especially for its furry friends.

🐾 COME

Strap a pet life jacket on Rover and join the many humans who float down the **Blackfoot** and **Clark Fork Rivers** with their pals. During the summer, downtown is lively with festivals and events, many of which welcome dogs on leashes. If you visit in August, time your trip for **PetFest,** held every August in Caras Park, downtown on the banks of the Clark Fork River, and featuring exhibitions, pet adoption, food vendors, and a Weiner Dog Dash.

🐾 UNIQUE ACTIVITY

Bring your four-legged friend along for good luck when you folf (Frisbee golf), a popular activity in Missoula and a great activity for a novice because the folfers are friendly and helpful. Or is that felpful? Blue Mountain and Pattee Canyon are among the dog-friendly courses.

Emergency Veterinarian
Pet Emergency Center—emergencyvetmissoula.com; 406-829-9300

🏠 Stay
All Pups Welcome

■ *Holiday Inn Missoula (Downtown):* Bone biscuit upon check-in. Dog walking and dogsitting can be arranged with prior notice. No size/number restrictions. Fee. himissouladowntown.com

■ *Doubletree by Hilton Hotel Missoula Edgewater:* No size/number restrictions. Fee. doubletree3.hilton.com/en/hotels/montana/doubletree-by-hilton-hotel-missoula-edgewater-RLMV-DT/index.html

Portland, Oregon

Whether you're a hiker with a hound, a pedestrian with a pooch, or a beer lover with a bowwow, Portland has you covered. Man's best friend can have a howling good time in this eco-conscious metropolis that appeals as much to hipsters as outdoor enthusiasts. Mix PDX's vibrant downtown scene and progressive culture with its proximity to Mount Hood, Columbia River Gorge, the Oregon coast, and wine-producing Willamette Valley for the ultimutt destination, especially on those days when Fifi doesn't need her slicker.

PLAY

Portland earned barking rights for its 5.7 off-leash dog parks per 100,000 residents, which ranked it first for number of dog parks in a national study done by the Trust for Public Land. And that was before the City of Roses added its whopping 33rd off-leash area, **Fields Neighborhood Park,** in the happening Pearl District in 2013. If you're staying in Portland's Central City, **Wallace Dog Park** and **Couch Park** are most convenient.

Take Brutus, on leash, along the easy hiking paths on the **Eastbank Esplanade** or to **Forest Park,** the largest wooded urban park in the United States, boasting more than

70 miles of walking and hiking trails. As furbulous as Portland is, side trips are a must. A jaunt to the Oregon coast is only 90 minutes. Most of Oregon's dog-friendly beaches allow pets on a maximum-six-foot leash, and some let Rover romp under voice control. Oregon state parks and state beaches require a leash. For beaches outside the boundaries of an Oregon state park, such as popular **City of Cannon Beach,** no leash is required, but you must maintain physical control. **Mount Hood,** with fabulous scenery and hiking, is less than two hours away. Or take a drive through the spectacularly scenic Columbia River Gorge. Willamette Valley's **Elk Cove Vineyards** and **Sokol Blosser Winery** are two of the wineries that allow leashed pooches in their outdoor areas.

🐕 SIT

If you need to part with your pet, there's doggy day care available at **LexiDog Boutique & Social Club,** which provides overnight boarding, grooming, retail, and space for a birthday pawty too, at its two locations in the Pearl District and Macadam. Both you and your pooch can enjoy the **Sniff Dog Hotel.** Doggie day care, boarding, and grooming are offered, but there's also a café for humans, so you can nosh while your posh pet gets a massage from a certified small-animal massage therapist. There's outdoor seating at the café, which also hosts happy hour Mondays through Saturdays, 5 to 7 p.m. You can mingle with other pet parents while your fur babies play in the indoor park for free.

Both you and your pooch can enjoy the Sniff Dog Hotel . . . you can nosh while your posh pet gets a massage.

🐕 HAUTE DOG

Whether your pooch is a furry fashionista or a trekking tyke, boutiques like **Furever Pets** (Northeast Portland) and **The Hip Hound** (Alphabet District) carry upscale apparel, outdoor gear, plus holistic and natural food and treats. It's no coincidence that **NoPo Paws** opened on Earth Day (2011). The North Portland store carries locally made and environmentally friendly pet supplies plus a great selection of holistic, raw, and organic pet foods. At **Green Dog Pet Supply** in Beaumont Village, pick up environmentally friendly pet supplies and gifts as well as organic and natural food and treats.

🐕 CHOW TIME

When Fido is in the mood for a bowl of Ham "Barker" Helper, order from the doggie dining menu at **Tin Shed Garden Cafe,** in Alberta. The restaurant always provides complimentary water and cookies to four-legged guests. You don't have to be a Lab to get a seat at **Lucky Labrador Brew Pub,** which allows dogs at all four of its Portland locations and features beers with names like Blue Dog Pale Ale, Dog Day IPA, and Winter

Wonder Dog. When you need a pick-me-up, head to **Barista,** a coffee shop in the Pearl that allows pets inside. **Count Bluehour,** in the Pearl District and one of PDX's best restaurants; **Amnesia Brewery; Lovejoy Bakers; Songbird Neighborhood Eatery,** where you can enjoy a view of Mount Tabor; and **McCormick & Schmick's,** in the scenic RiverPlace marina with a glorious view of the Willamette River, are among the many Stumptown restaurants to allow pooches on their patios.

Stay All Pups Welcome

■ *Hotel Monaco Portland, a Kimpton Hotel (Southwest Portland/Downtown):* Greetings on its Pet Welcome Board, food and water bowls and a dog bed for use during stay, bottle of water and treats, ecofriendly Dispoz-A-Scoop cleanup bags. Available for a fee are petsitting, grooming, and walking services and pet psychic sessions. No number/size restrictions. monaco-portland.com

■ *Vintage Plaza, a Kimpton Hotel (Downtown):* Your pet's name on welcome chalkboard; pet bed, place mat, food and water bowls, pickup bags, and toys for use during your stay. Upon request, will take a photo of your pet at check-in and email it to you. Concierge can assist with dog walking, pet playtime, petsitting, grooming, massage, veterinary needs, local dog-friendly parks, and other venues

that welcome your pet. No number/size restrictions. vintageplaza.com

■ *RiverPlace, a Kimpton Hotel (Downtown):* Dog bed, food and water bowls, and pickup bags. No number/size restrictions. riverplacehotel.com

■ *Jupiter Hotel (Lower Burnside, Central Eastside, Buckman):* Partnered with LexiDog to equip all 81 rooms with an ecofriendly dog bed made from recycled products, food and water bowls, a stylish leash, discounted LexiDog Doggie Daycare coupons, toys, snacks, potty bags, and other treats. No number/size restrictions. dogfriendlyjupiterhotel.com

■ *The Nines, Portland (Downtown):* Bed and bowls. No number/size restrictions. Fee. thenines.com

■ *The Heathman Hotel (Downtown):* Pampered Pet Package includes complimentary office visit and pet exam voucher valid at any Banfield Pet Hospital nationwide; "Bark of Sleep Pet Bed Menu" offering choice of three beds, goody bag at check-in, Banfield Pet Hospital collapsible water bowl, and collar-attachable bag dispenser, complimentary area walking guide for two- and four-legged guests. No number/size restrictions. Fee. portland.heathmanhotel.com

■ *Westin (Downtown):* Westin Heavenly dog bed, food bowl and mat, "Dog in Room" privacy sign, doggie welcome amenity upon arrival. No number/size restrictions. westinportland.com

■ *Ace Hotel:* Dog bowls and pickup bags. Treats at the front desk at check in. acehotel.com/portland

COME

Portland is famous for its biking, so enjoy a **Historic Downtown Tour** from Pedal Bike Tours, which rents to bipeds who want to put their barker in a tiny basket on the front or on a trailer in the back. Pets are welcome at the **Portland Saturday Market,** in the historic Old Town, one of the most popular shopping destinations for local handcrafted goods, including items for Fifi. Run, walk, or stroll in **Doggie Dash,** an annual fund-raiser for the Oregon Humane Society, which has taken place every May for more than 25 years. Put your pooch in a handlebar basket or in a kiddie cart on the back of your bike and participate in the **Tour de Lab,** put on every September by Lucky Labrador Brewing Company to raise money for DoveLewis Emergency Animal Hospital. In April, the **Northwest Pet and Companion Fair,** the largest pet expo in the Northwest, takes place over two days at the Portland Expo Center.

> *Insider Tip*
>
> "I love taking Hans, my seven-year old black Pug, to **Mount Tabor** in Southeast Portland. The park is hilly and forested, big enough to have new areas to explore each time, and has a nice off-leash area. If Hans has a lot of energy to burn, there are some steep steps that run between the reservoirs on the west-facing side of the park. When you get to the top, your reward is a sweeping view of the city!"
> — CASEY OGDEN

UNIQUE ACTIVITY

Let Fifi stop and sniff the roses at the **International Rose Test Garden,** which welcomes well-behaved dogs on leashes with guardians who clean up after them. You and your pampered pooch can explore the 4.5-acre park, founded in 1917, whose rose plants number around 10,000. Open year-round and free. rosegardenstore.org/international-rose-test-garden.cfm

Emergency Veterinarian
VCA Southeast Portland Animal Hospital—vcahospitals.com/southeast-portland; 503-255-8139

Seattle, Washington

No one blinks twice when the little one being pushed in the stroller through Pike Place Market has four legs instead of two. That's how it is in Seattle, which boasts more dogs than children, making canines the jewel of the Emerald City. The benefits trickle down to travelers, whose furry friends are mollycoddled by hotels, allowed inside some restaurants on the DL, although officially forbidden, and openly welcomed at many tourist attractions. Seattle's spectacular summers make June through September the best time for a petcation in the Pacific Northwest's largest city, known for its many dreary days. Then again, in Seattle, dogs bring sunshine.

PLAY

Princess will have plenty of playmates at the top dog park, **Warren G. Magnuson Park.** Spanning 9 acres and fully fenced, it's the largest and most popular of Seattle's fourteen off-leash areas, and boasts multiple sections (including one for small/shy pups) and a winding path that leads to Lake Washington, where dogs can go for a swim. Also well liked is **Golden Garden**'s 1-acre, off-leash area, as much for its view of Puget Sound as for the covered area that shields you from the rain. Leashed-dog-friendly hiking trails beckon at the **Washington Park Arboretum** on the shores of Lake Washington; on the

Burke-Gilman and **Elliott Bay Trails;** and at 300-acre **Seward Park.** Fido isn't allowed at organized athletic fields, beaches, or children's play areas in Seattle parks.

🐕 SIT

When it's time to clean up Fido, head to **The Grooming Spa** in Greenlake or **The Wash Dog, A Bath House & Spa for Pets,** in West Seattle, both offering self-service and full grooming. **Dog Mania Seattle** offers grooming and doggie day care in the Mount Baker

🏠 Stay All Pups Welcome

■ *Alexis Seattle, A Kimpton Hotel (Downtown):* Pet treats, food and water bowls, distilled water, designer doggie bed for use during stay. Petsitting, walking, and grooming services may be arranged through front desk staff or concierge for a charge. No number/size restrictions. alexishotel.com

■ *Monaco Seattle, A Kimpton Hotel (Downtown):* A Very Important Pets register is set up upon check-in. Bowls and special bed are provided for use during stay, and bottled spring water, treats, and disposable pickup bags are on hand. Concierge and front desk staff can arrange for special pet services and amenities, such as petsitting, dog-walking referrals, and personalized doggie itinerary. No number/size restrictions. monacoseattle.com

■ *Vintage Park, A Kimpton Hotel (Downtown):* Food and water bowls and pet bed for use during stay, bottle of spring water, treats, disposable pickup bags. Concierge and front desk staff can arrange for special pet services and amenities, such as petsitting, dog-walking referrals, and personalized doggie itinerary. No number/size restrictions. hotelvintagepark.com

■ *The Fairmont Olympic Hotel (Downtown):* In-room dining menu for pets. No number/size restrictions. Fee. fairmont.com/seattle

■ *Four Seasons Seattle (Downtown):* Bed, bowls. One dog/20 lb max. fourseasons.com/seattle

■ *Grand Hyatt Seattle (Downtown):* Personalized dog tag, food and water bowls, wee pads, special door notification for

housekeeping. One dog/50 lb max. Fee. grandseattle.hyatt.com

■ *W Seattle Hotel (Downtown):* P.A.W. (Pets Are Welcome) program features dog walking, grooming services, petsitting, pet toys, pet turndown treat, W pet bed. No number/size restrictions. Fee. wseattle.com

■ *The Westin Seattle (Downtown):* Westin Heavenly dog bed, food bowl and mat, "Dog In Room" privacy sign, doggie welcome amenity upon arrival. No number/size restrictions. westinseattle.com

■ *The Woodmark Hotel & Spa (Lake Washington):* Use of a cushy pet bed, food and water dishes, plus a walking map, bottled water, leash, tennis ball, and doggie biscuits. No number/size restrictions. thewoodmark.com

area. **Central Bark,** in an 8,000-square-foot facility on the edge of downtown, offers day care, grooming, and boarding with webcams so you can see what your pal is up to.

HAUTE DOG

You won't find any leftovers at **Scraps Dog Bakery,** above the Whole Foods store in Belltown, just fresh baked goods, high-quality accessories, stylish sweaters, and healthy food and treats. At **Rex Capitol Hill,** pick up collars and leashes, toys, treats, and high-quality natural foods, including raw ones. **Mud Bay,** with 24 outposts in the Puget Sound area, specializes in healthy food, supplements, and supplies.

CHOW TIME

Well-behaved four-legged diners who stay off the furniture are welcome inside **Norm's Eatery & Ale House** in Fremont, which offers a daily Doggie Bowl Special for humans as well as "dog burgers" and Bowser beer for their best friends. Several restaurateurs turn a blind eye to dogs inside their establishments as long as pups and their people show manners. **Ristorante Picolinos** (Ballard), **Il Bistro** (Downtown), **Le Pichet** (Downtown), **Bahn Thai** (Queen Anne), and **Greenlake Bar & Grill** (Green Lake) are among the more than 100 eateries to allow hounds to join their humans on the patio. In the Pinehurst-Northgate area, **BARK! Espresso** teamed up with next-door neighbor **Great Dog,** which offers doggie day care and overnight boarding, to create the **Hound Hang Out.** Patrons can relax in the lounge at Great Dog and access BARK! through a special window.

You'll see many dogs at Pike Place Market, where the vendors love four-legged visitors.

COME

There's no shortage of activities to enjoy with your favorite canine companion. Glide in a seaplane above Seattle on a **Kenmore Air Scenic Flight Tour.** Take in the fantastic views and splendor of the Olympic Mountains and Puget Sound as you meander around 9-acre waterfront **Olympic Sculpture Park.** Enjoy a view of the city from the water on Seattle Ferry Service's **Sunday Ice Cream Cruise.** You'll see many dogs at **Pike Place Market,** where the vendors love four-legged visitors. Dogs are allowed through the main arcade but not inside buildings. Stop at the **Adventure Days!** stall to buy Fifi handmade, all-natural treats. Because of the crowds at the market, a stroller or tote bag for small dogs is highly recommended.

A dog needs a social secretary to sort through all the furbulous pet invitations. Every Wednesday from June through September, pet parents and their pooches flock to the tony **Woodmark Hotel & Spa,** on the shore of Lake Washington, for Yappier Hour. Every July *City Dog* magazine puts on **Dog Day on Elliot Bay,** a scenic cruise along Seattle's waterfront to Blake Island, a 475-acre state park with miles of uninhabited beaches and trails to explore, followed by a feast. Seattle Humane Society's **Tuxes & Tails,** a gala and auction, is held in May, and the organization's **Walk for the Animals** and **FidoFEST** in September.

> ## Insider Tip
>
> "Seattle's Washington Park Arboretum, a 230-acre oasis along part of Lake Washington Boulevard, is a paradise for our Chloe, a 13-lb Cavalier King Charles Spaniel, at any time of year. The one part you can't visit with your leashed pup is the exquisite Japanese Garden, but Seattle, happily, has a second, equally beautiful Japanese garden just south of downtown; leashed dogs are welcome at **Kubota Garden.**"
> — MARY-ALICE POMPUTIUS, *dogjaunt.com*

UNIQUE ACTIVITY

Treat your posh pal to a fine dining experience at the **Dining Dog Café & Bakery,** a canine-only restaurant in nearby Edmonds, serving four-course meals that include doggie cocktails (Barkarita and Chowtini), appetizers, entrées, and desserts in an elegant setting, complete with soft music, gold platters, chandeliers, low benches, and plush pillows. Open Thursday through Saturday. Reservations necessary for pawty of six or more. Takeout available. diningdog.com

Emergency Veterinarian
Animal Critical Care and Emergency Services (ACCES)—criticalcarevets.com; 206-364-1660

Yakima Valley, Washington

Yakima Valley in Washington State prides itself on its wine, love for dogs, and 300 days of sunshine, all of which combine to create a fun-filled environment highlighted by events and Fido-friendly activities. The valley, located within a two-to-three-hour drive of Seattle, Portland, and Spokane, appreciates pooches so much that its visitors bureau encourages locals and travelers to send in a photo of their pooch and a story about their adventure in Yakima for its website, WineDoggies.com.

🐾 PLAY

When nature calls, head to the **Greenway,** fondly called the Jewel of Yakima, a collection of parks, paths, and natural areas along the Yakima and Naches Rivers. Fifi can canvass 10 miles of paved paths while on leash. When she needs more freedom, let her off leash inside the 1-acre, fenced dog park at **Sherman Park,** one of the Greenway's three parks. Take your leashed pup on a scenic hike along a Yakima River suspension bridge at the **Umtanum Creek Recreation Area,** at the northern end of the Yakima River Canyon. Among the many other hiking options: **Cowiche Canyon Trail; Dog Lake Trail,** just past White Pass mountain and offering a spectacular view; the picturesque **Tieton River Trail; Edgar Rock Trail;** and **Little Bald Mountain Trail.** Leash required on all.

🐕 SIT

The Paw Spa is a mobile dog-grooming salon, owned and operated by a certified master groomer, that brings its services to you. Pets receive a five-minute soothing hydro massage, followed by a facial treatment and aromatherapy in a relaxing atmosphere; treats and bottled water are provided. Grooming is also available at **Yakima Tropical Fish & Pet Village,** family owned and operated for more than 40 years. For doggie day care, **Barking Barnyard, K9 Country Club,** and **Little Paws Playhouse** are available.

🥫 HAUTE DOG

Pick up food, treats, collars, leashes, and other supplies at **Pet Pantry.**

🦴 CHOW TIME

When it's time to say bone appétit, head to **River Ridge Restaurant,** where you can often find dogs on the 1,600-square-foot deck overlooking the golf course; **Russillo's Pizza and Gelato,** which has a great outdoor boardwalk dining area; **Second Street Grill;** or **Tony's Steakhouse** are just a few of the restaurants that allow pooches on their patio.

🐾 COME

Yakima Valley produces more than one-third of eastern Washington's wine and 98 percent of the region's grapes. Oenophiles can take their well-socialized furry friends to wineries, some of which will let dogs inside the tasting room, but you should ask first. Rover can roam the grounds at **Two Mountain Winery** off leash but must be leashed inside the tasting room. **Airfield Estates** says yes to pups in the tasting room, on the patio, and on the grounds. **Apex Cellars** provides water and treats for Fido. Have a picnic with your pup on **Bonair Winery**'s large, grassy grounds. **Paradisos del Sol** offers dogsitting services outside the tasting room while you imbibe. Many of the wineries have a resident dog or two. **Sleeping Dogs Wine**'s canine valet, Aurora, greets people and their pets.

Almost daily, you'll see friendly dogs on leashes walking with their humans at the **Central Washington Agricultural**

Stay
All Pups Welcome

■ *Canyon River Ranch Lodge (Ellensburg):* Two dogs/small or medium sized. Fee. canyonriver.net/

■ *Cherry Wood Bed, Breakfast and Barn (Zillah):* This working farm provides a dog bed in your tepee and has a kennel for when you go out on a wine ride. No number/size restrictions. Fee. cherrywoodbbandb.com

■ *Holiday Inn Yakima (Downtown Yakima):* Dog treats upon check-in. No number restriction/smaller dogs. Fee. ihg.com/holidayinn/hotels/us/en/yakima/ykmyw/hoteldetail

Museum, where interactive exhibits of living history are on display. The **McAllister Museum of Aviation, Yakima Area Arboretum, Yakima Farmer's Market, Cobblestones Gifts & Antiques,** and **Inklings Bookshop** are among the other establishments that allow leashed dogs. Your tyke can come along with you as you pick raspberries, blueberries, apples, pears, peaches, cherries, apricots, plums, squash, and other fruits and veggies at **Yakima All Natural U-Pick Berries and Fruit.** Pick up Fido Fruits, made from 100 percent Washington apples, at the dog-friendly Yakima Valley Visitor Information Center (off I-82), which also provides a water bowl, dog biscuits, and designated doggie rest stop with bags and a waste can.

> ## Insider Tip
>
> "I love to start my mornings taking Murphy, my Golden Retriever, on a trek along the **Cowiche Canyon** trails just north of town. Nearby you see vineyards and apple orchards, and the view is reminiscent of the countryside outside Florence, Italy. The cherry on the cake is that in the distance loom Mount Rainier and Mount Adams. It's like heaven, and Murphy, who is the resident house dog at City Hall, enjoys snooping around the rocks and brush."
> — TONY O'ROURKE, *Yakima City Manager*

Among the annual pet events, Wags to Riches Animal Rescue's **Spaghetti and No Balls Dinner** takes place in February. **See Spot Run 5K Walk/Run** is in April. **Canine & Wine Walk,** to benefit Yakima Pet Rescue, starts at Cherry Wood Bed, Breakfast & Barn and stops at selected wineries the Saturday before Mother's Day. A favorite for dogs is **Paws in the Pool** at Franklin Pool, where pets are allowed to swim as the pool celebrates its last day of the season, to benefit the Humane Society of Central Washington. The society also puts on the grand **Fur Ball Gala & Auction** in October.

(FIDO) UNIQUE ACTIVITY

Enjoy a day river rafting on the Yakima River with your favorite canine companion. Dog-friendly **Rill Adventures** in Thorp offers self-guided trips and experienced guides, and supplies a personal flotation device for your pal. rillsonline.com/rivers.php

Emergency Veterinarian
Tieton Drive Animal Clinic—tietondriveanimalclinic.com; 509-452-4138

Southwest & Southern Rockies

Albuquerque, New Mexico

The television series *Breaking Bad* put Albuquerque on the pop-culture map, but it's the pup culture in this New Mexico city that lives on. In Duke City, Duke has a choice of 13 off-leash dog parks and can go to concerts, ball games, and farmers' markets. A pet consignment boutique sparkles at **ABQ Dogtown,** which sells high-quality food and treats and offers a self-service dog-wash area. Canines can get their kicks on Route 66, the historic road now called Central Avenue in ABQ. Pooch-pleasing stops along the main drag include: in trendy Nob Hill, **Dawg Gone Good,** a boutique, bakery, and paw spa; **Kellys Brew Pub,** which has dog food on the menu; **Flying Star Café,** which boasts "petios" (dog-friendly patios or sidewalk seating) at six of its seven ABQ outposts; **O'Niell's Pub,** which has a dog-watering station; the **Grove Café & Market** in East Downtown; and **Hotel Parq Central.** Other dog-friendly hotels include **Hotel Andaluz** and **Hyatt Regency Tamaya Resort and Spa,** just 30 minutes north of the city in Santa Ana Pueblo. Fido can hike trails at **Elena Gallegos Picnic Area** and **Albert G. Simms Park** on leash, but the ultimutt is **Paseo del Bosque Trail,** a scenic, 16-mile paved path along the Rio Grande's cottonwood-lined bank. **Tingley Beach** (man-made) allows pups on leashes but no swimming.

Aspen, Colorado

Jet-set pets can live in the lap of luxury in Aspen. This ritzy Colorado ski resort attracts the rich and famous, who come in on private jets in the winter, but also dazzles during the spring, summer, and fall, when cultural events and adventure options take center stage. Canines are coddled year-round. Nearly every shop and business on street level dispenses doggie treats. And if Rover's rhythm is misaligned after he checks into the Little Nell hotel, a Puppy Jet Lag Kit is available.

PLAY

Purse dogs are fetching, but for furry friends who like to frolic, there are plenty of opportunities. **Wagner Park,** across from the pet-friendly Limelight Hotel, is the ultimutt place for pooches to socialize. Dogs can be off leash, the same as at **Koch Park.** And on the southeast side of town, **Smuggler Mountain Road** doubles as a challenging hike for bipeds and an official off-leash dog park. You'll see pups off leash at other parks (except for family-oriented Herron Park), because the leash laws are lightly enforced as long as hounds are under voice control.

For an easy hike, hit the **Rio Grande Trail,** where Fido will appreciate the swimming holes in the Roaring Fork River. A more challenging trek is the **Ute Trail,** but it's worth the effort to enjoy the view when you and your best friend reach the summit.

If your ally is up for a bit of adventure, book a private trip with **Aspen Whitewater Rafting** or go stand-up paddling. In the winter, book a recreational skijoring (cross-country skiing while being pulled by your dog, or dogs) lesson with **Skijor-N-More**'s Louisa Morrissey, who has had Pomeranians to Mastiffs in her classes. Dog-friendly trails for cross-country skiing, snowshoeing, skijoring, and dog sledding can be found on **Bernese Boulevard,** which goes around the perimeter of the Aspen Golf Course, **Labrador Lane** (Snowmass Golf Course), **Rio Grande XC Trail, Maroon Creek Road** toward Maroon Belles, **Marolt Trail,** and **Independence Pass Road.**

🐕 SIT

After a long hike, take advantage of the self-service dog-wash area at local fave **Rocky Mountain Pet Shop,** which carries food, treats, toys, and supplies. Or leave it to the master groomer at **Barking Beauties Dog Spa.** Help a homeless pet by utilizing the services at **Aspen Animal Shelter,** where doggie day care, boarding, grooming, and a store generate revenue. The shelter also has a Rent-a-Pet program that allows visitors to take an adoptable dog out for a day of fun. Travelers have been known to take a furry friend home.

In the summer, Silver Queen Gondola whisks you and your posh pal to the 11,212-foot summit of Aspen Mountain.

Stay All Pups Welcome

■ *The Little Nell (Downtown):* Personalized brass identification tags, food and water bowls, bed, pet menu selections, epicurean treats, a handbook of guidelines for pet and pet owners, recommended pet-friendly hiking trails and groomers, dog walking and dogsitting on request. Puppy Jet Lag kit available. No number/size restrictions. Fee. thelittlenell.com

■ *Sky Hotel, A Kimpton Hotel (Downtown):* Pet's name on welcome board in lobby, bed, bowls, cleanup bags, and walking map. Dog walking/sitting available. No number/size restrictions. thesky hotel.com

■ *St. Regis (Downtown):* Bed and bowls. Four small dogs or two large dogs. stregis.com/aspen

■ *Aspen Meadows Resort (Historic West End):* Two dogs/no size restriction. Fee. aspenmeadows.com

■ *The Limelight Hotel (Downtown):* Bowls and place mat. Across street from off-leash Wagner Park. Two dogs/no size restriction. Fee. limelight hotel.com

HAUTE DOG

Canine couture can be found at **C. B. Paws,** which also has luxury accessories for pets weighing 2 to 200 pounds, beds, carriers, and homemade cookies. Aspen Animal Shelter's pet shop carries jackets, booties, beds, dog food, collars, leashes, dog sleds, and works by animal artist Ron Burns, artist in residence at the Humane Society of the United States.

> ### Insider Tip
>
> "Anytime I'm feeling the need for social interaction, I grab a shelter dog and walk a lap around town. I eat lunch outside at **Peach's Corner Café,** where I'm bound to run into many locals and tourists. I not only get to enjoy excellent conversation, but often end up finding a loving, responsible home for my companion for the day."
> — SETH SACHSON, *Aspen Animal Shelter*

CHOW TIME

Well-behaved dogs lounging at their humans' feet are a common sight at many restaurants. However, some eateries may make you abide by the rule of tying your dog up outside the patio area. Either way, waiters generally deliver a bowl of water to your sidekick without being asked. Al fresco dining is popular at **Ajax Tavern; Casa Tua,** great for pooch and people watching; **Above the Salt; Il Mulino; Poppycock's Café** (a breakfast fave); and **Terrace Bar** at the Little Nell. In the winter, pooches with panache gather for their own après ski in the **Living Room** at the Little Nell.

COME

Aspenites put on their seventies disco finery for the annual **Dancing for the Dogs and Cats,** an evening of dinner, drinks, disco dancing, and live and silent auctions held every July to benefit the Aspen Animal Shelter. Every January, furry fashionistas strut their stuff at the **Wintersköl Canine Fashion Show.**

UNIQUE ACTIVITY

In the summer, **Silver Queen Gondola** whisks you and your posh pal to the 11,212-foot summit of Aspen Mountain. Pups ride free, but you'll want to spend five bucks on a souvenir dog gondola pass with your furry friend's photo. At Aspen Mountain, dine on the patio at **Sundeck Restaurant,** meander along **Richmond Ridge** (the trail begins behind the gondola), or hike 4.5 miles down to the bottom.

Emergency Veterinarian

Aspen Animal Hospital—aspenanimalhospital.com; 970-925-2611 ▪ After hours: Valley Emergency Pet Care (VEPC)—970-927-5066

Austin, Texas

Rover has reached rock-star status in Austin, the state capital that bills itself as the Live Music Capital of the World. Raucous Sixth Street once symbolized this college town, which has blossomed into a hip, artsy city and major player in the music, film, and tech worlds. With more than 250 music venues, live sounds are everywhere, including the airport. The same can be said for canines, which have clawed their way to the top of the charts. More than a million bats may call Austin home, but dogs are everywhere from outdoor concerts to restaurant patios to stores. Home Depot is the favorite place for one local's three pooches, which ride on a blanket in the bottom of a cart and think they are the greeters. You can build a lasting bond with your favorite canine companion while enjoying beautiful music together in Austin.

🐾 PLAY

Before every hipster had a hound, **Red Bud Isle Park** was an underutilized piece of paradise, a 13-acre oasis positioned on a peninsula surrounded by Lady Bird Lake (formerly Town Lake), just below the Lake Austin dam. Now it's gone to the dogs, literally: It's the jewel of Austin Parks and Recreation Department's 11 off-leash areas. Be prepared for the long wait for parking, just a few minutes from downtown. Dogs can swim, and there's a short loop trail. Also popular, **Norwood Estate** at Town Lake Metropolitan Park and **Auditorium Shores.** On the banks of Lady Bird Lake and just west of the First Street Bridge, the 81-acre Auditorium Shores plays host to outdoor concerts, festivals, and other events. The off-leash area includes a place for Daisy to take a dip. All off-leash areas are open daily from 5 a.m. to 10 p.m. unless otherwise posted.

You'll need to leash your loved one if you go on the **Lady Bird Lake Hike and Bike Trail,** Austin's most popular path, offering 10 miles of scenic trails along the lake downtown. Don't be afraid to pose your pet next to the Stevie Ray Vaughan statue at the lake. You won't be the first. Although leashes are required, furry friends fall for the **Barton Creek Greenbelt Reserve,** where they can sniff the well-used 7.2-mile trail and take dips in the swimming holes along the creek. There's a large off-leash area inside **Walnut Creek Metropolitan Park,** but you'll want to explore the miles of winding, hilly trails with your pup on leash.

Furry friends fall for the Barton Creek Greenbelt Reserve, where they can sniff the well-used 7.2-mile trail.

🐕 SIT

Austin's music scene isn't just for bipeds. **Southpaws Play-school** in South Austin, which offers climate-controlled, free-range canine day care, uses music to help stimulate positive play and relax its charges. Also in South Austin, **Austin Dog-town** offers boarding, day care, and grooming, while **Jackie's Stay and Play** does the same in the Cherrywood neighborhood. **Mud Puppies,** with two Austin locations, offers play care, boarding, grooming, training, and a self-service dog wash. **Groomingdale's of Austin** offers grooming and, for pups 20 pounds or less, day care.

🌭 HAUTE DOG

Dogadillo, in the dog-friendly Hill Country Galleria, carries apparel, premium food and treats, and an amazing selection of cool collars. **Lofty Dog Village,** in the Village Shopping Center in North Austin, offers super-premium food and treats, locally made goods, unique toys, designer bedding, custom feeders, clothing, and accessories. **Tomlinson's,** with seven locations in the Austin metro area, carries natural, raw, and holistic pet foods, as well as quality pet toys, supplies, and accessories. **Bark 'n Purr Pet Center,** in Rosedale, also sells high-quality food and delivers with a minimum purchase.

🐾 CHOW TIME

There's no need to leave the leggiest member in your party behind when you want to eat and hear live music. In happening South Austin, **Freddie's Place** brings treats and water bowls and has live music Thursday through Sunday. **Uncle Billy's Brew & Que,** on Barton Springs Road, Austin's funkiest restaurant row, within walking distance of Zilker Park's off-leash area and Barton Creek Reserve, also makes sure tykes don't go thirsty and has live music on Saturdays and Sundays during spring and summer. Hound-friendly **Austin Java Tarrytown** has wine tastings on the first Friday of the month, and occasionally the Barton Springs location has live music. Other pooch-pleasing restaurants in South Austin include **Bouldin Creek Café** and the entire first floor of **Red Porch.** Downtown, al fresco dining with your dawg is available at **Lucy's Retired Surfer Bar & Restaurant.** Its Yappy Hour menu includes Surf Dog Delight, the three-ounce Lucy burger patty, and Canine Kahuna (grilled boneless, skinless chicken breast). **The Dog & Duck Pub, Carmelo's Ristorante Italiano, Snack Bar** in SoCo, **Cipollina** in West Austin, and **ZAX Restaurant and Bar,** close to the popular Auditorium Shores off-leash dog park, also welcome four-legged guests.

For your good boys and good girls, there's **Groovy Dog** bakery in the Westgate Shopping Center and **Woof Gang Bakery Austin** in the Clarksville neighborhood.

🐾 COME

Bring your blanket and cultured canine on leash to Austin Symphony Hartman Foundation's free **Concerts in the Park,** held Sunday evenings in front of the Long Center City Terrace from early June to late August, and to Zilker Park for **Blues on the Green,** Austin's largest free concert series, held every other Wednesday from late May to early August.

No one from Austin's Convention & Visitors Bureau will discourage you from bringing your leashed, four-legged sightseer on its two free, guided walking tours of downtown to learn about the city's history. However, if the guide takes a detour inside one of the buildings, your pal cannot enter. Tours depart from the south entrance of the Texas Capitol, which dates back to 1888 and is among the nation's most illustrious state capitol buildings.

Stay All Pups Welcome

■ *Omni Austin Hotel Downtown:* Two dogs/25 lb each max. Fee. omnihotels.com/austin

■ *Driskill Hotel (Downtown):* Pampered Pets Program provides custom bed, designer dishes and mat, bottled spring water, gourmet pet treats, souvenir toy, doggie business bags, Driskill-logo leashes and collars for loan or purchase, and a map with pet-friendly areas. Two dogs/35 lb each max. Fee. driskillhotel.com

■ *Four Seasons Hotel Austin (Downtown):* Amenities include a dog mat, food and water bowls, dog biscuits, room service pet menu. Three dogs/25 lb each max. fourseasons.com/austin

■ *Aloft Austin at the Domain:* Arf pet program offers a dog bed, bowl, woof-alicious treats, and toys. Two dogs/40 lb each max. aloftaustinatthedomain.com

Dogs on leashes can nose around at **Cedar Park Farmers' Market,** located at Lakeline Mall in North Austin, on Saturdays from 9 a.m. to 1 p.m., and **Mueller Farmers' Market** at the Browning Hangar on Sundays from 10 a.m. to 2 p.m. Of course, there's live music at both. Your paw-footed pal is also welcome, on leash, at **Zilker Botanical Garden** inside **Zilker Park,** where there is also an off-leash, unfenced area on the Great Lawn. And you can bring your side-kick on a horse-drawn carriage tour with **Austin Carriage** and to the annual **Bat Fest,** held the weekend before Labor Day.

Insider Tip

"There's a great patio culture here. My favorite place to go with Darren, my Australian Cattle Dog/Border Collie mix, is the **Bouldin Creek Café** in South Austin. It's a great place just to sit and enjoy vegetarian food, relax, and have a cup of tea. Darren loves to lounge at my feet and wait to see to see if I'm going to share my vegan cornbread with him."
— KIM ROCHE

Social functions for furry friends are numerous. **Dogadillo** throws a monthly Yappy Hour at its boutique the second Tuesday of every month, featuring a guest speaker from the pet world. Dog trainer Nancy Cusick-Finck's Yappy Hour takes place the last Friday of the month at **Irie Bean Coffee Bar** on S. Lamar Blvd. Lofty Dog in the Village hosts **Poochinis & Peticures** on the first Thursday of every month, as well as other regular events. Annual events include **Dogtoberfest** at the Domain in October; **Barkitecture,** a fund-raiser showcasing doghouses, put on every fall by Animal Lovers of Austin, Inc.; and **Jo's Annual Easter Pet Parade and Costume Contest,** held the Saturday before Easter to benefit a local pet charity. But the biggest is Service Dog Inc.'s **Mighty Texas Dog Walk,** a scenic stroll that attempts to set world records (so far it has five Guinness World Records), which takes place in the spring and draws 12,000 bipeds.

UNIQUE ACTIVITY

Go batty with your bowwow. Dogs are welcome on the **guided bat tours** led by **Congress Avenue Kayaks** around Congress Avenue Bridge, where up to 1.5 million Mexican free-tailed bats make their home from mid-April until October and emerge at dusk to eat insects. Tours take place on Fridays and Saturdays (Sundays also during BatFest) from May to August, the prime viewing month. Don't worry about your dog's safety around bats. "There is very little risk if your pet is vaccinated against rabies," says Dr. Deborah J. Besch, DVM, of Austin Vet Hospital. "The people probably need to be more worried because they haven't been vaccinated." congresskayaks.com

Emergency Veterinarian
AM/PM Animal Hospital—ampmanimalhospital.com; 512-448-AMPM (2676)

Colorado Springs, Colorado

The altitude isn't the only thing that will make you gasp in Colorado Springs, located in the middle of the state. Magnificent Rocky Mountain scenery can take your breath away, and it provides the perfect backdrop for you and your favorite canine companion to experience a multitude of outdoor attractions together in the Springs, home of the purple mountain majesty that is Pikes Peak, America's mountain. Colorado Springs, headquarters for the U.S. Olympic Training Center, boasts more than 300 days of sunshine and is popular from May through September.

PLAY

Your pooch can have a tail-waggin' time at off-leash, voice-command **Bear Creek Dog Park,** approximately 25 acres of nirvana with multiple trails, a creek, and a fenced area for small dogs. **Palmer Park** also has a fenced off-leash dog park, on the site of an old baseball field, .3 miles from the Maizeland entrance. Other fenced off-leash dog parks can be found at **Cheyenne Meadows Park** (south portion; native grass area), and **Rampart Park,** just east of the baseball diamond.

But if your favorite canine companion likes to trek and you want to soak up spectacular scenery, skip the off-leash dog parks (except for Bear Creek) and head for the off-leash hiking trails. As long as Fido is under voice control, he can ramble unrestrained at **Red Rock Canyon Open Space** (designated Dog Loop trail areas south of main parking lot), located along US 24; the ever popular **Palmer Park** (Yucca Flats), in the middle of the city with spectacular views of Pikes Peak; and **Garden of the Gods Park,** a registered National Natural Landmark. The designated off-leash area is east of Rock Ledge Ranch Historic Site. For the rest of Garden of the Gods, which boasts 15 miles of trail, a six-foot leash is required.

When visiting city parks and trails, keep Fido on leash. Unless posted, Fido is welcome on all hiking trails in the area, though there are restricted trails in the Manitou Springs Incline and state parks. Pace yourself and your pal when you tackle the **Section 16/Palmer Trail Loop,** a popular 5.5-mile hike north of the Bear Canyon that offers terrific views of Garden of the Gods and Red Rocks Canyon. On the **Seven Bridges Trail** in North Cheyenne Canyon (Pike National Forest), you may opt for the seven wooden bridges crossing the North Cheyenne Creek, but your pup can get his paws wet.

Pets are permitted to hike Pikes Peak, the country's most visited mountain. Trails range from 4 to 26 miles. Hounds are suited for the **Crags Trail,** an easy-to-moderate hike about 4 miles round trip that puts you atop a mountain with spectacular vistas of the Rocky Mountains and Crystal Reservoir. Slightly more difficult is **Catamount Trail.** Because of the wildlife around, pets must be on leashes. Canines up for a real challenge can tackle **Barr Trail,** which takes you to the summit, 14,115 feet above sea level.

SIT

After romping in creeks, stop by **Wag N' Wash Healthy Pet Center,** which has self-service wash areas and grooming at three locations in the city. DIYers can knock off two things at once at **Smudge Car & Dog Wash.** A bonus is the two fenced dog parks for air drying or just running around. After grooming at **Old Town Pet Salon & Barkery,** pups can enjoy cookies, muffins, and cakes from the doggie bakery. **Lucky Dog Resort and Dog Training School,** with locations in Colorado Springs South and Central, offers day care, training, boarding, grooming, and agility training, plus webcams so you can watch your paw-footed pal. Day camp, boarding, grooming, and webcams are also available at **Camp Bow Wow.**

HAUTE DOG

Whether your bowwow needs a biker jacket (pleather, no leather) and sunglasses, or you need a pet sling to tote your tyke, **Gigi's** in Manitou Springs, just 6 miles west of downtown Colorado Springs, carries it. The boutique has coats to fit pooches from teacups to Great Danes, as well as pet-themed gifts and breed-specific merchandise. In Old Colorado City, **Republic of Paws** sells all-natural food and treats, toys, carriers, collars, grooming products, and vitamins and supplements. Wag N' Wash Healthy Pet Center has shops at all three of its outposts that allow you to outfit your pooch in outdoor apparel and gear. They also have doggie bakeries with fresh-baked goods.

CHOW TIME

Nosh on the patio of **Nosh** in downtown Colorado Springs. Your dawg can also join you outside at **Phantom Canyon Brewing Co.,** located in the 1901 Cheyenne Building; at **Pizzeria Rustica** in Old Colorado City; and at **Dogtooth Coffee Company.** In Manitou Springs, **Coquette's Bistro & Bakery,** which draws both locals and tourists, and the **Stagecoach Inn,** featuring a creek-side patio, welcome dogs.

COME

Your dog is welcome at so many attractions that you'll have a hard time narrowing down what to do with Rover by your side. **Royal Gorge Bridge & Park** near Cañon City suffered extensive damage during a 2013 fire, but you two can still walk across one of the highest suspension bridges in the world (956 feet high and stretching 0.25 mile across the canyon). At Garden of the Gods, pets on leashes are permitted in the store and on the restaurant patio at **Garden of the Gods Trading Post,** in the southwest corner of the park, and at the **Garden of the Gods Visitor & Nature Center.** There are baggie stations in both locations.

Stay All Pups Welcome

■ *The Broadmoor:* Pitty Pat Pet Club provides bedding, bowls, a treat, complimentary Broadmoor ID tag, "best friend in residence" door hanger tag, designated lawns for pet walking, Pitty Pat Pet Menu, local maps to pet parks and scenic pet-friendly walking areas, and contact information for hotel's preferred pet specialists, including walking, petsitting, and veterinarian services. Broadmoor Pet Boutique sells a unique array of pet products. Two dogs/no size restriction. Fee. broadmoor.com

■ *Cheyenne Mountain Resort:* Bed & Biscuit Club offers bowls, washable dog blanket, eco-friendly dog toy, treats, courtesy cleanup bags, plus a stylish logoed dog tag, all yours to take home. Provides info on local pet services, including veterinarians, pet shops and groomers. Two dogs/under 80 lb each. Fee. cheyennemountain.com

■ *Radisson Hotel Colorado Springs Airport:* Food and doggie bags upon arrival. One dog/50 lb max. Fee. radisson.com/colorado-springs-hotel-co-80916/colospri

In historic Manitou Springs, an artisan community of 5,200, you'll find wide sidewalks, parks, and creeks ideal for dogs; water bowls outside shops; and pickup bags sprinkled throughout. Dogs must always be on leashes. The **Cripple Creek District Museum** allows well-behaved pets on leashes or carried in the buildings, which are filled with gold-rush history. Check out **Manitou Cliff Dwellings,** where leashed pets are permitted in the ruins and museums. Small dogs that can be carried can explore **Miramont Castle Museum,** an 1895 mansion that is on the National Register of Historic Places.

Wilderness Aware Colorado Whitewater Rafting has two lockable and shaded dog kennels that are free for your use while you go whitewater rafting.

Insider Tip

"We live in one of the most beautiful places on earth with many choices for dog fun, including Garden of the Gods, Cheyenne Canyon, Red Rock Canyon Open Space, and the Broadmoor. As owner and photographer of Blue Fox Photography, I have crafted human and canine portraits in all of these breathtaking locales. But our very favorite getaway is **Bear Creek Park.** Set in the foothills of Pikes Peak, it is a natural wonderland with long trails, shallow brooks, rock outcroppings, grassy knolls, and sun-dappled stands of Aspen. A perfect dog playground with lots of dog friends! My Westies, Mick Wagger and Lucy, strain at the leash to get through that gate!"
— WENDY PEARCE NELSON

Top-dog annual events are the Humane Society of the Pikes Peak Region's **Fur Ball,** usually held on the fourth Saturday in April at Cheyenne Mountain Resort, with a gourmet dinner, Pet Parade (that features adoptable shelter dogs and cats), silent and live auction, and a paddle raiser; and in the fall, there's **Pawtoberfest,** a 5K run/3K walk followed by a festival.

UNIQUE ACTIVITY

You and your leashed sidekick can enjoy "the Grandest Mile of Scenery" in Colorado. Located in South Cheyenne Canyon, Seven Falls cascades 181 feet in seven distinct steps down a solid cliff of naturally carved Pikes Peak granite. Trot up 224 steps alongside the falls, or catch a ride in the in-mountain elevator to the Eagle's Nest. Two hiking trails are open May through October. The reservoirs and café are off limits to Fido, but he's welcome in the shops. Watering and baggie stations are available. sevenfalls.com

Emergency Veterinarian
Animal Emergency Care Centers: animalercare.com; 719-260-7141 (North Colorado Springs) or 719-578-9300 (South Colorado Springs)

Dallas, Texas

"Big D" can just as easily refer to big dogs as it does to Dallas, the sprawling Texas metropolis where the conveniences of urban living extend to canines. Lounges for hounds, swimsuit contests for canines, and a free bark account at the local bank are just some of the offerings. This area also boasts the nation's largest Urban Arts District, 14 entertainment districts, pooch-friendly patios at restaurants, and a wealth of hotels that cater to four-legged guests.

PLAY

Dallas requires dogs to wear a tag showing that they are currently vaccinated against rabies in order to use any of its off-leash parks. Among the fave dog parks is **Bark Park Central,** under US 75 and convenient to downtown. Covering 1.2 acres, it features doggie watering holes, doggie showers, and a great downtown view. Close to dog-friendly restaurants and bars, it's open 5 a.m. to midnight (closed Mondays). The downside is if you're looking for shade, you have to stand under the freeway overpass. There's also an off-leash dog run at **Main Street Garden** in downtown Dallas.

    NorthBark in North Dallas scores high with its trails, man-made pond, washing station, and plenty of parking. Open from dusk to dawn and closed Tuesdays, the

5.75-acre park also has separate areas for big and small dogs. **Wagging Tail Dog Park** also has two separate areas, a concrete loop walking trail, shade trees, and a deck over-looking White Rock Creek, but very limited parking. In East Dallas, **Mockingbird Point Dog Park** provides direct access to White Rock Lake, where some humans let their pups cool off, but watch out for fishhooks and other supplies that can harm paws. The dog park also links to the 9.4-mile **White Rock Lake Park Loop Trail,** a favorite path that runs along the scenic shoreline, where you'll have to leash your hound.

In all, Dallas packs in more than 100 miles of hiking and biking trails. Hounds on leashes are welcome on all, and waste pickup is required. Another favorite trek is the 3.5-mile-long **Katy Trail,** situated between the Uptown and Oaklawn neighborhoods just north of downtown Dallas. It begins just north of the American Airlines Center and ends at Central Expressway. Look for dog-height water fountains at the David's Way Plaza and Thomsen Overlook.

Urban Dog Run, in downtown Dallas, is popular, too, because of its proximity to Main Street Garden.

SIT

Cool canines and their people hang at **The Pooch Patio** (Oak Lawn), which offers a beer/wine/coffee bar, doggie day care, boarding, webcams, full-service grooming, self-service wash area, boutique, bakery, and leash-optional patios with heaters and fans, outdoor televisions, and stereo. Yappy Hours take place daily from 4 to 7 p.m. and all day Sunday. Muttmosas, anyone? Soothing facials, pawdicures, and highlights are among the highlights at **Lucca Bella Doggie Spa & Boutique** in Oak Lawn, which also offers doggie day care and webcams. The **Petropolitan,** in downtown, also offers grooming and spa services, play areas, a boutique, and urban hikes for tykes, while **Woof Gang Bakery & Grooming** in Plano offers what the name states.

HAUTE DOG

Distinguished dogs will adore Lucca Bella Doggie Spa & Boutique's **Doggie Meets Décor** boutique, featuring canine couture, jewelry, bedding, toys, spa products, accessories, all natural gourmet treats, food, and

Insider Tip

"One of the most dog-friendly areas of Dallas is the **Bishop Arts District** in Oak Cliff. In addition to several restaurants like **Ten Bells Tavern** and **Bolsa,** there are a number of retailers like **Dirt** flower shop and **Strut** clothing store that welcome dogs. And every year during the Mardi Gras festivities, there's a **Krewe of Barkus** parade especially for dogs. My Pekingese, Chewy, and I make a point to stop in at **Green Pet** for treats and toys when we are shopping in Bishop Arts."
— YVONNE YBARRA, *dallasdoglife.com*

wine. The **Bark Boutique** at the Pooch Patio carries toys, treats, leashes, collars, clothing, cards, books, and more. **Downtown Pawz** prides itself on its all-natural food selection and provides services such as dog walking, bathing, and grooming. **Avenue Barket** (Lower Greenville) carries premium natural and raw food, all-natural treats, supplements, and remedies. Organic, natural, and raw food, plus stylish sweaters, are available at **Lucky Dog Barkery** (University Park).

CHOW TIME

A multitude of Dallas eateries allow you to bring your pals with you when you dine al fresco. **Mutts Canine Cantina** takes it a step further by featuring a 1-acre, members-only, off-leash park with full-time attendants, along with an on-leash, dog-friendly outdoor patio (doggie menu available) and beer garden open to the public. Nonmembers can pay per visit. Picnic tables, fire pits, and live music create a fun atmosphere at **Lee Harvey's** in South Dallas, where the action is turned up a notch on Sundays and pooches

Stay All Pups Welcome

■ *Hotel Palomar Dallas, a Kimpton Hotel (Dallas Park Cities/ Lakewood):* Bowls, bed, guestroom honor bar offering dog treats; treats, bottled water, and plastic pickup bags available at front desk; reserved grassy area for pets with waste-bag dispenser and disposal. Petsitting, grooming, walking, and veterinary services may be arranged through concierge. No number/size restrictions. hotelpalomar-dallas.com

■ *Hotel Lumen, A Kimpton Hotel (Dallas Park Cities):* Bed, food and water bowls, treats. No number/ size restrictions. hotellumen.com

■ *The Ritz-Carlton, Dallas (Uptown):* Insignia bed, homemade cuisine (based on the dietary needs of each pet), biodegradable waste bags with a leash attachment, signature Ritz-Carlton dog toys, and portable food and water bowls. No number restriction/ 25 lb each max. Fee. ritzcarlton.com/dallas

■ *Rosewood Mansion on Turtle Creek:* Crystal food and water bowls, treats, and a custom-embroidered blanket. Can arrange petsitting, walking, and grooming services. Often the bellmen or front desk attendant will walk a dog for guests. No number/ size restrictions. Fee. rosewoodhotels.com/en/mansiononturtlecreek

■ *W Dallas–Victory (Victory Park):* P.A.W. (Pets Are Welcome) program provides custom W pet bed, food and water bowls with floor mat, pet-in-room door sign, toy, treat, W Hotels pet tag, cleanup bags, special treat at turndown. Concierge can arrange dogsitting, walking, veterinarian, grooming services, and more. One dog/40 lb. Fee. wdallasvictory.com

can socialize off leash. **Toulouse Café and Bar, Katy Trail Ice House,** and **Company Café** are three options to hit after the Katy Trail. There's also a Company Café in Lower Greenville. Additional choices include **Bolsa** (Oak Cliff), **Bread Winners Café and Bakery** (Uptown and Inwood Village), **Fireside Pies** (Lower Greenville), **Cane Rosso** (Deep Ellum and White Rock), **Y. O. Ranch Steakhouse** (West End), which gives a dog a bone, and **Iron Cactus.** Haute dogs can cool off with dogsicles at **Eden Restaurant and Pastries.** And fresh-baked doggie treats can be found at **Three Dog Bakery** (Plano and South Lake).

COME

Parks, such as **Klyde Warren,** welcome pooches on leash at their outdoor concerts, which happen frequently in summer. All outposts of **Half Price Books,** which has canine adoptions at its flagship store in Lake Highlands, welcome pets. **Dallas Farmers' Market** and **Dallas Heritage Village,** the largest collection of 19th-century pioneer and Victorian homes and commercial buildings in Texas, don't mind if you bring your little one to their outdoor sections either. In April, the annual **Dog Bowl** takes place at Cotton Bowl Stadium at Fair Park.

A multitude of Dallas eateries allow you to bring your pals with you when you dine al fresco.

The free event features an animal-only agility course, pet/human look-alike contest, giveaways, exhibits, pooch portraits, canine crafts, vendors, vets, and live music. The annual **Bark for Life for Dallas,** a fundraising event for the American Cancer Society, takes place in May. **Dallas Pet Expo** happens every June at the Automobile Building in Fair Park, and **Dog-A-Palooza** occurs in Garland in August.

UNIQUE ACTIVITY

Restaurant-hop with your well-behaved, four-legged pal on the **McKinney Avenue Trolley** to lively Uptown, where pooches are permitted on many restaurant patios. Afterward, catch the trolley downtown and walk to Klyde Warren Park, a 5.2-acre deck park built over Woodall Rodgers Freeway, complete with **My Best Friend's Park,** a dog park where pooches can chase water that randomly pops up from an in-ground fountain. You and your pal can work up an appetite before patronizing one of the many food trucks at the park, which opened in 2012. The air-conditioned and heated, restored vintage trolleys run 365 days a year and are free. mata.org

Emergency Veterinarian
Emergency Animal Clinic—emergencyanimalclinicdallas.com; 972-994-9110 ▪ E-Clinic—214-520-8388

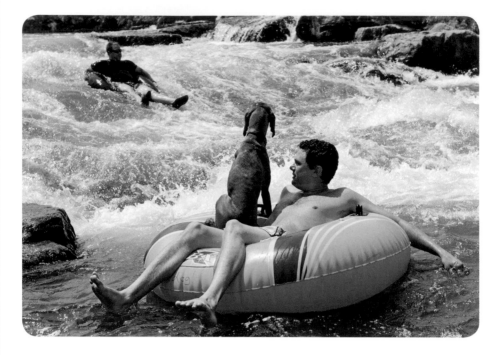

Denver, Colorado

Apet boutique at Denver International Airport is the first signal for travelers to Colorado's Mile High City that pets are well received in a state capital that fuses urban style and outdoor escapades. Your canine companion can nose around on a hiking trail in the morning, enjoy a spa treatment in the afternoon, and join you for an evening brew at a combination bar/dog park in this young, active city at the base of the Rocky Mountains.

PLAY

Because Denver is nestled at the base of the Rockies, not in them, the city boasts a milder than expected climate that is Fido friendly, too. Ten off-leash dog parks, all open either from dawn to dusk or 5 a.m. to 11 p.m., are sprinkled throughout the city. Pit bulls are banned at all of them. Among the most popular is **Stapleton Dog Park,** a 3-acre sand park with fountains for hounds, but no separate section for small dogs.

In nearby Aurora, the **Dog Park at Cherry Creek State Park** draws crowds, especially on the weekends. Canines can cool off in the creek and run to their heart's content on the 100 acres. But be prepared to pay for your pooch's pleasure. You'll need to purchase a Parks Pass for vehicle entrance, plus pay a separate fee to use the off-leash area.

It's a good idea to bring cash, because debit and credit cards are accepted only when the gate is open. Gate hours vary depending on the time of year. Cherry Creek also allows leashed dogs on 14 of its 20 hiking trails. Like Cherry Creek, the popular off-leash area at **Chatfield State Park** will cost you. But it's worth it for your favorite canine companion to enjoy 69 acres of open space, including two ponds and miles of paved and unpaved walking trails. Fave hiking trails to walk Rover on leash are the 6.8-mile **Platte River Greenway Trail** in Adams County, which follows the river and features sandbars that connect to sandy beaches, and the 14-mile **Sand Creek Regional Greenway.**

For the ultimutt social scene, there's **Washington Park,** called Wash Park by the locals. Dogs, squirrels, and geese (and their droppings) are in abundance at the 165-acre park, which dazzles with two lakes, a pond, dog-friendly trails (a 2.6-mile path circles the park), and colorful flower gardens, including a reproduction of Martha Washington's garden at Mount Vernon. Leash laws are enforced.

SIT

If you need doggie day care while you head to Coors Field for a baseball game, a Denver museum, or another non-pet-friendly attraction, services are available downtown at **BARK! Doggie Daycare + Hotel + Spa.** At **Dog Savvy,** your pooch can enjoy a blueberry facial, aromatherapy, or pawdicure from a pro, or you can utilize the do-it-yourself wash area, before you two kick back on the front patio and watch the happenings in downtown's Larimer Square, a trendy section of Victorian buildings on the Mile High

Stay All Pups Welcome

■ *Hotel Monaco, A Kimpton Hotel (Downtown):* Food and water bowls, dog bed, pickup bags, map. Concierge can arrange petsitting, grooming, and walking services. No number/size restrictions. monaco-denver.com

■ *Four Seasons Denver (Downtown):* Provides beds, bowls and place mats. No number

restriction/25 lb each max. fourseasons.com/denver

■ *Ritz-Carlton, Denver (Downtown):* Food and water bowls, treats. Culinary team can create customized meals for dogs. No number/size restrictions. Fee. ritzcarlton.com/denver

■ *The Brown Palace Hotel and Spa*

(Downtown): Puppy Love amenities include dog bowls, bed, "Pet in Room" sign, Bone Appétit treat with all-natural dog biscuits. One dog/no size restriction. Refundable deposit. brownpalace.com

■ *Sheraton Downtown Denver Hotel:* Sheraton Sweet Sleeper dog bed, bowls, mat. One dog/40 lb max. sheratondenverdowntown.com

City's oldest and most historic block. There's also lodging, doggie day care, and a dog spa at **Digstown** in Stapleton. **U-Shampooch Dog Wash,** in Stapleton's 29th Avenue Town Center, offers self-service wash and retail areas.

HAUTE DOG

Fliers passing through Denver International Airport can land at **Jet Pets Boutique,** on the mezzanine level of Concourse B, where doggie apparel, leashes, collars, carriers, and toys are sold, as well as T-shirts, clothing, and bumper stickers for pet lovers. Shop for your furry fashionista at **Dog Savvy,** which sells merchandise ranging from posh to practical, plus all-natural foods and doggie oatmeal–peanut butter cookies with yogurt frosting. **Mouthfuls,** in the trendy Berkley neighborhood, not only carries its own products like Doggone Fresh Breath Mints for dogs, but specializes in nutritious and safe foods for dogs and cats, and is known for its treat-tasting bone bar and bakery case full of homemade goodies. **Two Pals & a Pup Pet Bakery and Bowtique,** in the exclusive Cherry Hill North center, also provides all-natural, organic, fresh baked treats for your pooch, and in the winter has a terrific selection of winter apparel designed to keep distinguished dogs warm.

> ### Insider Tip
>
> "Each year my Weimaraner, Inkka, and I celebrate her birthday by hanging out in our neighborhood, Cherry Creek, just 3 miles from downtown Denver. The entire area is VERY dog friendly. In Cherry Creek North, while I shop, sip a coffee, and check out artwork, Inkka laps up fresh water at each shop, gets dog bones from the merchants, and cools off in the fountains. The finale is the homemade birthday cake we pick up from **Two Pals & a Pup**—the perfect way to celebrate my girl Inkka!"
> — RACHEL BENEDICK

CHOW TIME

You'll be able to tote your tyke to a muttitude of restaurants and bars, but know the rules. Dog-friendly breweries and bars without kitchens welcome dogs into their fenced-in patios, and often inside the building as well. For a restaurant with a kitchen, be prepared to tie your tail wagger to the railing next to you, but on the sidewalk side, not the restaurant side. Regardless, beer and bowsers bond beautifully in Denver. Enjoy a cold one with your dawg at **Bark Bar,** a watering hole with a fenced-in, 4,000-square-foot, off-leash play area in West Highland. **Ugly Dog Sports Café** in North Denver, where "Milk-Bones flow as freely as pitchers of Coors Light," allows dogs inside, and it has its own outdoor dog park, too. Dogs are welcome inside and outside at **Denver Beer Company,** where food trucks do great business, a nice stopover after Fido swims in the nearby Platte River.

Dog-friendly restaurants include **SteakBar** in the Lower Highlands, **Black Pearl Restaurant, Racines,** and **Old Capitol Grill** in Golden, 20 minutes outside of Denver. In LoDo, **Marg's Taco Bistro** provides fresh water (with ice when it's hot) to dogs leashed outside, and **Illegal Pete's** allows pets, too. When the mercury rises, keep your dog cool with doggie ice cream or yogurt at **Skoops Ice Cream and More.**

❁ COME

Bring a blanket or folding chair and your dog to the free outdoor concerts at **City Park Jazz,** held rain or shine every Sunday from early June to early August, at Denver's City Park Band Shell on Ferril Lake. Fifi can prance down the mile-long **16th Street Mall,** a promenade packed with outdoor cafes, shops, and attractions in the heart of Denver, or take a stroll through happening LoDo, where merchants leave water bowls outside. The LoDo District self-guided, historic building **walking tours** are perfect for man and man's best friend, and every August the **LoDo Dog Days of Summer** party is held at the **Riverfront Dog Park.**

Dog-friendly breweries and bars without kitchens welcome dogs into their fenced-in patios, and often inside the building as well.

In the summer, haute dogs and their humans can hang at **Patio Pooches,** a special section on the patio of 16MIX, a hip, outdoor cocktail lounge at the pet-friendly Sheraton Downtown Denver Hotel, complete with customized pet beds, water bowls, and complimentary Brew Bones, dog biscuits made of recycled hops from many of the local breweries.

Annual events include the **Taggin' Waggin' Pet Fair,** every June in O'Kane Park in Lakewood, with contests, vendors, demonstrations, vaccinations, and licensing; **Lucky Mutt Strut,** a 5K run or walk in May to benefit the no-kill shelter MaxFund; and in October, **Elitch Gardens Fright Fest Pet Parade** to benefit Denver's Dumb Friends League.

❤ UNIQUE ACTIVITY

Get creative with your canine at **Paw Prints & Cocktails,** a pet-friendly painting class offered at Ark Pet Art Gallery in Denver's Art District on Santa Fe. All events help raise funds and awareness for local pet-related charities. pawprintsandcocktails.com

Emergency Veterinarian
VCA Alameda East Veterinary Hospital—vcahospitals.com/alameda-east; 303-366-2639

Durango, Colorado

I t is said in Durango that the toys on one's car are worth more than the car itself. We're talking bikes, skis, and kayaks in this outdoorsy southwestern Colorado mountain town in the Four Corners region. Bordered by the scenic San Juan National Forest, Durango, which translates to "water town" in Basque, gets its name from the river that runs through it, El Rio de las Animas Perdidas (River of Lost Souls), better known as Animas River. Fido can enjoy adventure-filled days year-round and spend nights curled up in a historic hotel in downtown Durango, a district that is listed on the National Register of Historic Places. You'll see Zuke's all-natural, made-in-the-USA treats everywhere, because the company is headquartered here.

🐾 PLAY

Fido can amaze you with his dog-paddle skills when you play fetch with him at the 5-acre **Durango Dog Park,** located along the riverbank at the base of Smelter Mountain, and just a bone's throw from the pet-friendly DoubleTree by Hilton hotel. Pooches are also permitted off leash, as long as they are within sight and under voice control, in **La Plata County, the San Juan National Forest,** and **Weminuche Wilderness Area.**

Among the 300-plus miles of hiking trails within a half hour of downtown

Durango, favorite paths include the **Animas River Trail,** a nearly 7-mile-long scenic paved trail on the banks of the river that winds in and out of parks and over several bridges; the **Horse Gulch** trail system; **Vallecito Lake;** and the famous **Colorado Trail.** Plans call for an extension of the Animas River Trail to 12 miles.

Rent a pontoon from Doc's Marina and take your favorite canine companion for a couple of hours or all day on **Vallecito Lake,** 22 miles northeast of Durango, and tucked inside a secluded valley 8,000 feet above sea level. In the winter, cross-country ski and snowshoe with your pal on Vallecito's 9 miles of groomed trails.

Insider Tip

"We have three dogs—Belle, a Blue Heeler/Australian Shepherd mix, Baretta, an Italian Spinone that will do anything for pasta, and Daisy, a Bulldog not as active as the others—five cats, fourteen horses, and two mules. Belle and Baretta like to hike. **Horse Gulch** has all different types of trails, so there's something for everybody: If you're a senior citizen and just want to walk your dog on a trail that isn't difficult, you can do that. If you're young and agile, you can take your dog on a mountain bike ride, and if you have a horse, you can take it on the same trails."
— SANDY BRUCE

SIT

After a morning on the trails, dogs can clean up near the historic downtown at **Dog Gone Gorgeous** or **Healthy Hounds and Fat Cats,** where self-service dog-wash areas and professional grooming are available, along with doggie day care, boarding, and retail. Also nearby is **Wagging Tails Pet Salon & Boutique** in Bayfield, 20 miles east of Durango. If you ride the Durango & Silverton Narrow Gauge Railroad or plan for a non-pet-friendly adventure, doggie day care is available at **Dogs Rock,** which provides pickup and drop-off service; and **Durango Pet Resort,** which offers three indoor/outdoor play areas.

HAUTE DOG

Pick up sweaters, coats, collars, leashes, and raw, dried, and wet pet food at **Creature Comforts.** Healthy Hounds and Fat Cats also carries winter coats, toys, premium foods, and the essentials. And downtown **Pet Haus** offers high-quality food, unique products, and winter apparel.

CHOW TIME

Pets are welcome at many outdoor cafés, such as **Cyprus Café** and **Linda's Local Food Café,** and at picnic areas. Your sidekick can expect water and treats at **Guido's Favorite Foods** downtown, where **Nini's Taqueria** and **Serious Texas Bar-B-Q** are also dog friendly, as are **Ska Brewing Company** and **Cold Stone Creamery.**

😵 COME

Water bowls outside downtown retail shops are the norm, and some businesses, such as **Jitters' Java** drive-thru coffee kiosk on the corner of Eighth Street and Camino del Rio, **Maria's Bookshop,** and **Southwest Sound,** offer treats.

The annual Snowdown Winter Celebration, which takes place in late January or early February, features the **Snowdown Canine Fashion Show.** La Plata County Humane Society puts on its annual **Bark & Wine** silent auction fund-raiser the third Saturday in October.

🐾 UNIQUE ACTIVITY

You and your pal can see how Durango celebrates four-legged friends in public art by checking out **bronze canine sculptures,** created by local artist Patsy Davis, scattered around town. "Cash" is an appropriately named Labrador Retriever in front of Pine River Valley Bank, and "Semper Fi," prominently located in front of the Durango Police Department, is a German Shepherd that pays homage to search and rescue dogs. There's also "Napoleon," a jumping Labrador Retriever, at the Labyrinth Meditation Garden at Mercy Regional Medical Center, but unfortunately you can't take your pal. pdavissculpture.com

Emergency Veterinarian
Riverview Animal Hospital—riverviewanimal
.com; 970-247-8545

🏠 *Stay* All Pups Welcome

■ *Strater Hotel (Downtown):* One dog/25 lb max. Fee. strater.com

■ *Rochester Hotel and Leland House (Downtown):* Wagging Welcome Package provides Durango welcome bag, Zuke's dog treats, coupons to local kennels and groomers, Durango dog-friendly information, leash, doggie bags, bed. Two dogs/no size restriction. Fee. rochesterhotel.com

■ *DoubleTree by Hilton (Historic Durango):* Food and water bowls, mat, treats. No number/size restrictions. Fee. double tree3.hilton.com/en/hotels/colorado/doubletree-by-hilton-hotel-durango-RLDU-DT/index.html

■ *Apple Orchard Inn (Hermosa):* One cottage designated for dogs, and kennel available. One dog/no size restriction. Fee. appleorchardinn.com

Grand Canyon National Park, Arizona

An awe-inspiring trip to the Grand Canyon is all the more special with man's best friend. At 277 river miles long, up to 18 miles wide, and a mile deep, this northern Arizona wonder, one of the Seven Natural Wonders of the World, lures close to five million visitors annually and, rare for a national park, allows dogs on some of its paths. As long as Fido is on leash, he can sniff along the trails above the South Rim, including the mostly paved **Rim Trail** and paved **Greenway Trail,** about 12 miles in all. Enjoy a picnic at **Shoshone Point,** an easy 2-mile out-and-back trail with a superb canyon view. (A special-use permit is required for this popular wedding spot.) Hounds are also welcome in **Mather Campground, Desert View Campground, Trailer Village,** and throughout the developed areas. Kennel services on the South Rim, operated by Xanterra Parks & Resorts and near Maswik Lodge, offer day care and overnight boarding. Reservations are recommended. No pets are allowed in the "inner canyon" (below the rim) where wildlife roams, in park lodging, or on park buses. However, rangers love to have well-behaved dogs join their humans on the outdoor ranger walks and talks. Pet-friendly lodging is available at the **Canyon Plaza Resort, Grand Hotel,** and **Red Feather Lodge,** and in Sedona for more upscale accommodations.

Houston, Texas

Houston can boast that it's America's fourth most populated city, yet its southern hospitality gives it a small-town feel. But it is the hospetality shown to your dog that will have Fido wagging his tail. Pooches are welcome at some of H-town's best restaurants, dog parks possess an enviable amount of features for furry friends, and hotels lavish canines with so many creature comforts.

🐾 PLAY

Bayou City boasts a bevy of amenity-filled, off-leash dog parks of all sizes. Spread over 20-plus acres is **Congressman Bill Archer Bark Park** in West Houston. Open from 7 a.m. to dusk, the park boasts doggie showers and separate sections for large and small dogs, each with its own walking trail, agility equipment, bone-shaped swimming pond, and water fountain. Pet parents will put aside political-party affiliation to have their favorite furry canine companions enjoy the nearly 9-acre **Millie Bush Dog Park** (West Houston) in George Bush Park, named after the former President's dog and featuring three ponds, granite trails, doggie fountains, and showers. Also open dawn to dusk. The popular, 2.76-acre **Danny Jackson Family Dog Park** (Inner Loop) features small and large dog areas and a dog-wash area. Open 7 a.m. to 10 p.m. Downtown, **Discovery Green,** a

12-acre public park next to the George R. Brown Convention Center that's open from 6 a.m. to 11 p.m., has two dog runs for small and large pooches.

About an hour from downtown is Galveston, where leashed dogs can romp on the beaches at **Big Reef Nature Park, Galveston Island State Park,** and **Stewart Beach.** Pups must also be restrained on hiking trails, such as **Brays Bayou Hike & Bike Trail** (17.9 miles) and the trails in **Herman Brown Park.** All parks in Houston allow leashed dogs.

SIT

When your plans call for you to spend the day in Houston's Museum District, doggie day care is available at **Molly's Mutt House** (Independence Heights), **The Pet's Play Palace** (West University), and **Urban Tails** (Midtown), all of which also offer overnight boarding and grooming. Urban Tails also has a Bow Wow Beach Club, complete with lifeguards. **Rover Oaks Pet Resort,** a little west of town near Reliant Stadium, and **The Best "Little Dog" House in Texas** downtown, also offering day care, boarding, and grooming, receive high barks.

HAUTE DOG

Apparel for dapper dogs can be found at **Rocky and Maggie's** in West Houston, which also carries beds and fresh-baked puppy pastries. **Natural Pawz,** with 13 locations throughout the Greater Houston area, specializes in providing all-natural food. A jaunt from downtown (but your pooch will appreciate both) are **Barker St. Gourmet Dog Bakery & Boutique** in The Woodlands, which creates gourmet dog treats including dog cakes, and **Woof Pet Bakery & Boutique** in Old Town Spring, where healthy treats are baked fresh daily.

Stay All Pups Welcome

■ *Hotel Derek (Uptown):* Dog beds, treats, and even personality-packed bandannas. Finicky eaters will appreciate the thoughtful, pet-friendly cuisine offered on the room-service menu. The property also provides complimentary dog-walking services. No number/size restrictions. Fee. hotel derek.com

■ *Hotel ICON (Downtown):* Bowls, play toys, and treats upon check-in. Four dogs/no size restriction. Fee. hotelicon.com

■ *Four Seasons Houston (Downtown):* Provides bowls for food and water, Four Seasons place mat, small toy. Two dogs/20 lb each max. fourseasons.com/houston

■ *Hotel Zaza (Museum District):* Fresh water and doggie treats at the valet desk. ZaZa dog beds, bowls, treats, stuffed ZaZa frog toy, and gourmet canine cuisine room-service menu. Two dogs/ 25 lb each max. Fee. hotel zaza.com/Houston

CHOW TIME

You and your pooch can enjoy Houston's vibrant culinary at oodles of restaurants that have al fresco dining. In the neighborhood of Montrose, known for its restaurants, **Mockingbird Bistro, Hugo's,** and **L'Olivier Restaurant & Bar** are among your options. At **Backstreet Café,** the delightful dog-friendly front patio is perfect for people watching. **Porch Swing Pub** (The Heights), and **King Biscuit Patio Café** (Woodland Heights) are noted for their patios. **Treebeards** (facing Market Square), **Tiny Boxwoods** (Highland Village), and **Ruggles Café Bakery** in Rice Village are pawpular choices. **Barnaby's Café,** named after the owner's childhood sheepdog, welcomes dogs at its original location on Fairview and at outposts in Woodway, River Oaks, and downtown, where you can take to-go orders across the street to the dog run and picnic tables at **Market Square Park.**

At **Winston's on Washington,** dogs receive water and mats. The gastropub also donates 100 percent of proceeds from its homemade dog treats to local animal organizations and hosts regular animal-related fund-raisers. **Boneyard Dog Park & Drinkery** (The Heights) provides 7,000 square feet for your well-socialized sidekick to frolic off leash while you enjoy a cold one and grub from one of the food trucks. The Boneyard also holds monthly events promoting pet adoption and has a permanent pet-adoption board.

COME

Most of the festivals and outdoor events in H-town are pet friendly. Just remember to keep your friend on a leash. Bark your calendar for these fun annual events: **Doggy Party on the Plaza, Howl-O-Ween Party, Pet-A-Palooza,** and **Mutts Meows and Margaritas.**

UNIQUE ACTIVITY

Pups on leashes are welcome at the **Houston Arboretum & Nature Center,** a free wildlife sanctuary spread over 155 acres, with 5 miles of nature trails, including forest, pond, wetland, and meadow habitats. Guardians must pick up after their pals. houstonarboretum.org

Emergency Veterinarian
VCA Animal Emergency Hospital Southeast
—vcaspecialtyvets.com/animal-emergency-southeast; 713-941-8460

Insider Tip

"Our four-legged kids—Callie, Big Ace, and Sydney, all chocolate Labs—have many choices for fun. One of our favorites is Millie Bush Dog Park, where there is a pond to cool off on those hot Houston days. We also try to bring cool collars with ice or cold wet bandannas to tie around their necks. Also, Houston has come a long way in allowing dogs on restaurant patios. One of our favorites is the Barnaby's on Shepherd. It's a great dog-friendly place to hang out. The staff is so nice and my Labs receive lots of attention."
— BIFF PICONE

Palo Duro Canyon State Park, Texas

Texas, where "everything is bigger," usually doesn't defer to others. But Palo Duro Canyon State Park, located in the Texas Panhandle near Amarillo, bills itself as the Grand Canyon of Texas. And like its larger counterpart, Palo Duro, the country's second-largest canyon, welcomes dogs as long as they are on a leash no longer than six feet and attended at all times. Stretching approximately 120 miles, as much as 20 miles wide, and with a maximum depth of more than 800 feet, Palo Duro boasts spectacular scenery and offers 30 miles of marked trails in the park, and a river for Fido to dip in. Because pooches aren't allowed in state vehicles (or inside park buildings), you can't take your pal on the Canyon Driving Tour, but you can take your own scenic drive. Leashed hounds are allowed in the campsites, but no leaving your little one tied to a table or tree. Pet-friendly lodging is available in Amarillo, 30 miles north, at the **Ambassador Hotel** and **Drury Inn & Suites.** For dining in Amarillo, **Macaroni Joe's** has a darling patio with a fountain and brings water to dogs. **Jason's Deli, McAllister's Deli,** and **Braum's Ice Cream** also allow pups in their outdoor sections.

St. George, Utah

Mormon pioneers gave St. George the nickname "Utah's Dixie" when they grew cotton in the warm climate. If only they could see this scenic southern Utah paradise now that it has turned into quite the vacation spot in the summer, fall when the crowds are gone, and pleasant winter. The natural beauty of the red rocks of Zion National Park and Snow Canyon State Park; the addition of luxurious, dog-friendly resorts; year-round golfing; Tuacahn, a unique amphitheater that welcomes pets; and a cornucopia of outdoor adventures keep you and your pooch happily occupied.

PLAY

Fido can choose where to kick up his paws off leash with other canines. **J. C. Snow Dog Park,** in the northwest corner of J. C. Snow Park provides separate off-leash areas for small and large dogs. There's also an off-leash dog run in the 4-acre **Firehouse Park,** a neighborhood park in the Dixie Downs area of St. George. But just east, in neighboring Washington City, **Dog Town Dog Park** has a snazzy stream for Rover to romp and cool his paws, separate areas for pups under and over 25 pounds, a pavilion, park benches, and picnic sites. As long as your pal is friendly and on a maximum-six-foot leash, he or she can join you in St. George's regular parks, too.

The city boasts more than 55 miles of paved, connecting hiking and biking trails, where you can take your pal for a jaunt on foot or bike, if your sidekick is small enough to fit in a basket. At gorgeous **Snow Canyon State Park** (10 minutes away), a picturesque 7,400-acre park with majestic views, or in the 62,000-acre **Red Cliffs Desert Reserve,** you'll find fewer crowds than Zion National Park (30 minutes away). Snow Canyon boasts many hiking trails, but pooches are only permitted on **West Canyon Road** (8 miles round-trip), an unpaved maintenance road whose last mile is within the walls of the narrow head of Snow Canyon, and **Whiptail Trail** (6 miles round-trip), a favorite of hikers, bikers, and joggers. The same goes at Zion, Utah's first national park. Fido can't exactly follow the paths where ancient native people and pioneers walked. He's only permitted, leashed, on the **Pa'rus Trail,** the easiest path but still incredibly splendid. Both parks allow hounds in the campgrounds if restrained at all times.

In neighboring Washington City, Dog Town Dog Park has a snazzy stream for Rover to romp and cool his paws.

SIT

When you want to explore more than the dog-friendly trails at Zion and Snow Canyon, doggie day care is available in St. George at **The Animal Tender,** which also does grooming, and at **Red Rock Pet Resort,** where Fifi can splash in the kiddie pool. Full-service grooming to breed standards is also available. If your pooch is one of those travelers who lets loose on vacation, have **La de' Paws** do a "creative groom." This state-of-the-art St. George pet salon also does basic full-service grooming with add-on spa treatments. Go all out with the Unleashed package, which includes a blueberry facial, massage, and pedicure. **All Fur Love** in Washington City also offers grooming in a cage-free environment. DIYers can use the self-service wash at **Lovin' Arms Pet Center** in St. George.

HAUTE DOG

While your favorite canine companion is getting primped at La de' Paws, visit the salon's boutique, which

Insider Tip

"At the **Downtown Farmers' Market** in beautiful Ancestor Square, in the heart of St. George, your best friend will find local crafters, jewelers, bakers, farmers, and some great food. Be sure to stop by and see Dewey, our golden Retriever/ Cocker mix. He has his own booth, selling his all-natural dog treats and promoting animal adoption. Pick up some burritos, pastries, breads, or crepes, and of course some treats for your best friend, and relax in a cool grassy area while listening to local musicians play!"
— CONNIE AND STEVE SUTTON

carries outfits, fancy collars, leashes, beds, and unusual and hard-to-find items, plus a case of doggie bakery items that will make even you drool. In Washington City, two doors down from All Fur Love, you'll find **Bone Appétit Natural Pet Pantry,** which specializes in holistic pet foods, treats, supplements, raw diets, and supplies. Lovin' Arms Pet Center also prides itself on its selection of high-quality, grain-free food and carries toys, collars, leashes, and other products.

CHOW TIME

Dining with your dog in St. George is more challenging than Zion's most difficult trail. **Café Rio Mexican Grill,** where you can order inside and take your food to an outdoor table, is the rare dog-friendly eatery.

COME

You'll want to bark your calendar for these annual events: **P.A.W.S. Tails on Trails Dog Walk** (usually scheduled in May) and **Pet Festival** at SunRiver, an active retirement community (usually in April). Throughout the year, several of the local pet adoption/rescue centers schedule **pet walk-a-thons and dinner galas** with available adoptions. Look for them on the calendar of events at AtoZion.com.

UNIQUE ACTIVITY

Pups small enough to be carried are welcome throughout the **St. George Dinosaur Discovery Site** at Johnson Farm, considered by many paleontologists as one of the ten best dinosaur track sites in the world. Larger dogs can wait with a guardian near the entrance, where they can still escape the heat. dinosite.org/

Emergency Veterinarian
After hours and weekends: Southwest Animal Emergency Clinic—southwestanimalemergency .com; 435-673-3191

Stay
All Pups Welcome

■ *Green Valley Spa and Hotel (St. George):* Two pets/no size restriction. Fee. greenvalleyspa.com

■ *Red Mountain Resort (Ivins):* Organic treats, bowls, walking and hiking trails. Two dogs/no size restriction. Fee. redmountainresort.com

■ *TownPlace Suites by Marriott (St. George):* Two dogs/no size restriction. Fee. marriott.com/hotels/travel/sguts-towneplace-suites-st-george

Santa Fe, New Mexico

Artists and other creative types are drawn to Santa Fe by the golden light that shines throughout this New Mexico city and the backdrop of the Sangre de Cristo Mountains. Dog lovers are attracted by the welcome given man's best friend on restaurant patios, in boutiques and hotels, at outdoor events, and certainly around historic Santa Fe Plaza, the heart of the nation's second-oldest city, known for its adobe architecture and culture. Many of the nearly 300 galleries invite cultured canines inside. Boasting the nation's third-largest art market, incredible spas, and some of the country's best air, Santa Fe also offers terrific hiking, skiing, whitewater rafting, and biking.

PLAY

You'll appreciate **Frank Ortiz Dog Park** almost as much as your bowwow, who can run free at Santa Fe's lone official dog park while you enjoy mountain and city views of the City Different. Just make sure your pooch is well trained—there are no fences at this beautiful, vast park—and, since there's only a seasonal drinking fountain, bring your own water. Open dawn to dusk. Another place for Fido to frolic is the **Santa Fe Animal Shelter and Humane Society,** which has two large, fenced, off-leash areas that not everyone knows about. As long as dogs are on leashes, they're allowed in city parks as well. Cathedral Park, however, is off limits.

Santa Fe is a hiker's delight, but keep in mind the altitude (7,000 feet above sea level in town), climate, and summer-afternoon thunderstorms when on the trails. A local favorite trek is the **Atalaya Mountain Trail,** a 4.6-mile journey that begins in the parking lot of St. Johns College and climbs to Atalaya Mountain's 9,121-foot peak, where views of the city and sunsets are fantastic. About a 20-minute drive from Santa Fe Plaza, high in the southern Rockies, you can hike among the aspens on the 10-mile, aptly named **Aspen Vista Trail,** where there are plenty of opportunities for your pup to socialize and for you to gaze at the lovely valley views. This relatively easy hike is a don't-miss in the fall when the leaves turn.

Other popular dog-friendly trails are the 4-mile, tree-covered **Borrego-Bear Wallow-Winsor Loop; Chamisa Trail,** a 10-minute drive from downtown; and **Big Tesuque,** a half-day commitment. Dazzling, 360-degree panoramic views can be experienced from the summit of the relatively new **Sun Mountain Trail.** If you want more of a challenge and have a full day, take on the 6.4-mile **Santa Fe Baldy Trail** in the Santa Fe National Forest, which leads to the highest summit (12,622 ft.) in the Pecos Wilderness. Also in the forest, you and your pal can enjoy a mellow hike on the 6.7-mile **Rio en Medio Trail** (the trailhead is in the tiny town of Tesuque, about 12 miles north of Santa Fe), which creeps through the forest along the edge of the creek to wonderful waterfalls.

In the winter, go snowshoeing with you pal on the **Aspen Vista Trail** (beginner), or **Winsor** or **Borrego Trails,** both intermediate. Or head out of town about two hours to **San Antonio Hot Springs,** in the Jemez Mountains northeast of Los Alamos.

SIT

While you explore the museums and art galleries of Canyon Road or attend a performance of Santa Fe's world-class opera, let Fifi socialize with other canines and get fluffed while she's at it. **Barks & Bubbles** offers doggie day care and playtime with webcam viewing, overnight facilities, and full-service grooming. Day care, boarding, and bathing are among the services at Santa Fe Tails, which has webcams and is noted for its dog-training academy. **Paws Plaza** has indoor/outdoor day care with canine chauffeur service, full-service grooming in about an hour with no cages, and a retail section with bones, books, and high-quality raw, dried, and canned food.

> ## Insider Tip
> "I like to take my dogs, Lucky, a West Highland Terrier, Chumley, a Bulldog puppy, Conway, a Labrador-pit, and Achilles, a Heeler, to **Dale Ball Trails,** at the top of Canyon Road. I always tell my customers to go there if they want a nice little hike with their dogs that's shady and not too hot."
> — FREDA KELLER, *El Farol*

HAUTE DOG

Pawsh pooches should visit **Teca Tu,** a pet emporium that carries its signature, colorful doggie coats, hand cut from Southwest Indian–inspired wool trade blankets, bound in cotton, and adorned with silver-tone conchas, along with apparel from Apache River and Ruff Wear, Southwest-motif collars and leashes, gourmet treats, toys, beds, grooming, and gifts for pet lovers. Specializing in baked goods made in the store daily for good boys and good girls, **Pooch Pantry Bakery and Boutique** also carries a sizable selection of high-quality, healthy dog food, and plenty of doggie clothes, leashes, collars, beds, and toys. **Zoe & Guido's Pet Boutique** carries classic to contemporary merchandise plus high-protein, grain-free, human-grade foods.

CHOW TIME

The leggiest member in your party can lounge at your feet when you dine al fresco at several restaurants in Santa Fe, and many eateries bring water for your pal. Among your options are **El Farol,** where pooches can sit under umbrellas; **La Casa Sena,** with its lovely courtyard in the historic Sena Plaza; **The Shed,** nestled in a back courtyard; **Burro Alley Café,** where there's a fountain on the patio; **Amaya's** bar at the pet-friendly Hotel Santa Fe, **The Hacienda and Spa,** and **Cowgirl BBQ,** where there is nightly entertainment.

Stay All Pups Welcome

■ *Four Seasons Resort Rancho Encantado:* Bed, bowl, and welcome treats. Two dogs/no size restriction. fourseasons.com/santafe

■ *The Inn of the Five Graces (Downtown):* Bed or kennel if requested, treats, food, bowls, toys, pickup bags, and a pampered pet activity sheet with suggestions for pet groomers, masseuses, and pet communicators. Dog-walking service upon request. One dog/medium size or smaller. Fee. fivegraces.com

■ *Rosewood Inn of the Anasazi (Downtown):* Baked doggie cookies. Dog walking and dogsitting can be arranged. Two dogs/50 lb each max. Fee. rosewoodhotels.com/en/innoftheanasazi

■ *La Posada de Santa Fe Resort & Spa (Downtown):* Bed & Biscuit package provides bed, bowls, biscuits, and more. Concierge has info on local pet activities and areas. Fee. No number/size restrictions. laposadadesantafe.com

■ *Hotel Santa Fe, The Hacienda and Spa (Downtown):* Doggie treat bag and map at check-in for where dogs can do their "business." Upon request, butlers will walk dogs for guests at the Hacienda. No number/size restrictions. hotelsantafe.com

✿ COME

Pups are welcome on Canyon Road, Santa Fe's famous art district, but each gallery has its own rules on letting them inside, so inquire before you enter. Some of the galleries you can count on to give your pooch water and treats include **Mark Sublette Medicine Man Gallery, Charles Azbell Gallery, Canyon Road Contemporary,** where Maggie the Mutt is the hostess, **Mark White Fine Art,** which also has a shady yard, and **Beals & Abbate Fine Art.** Take paws at the **Longworth Gallery,** which leaves fresh water outside its courtyard gates, and where you and your pal can sit in a cool, shady courtyard portal to catch your breath and enjoy the serenity of the old-growth trees and wisteria.

You'll see every sort of breed with their people at the **Santa Fe Bandstand** free summer concerts in the Plaza. Your paw-footed pal can join you on **Custom Tours by Clarice, Inc.**'s 90-minute tram tour that covers the history of Santa Fe, restaurants, and places to shop.

Downtown, water bowls typically line the streets in front of stores around the Santa Fe Plaza, and most retailers welcome four-legged customers. There's often something fun going on in the huge, colorful space at **Zoe & Guido's Pet Boutique.** Yappy Hour for small dogs and their humans takes place the last Friday night of each month, and small dog adoptions on the first Saturday. Book signings and seasonal parties, including an annual Halloween bash, take place year-round. Other annual events in Santa Fe include the **Barkin' Ball,** an October fund-raiser for the Santa Fe Animal Shelter that allows well-behaved pooches, and the **Pet Parade,** one of the summer's most popular events and part of Fiesta de Santa Fe, the oldest continuous community celebration in the United States, dating back to 1712.

Downtown, water bowls typically line the streets in front of stores around the Santa Fe Plaza.

✿ UNIQUE ACTIVITY

As the mascot at **Historic Walks of Santa Fe,** Andy, a tricolored Cocker Spaniel, welcomes you and your favorite canine companion on any of the tours. Known for its daily historical-cultural tour of America's oldest capital city, the company recommends calling in advance when you plan to bring your pooch. He can't go inside churches on the cultural tour but can on the historic Ghostwalker tour. historicwalksofsantafe.com

Emergency Veterinarian
Emergency Veterinary Clinic—vescnm.com; 505-984-0625

Scottsdale, Arizona

There's a good reason Scottsdale is called the Beverly Hills of Arizona. Here in the Arizona desert, pets with panache can enjoy a luxurious petcation highlighted by canine couture shopping sprees, pawties, a fur butter treatment or pawdicure at a doggie spa, and chauffeur service in a Bentley to doggie day care. The Valley of the Sun, which includes Scottsdale, Phoenix, and the surrounding area, is at its peak from January through April as those from other parts of the country flock in to escape winter. Baseball's spring training helps make March the busiest month. But you can count on resorts to pamper pooches year-round.

PLAY

Chaparral Dog Park is the best in show of Scottsdale's three off-leash dog parks, and near the pet-friendly FireSky Resort & Spa. Four acres (three are grass) of fun include play features, seating, water fountains, and separate areas for passive and active pups. Open 6 a.m. to 10 p.m. from November 1 to April 30 and 5:30 a.m. to 10 p.m. from May 1 to October 31. **Horizon Park**'s off-leash area is .66 of an acre and has a 10-by-20-foot shade structure and a people/dog drinking fountain. Open sunrise to sunset and closed Thursdays 9:30 a.m. to 12:30 p.m. for maintenance. **Vista del Camino Park**'s off-leash area is a 0.5-acre plot with shade trees, benches, doggie water fountain, and double-gated entry. Open 5:30 a.m. to 10 p.m.

You can take your sidekick to regular parks also, but a leash is a necessity. Mountains all around will put you in the hiking mood. Take plenty of water for you and your pal, especially from April to November when temperatures can hit triple digits. All of the parks are open sunrise to sunset, as trails can be dangerous in the dark. You two can commune with nature on a leisurely stroll or heart-pumping hike at Scottsdale's **McDowell Sonoran Preserve,** a unique stretch of 27,800 protected, scenic acres full of impressive geology, lush cactus forests, and diverse wildlife. **Camelback Mountain,** in neighboring Phoenix, offers breathtaking city views. The easy treks are **Bobby's Rock Trail** (.25 miles) and **Ramada Loop Trail** (0.125 mile), with **Cholla Trail** (1.6 miles) providing better vistas. The greatest and most popular challenge is **Echo Canyon** (1.2 miles), but you'll be dearly rewarded with panoramic vistas from 2,704 feet above sea level should you and your four-legged companion make the summit.

> ## Insider Tip
>
> "Scottsdale is famous for its warm, dry climate, and Zucca, my miniature Poodle, and I love to explore the surrounding desert hiking trails, as well as the grassy greenbelts that snake through the city. He especially loves the dog parks. Our favorite is the **Chaparral Dog Park,** where he can run free and socialize with other pawsome friends! The extreme summer temperatures are a challenge, however, so I am careful to keep him hydrated and out of the fierce heat at midday, when the pads of his little feet can burn in seconds on the hot pavement. The pet store carries all sorts of booties for protection, but Zucca shook his head and barked a firm 'no' when I tried to strap them on him!"
> — SUSAN POHLMAN

🐾 SIT

When spring training games, golfing, or a day at the spa is on your agenda, a chauffeur can fetch your distinguished dog in a Lamborghini or Bentley for day care at **D Pet Hotels Scottsdale,** which has three indoor dog parks, lavish boarding suites, grooming, massages, and retail with high-end organic food and other products. When Bella needs a makeover, take her to **Oh My Dog! Boutique + Spa** in the ultra-hip Southbridge section of downtown Scottsdale, where groomer extraordinaire Ivan Lugo gets shelter dogs ready for their close-ups; pet concierge Monica Bern, a certified canine massage therapist, handles services for locals and visitors; and the who's who of the area take their coddled canines for deep conditioning massages and custom hairstyles. **PAWS Salon,** downtown, also offers day care, cage-free boarding, grooming, and retail.

🦴 HAUTE DOG

While your four-legged friend is being fluffed at Oh My Dog! Boutique + Spa, you can shop for your furry fashionista. Darling Susan Lanci Designs; Pinkaholic, Petote, and Kwigy-Bo couture lines; Poochie Beverly Hills dog furniture; Gems4Paws jewelry; HuggleHounds toys; holistic food; natural treats; carriers, beds; and more are on display at this snazzy boutique, where you can also have a custom place mat made from a photo of your pampered pooch, buy a birthday cake or doggie cupcake, and treat your friend to frozen doggie yogurt. Embroidered sweaters and specialty dresses are available at **Mackie's Parlour Pet Boutique,** which carries designer dog duds, beds, bowls, collars, all-natural treats, toys, and customizable puppy jewelry (think crystal-bedecked hair clips and collar charms), doggie birthday cakes, and pupcakes.

🐾 CHOW TIME

Mountains all around will put you in the hiking mood. Take plenty of water.

Don't make a hot dog out of your paw-footed pal. When the weather is right, there are lovely restaurants where you two can sit on the patio. A downtown favorite is **5th and Wine.** Other popular eateries include **AZ88,** where an expansive patio overlooks Civic Plaza's fountain and greenery, **Barrio Queen, Orange Table, Dottie's True Blue Café, Temple Bar Sports Grill,** and **OHSO Brewery.** Pet-friendly hotels W Scottsdale and Saguaro Scottsdale welcome pooches in the outdoor area of their respective restaurants, **Sushi Roku** and **Distrito.** Also at the W, furry friends can hang out at the **Living Room** (the first floor lounge/lobby area). Those staying at the hotel can feast on dishes prepared by the chef of Sushi Roku. The hotel also offers Yappy Hours on special occasions. Each Halloween, the W hotel also throws a Howl-o-Ween event (see page 198). Any time of year you can treat your furry friend to a doggie cupcake made with eggs, honey, and vanilla, and topped with yogurt frosting at **Sprinkles Cupcakes** in downtown.

🐾 COME

Spend an afternoon at Scottsdale's Waterfront district along the north side of the historic Arizona Canal. Your precious small pal can be carried or pushed in a stroller at **Scottsdale Fashion Square,** where Neiman Marcus, Barneys New York, Gucci, Cartier, and Bottega Veneta are among the tenants. (Pooch-friendly shopping is also available in Phoenix at **Biltmore Fashion Park,** where stores leave water bowls for dogs, there's a grassy area to take paws, and the Arizona Humane Society has **Petique,** a pet adoption center and retail store with pet accessories and items for pet lovers. Social functions are plentiful. Pet-friendly **Montelucia Resort & Spa** in Scottsdale throws a Yappy Hour the last Thursday of the month from December to April. The W Scottsdale sometimes hosts Yappy Hours and also a **Howl-o-Ween** event, where dogs and their owners dress up and compete in a costume contest. Oh My Dog! Boutique + Spa hosts regular events. Fido the foodie will relish the annual **Dine with Your Dog,** which takes place in Greater Phoenix in early spring and benefits the PetSmart Paws Can Heal animal-assisted therapy program at Phoenix Children's Hospital. Arizona Humane Society hosts **Compassion with Fashion** (usually in late March), a luncheon and fashion show with a silent auction and adoptable pets.

UNIQUE ACTIVITY

Downward dog takes on new meaning when you do **doga,** which leads dogs and their people through a series of yoga-inspired poses and stretches, providing a unique, healthy bonding experience. Doga is offered the first Tuesday of every month from 7 p.m. to 8 p.m. at the pet-friendly W Scottsdale. wscottsdalehotel.com

Emergency Veterinarian
Emergency Animal Clinic—eac-az.com; 480-949-8001

Stay All Pups Welcome

■ *FireSky Resort & Spa, A Kimpton Hotel (Downtown):* Welcome board, bed, bowls, and leash for use during stay, pickup bags, walking map, pet exercise area within walking distance. Concierge can arrange services. No number/size restrictions. fireskyresort.com

■ *Fairmont Scottsdale Princess:* Princess Paws program provides bed, "pet-in-residence" doorknob hanger, bowls with mat, toys, and treats. Concierge has info on dogsitting and walking services. Two dogs/no size restriction. Fee. scottsdaleprincess.com

■ *Four Seasons Resort Scottsdale at Troon North:* "Bow Wow" amenity includes dog cookies, toys, bowls, Four Seasons water, pickup bags. Two dogs/30 lb each max. fourseasons.com/scottsdale

■ *W Scottsdale (Downtown):* P.A.W. (Pets Are Welcome) program provides custom W pet bed, bowls with floor mat, pet-in-room door sign, toy, treat, W Hotels pet tag, cleanup bags, turndown treat, and in-room dining menu. Concierge can arrange many services. One dog/40 lb max. Fee. wscottsdalehotel.com

■ *Hyatt Regency Scottsdale Resort and Spa at Gainey Ranch:* 4Paws program provides all-natural gourmet treats, toy, Labor of Love bed, bowls, suggested walking routes on property, 4Paws Beastro menu, pet-in-room door sign, cleanup bags and disposable gloves, list of special needs such as veterinarian and grooming services, pet market, and boutique. No number restriction/40 lb each max. at the resort's discretion. Fee. scottsdale.hyatt.com

Sedona, Arizona

As if the majestic red rocks for which Sedona is known are not enough to dazzle you, there is the fun you and your favorite canine companion can have when you visit this central Arizona gem. Whether you and your pooch are outdoor enthusiasts or just want to sit and stay, Sedona delivers with a slew of pet-friendly hotels, restaurants and cafés, hiking trails, a furbulous dog park, and shopkeepers who put out water bowls to make sure perambulating pooches keep hydrated in the desert climate. While spring and fall bring perfect weather and an abundance of festivals and events, summer means swimming holes with your buddy. The occasional snowstorm in the winter makes the famous red sandstone formations radiate even more. The spiritual flock here year-round to feel the energy from the four main "vortexes" in this town, which you and your dog will dig.

🐾 PLAY

Your buddy can socialize off leash with other canines at **Sedona Dog Park,** the city's lone dog park, located off of Ariz. 89A on Soldier's Pass Road in West Sedona. Gorgeous views, separate areas for smaller/older pups and large dogs, plus a fenced-in hiking area are among the highlights. The park is open April 1 to October 1, from 6 a.m. to 8 p.m., and October 2 to March 31, from 7 a.m. to 7 p.m., but your dog must have a city license to visit. You can take your furry friend to all parks in Sedona, but remember to keep your pal on leash. The renowned red rocks offer not just natural beauty but fantastic hiking trails, mountain biking paths, and swimming. Pooches on leashes are permitted on all of Sedona's more than 100 hiking trails. **Slide Rock State Park**'s swimming area is off limits to pooches, but you can let your leashed pup sniff along the hiking trails of this 43-acre park inside the stunningly beautiful Oak Creek Canyon. Strap a backpack on your hound and head to **Brins Mesa Trail #119** in the Coconino National Forest, where the trailhead is convenient to town and the views, well, you know, astounding. But the favorite in the forest is **West Fork Oak Creek #108,** 9.5 miles north of Sedona. Open year-round (in summer, 9 a.m. to 8 p.m., in winter, 9 a.m. to dusk), this heavily trafficked trail is an easy stroll but does have numerous stream crossings. If you go far enough, be prepared to wade and even swim with your pal.

SIT

When it's time to wash the red dirt off Fido, head to West Sedona. **Bark n' Purr Pet Center,** owned and operated by Joel and Jana Oestmann since 1976, offers professional grooming by appointment as well as boarding, pet supplies, and accessories. Around the corner, **Classy Critters** also grooms by appointment. Your pampered pooch can have a "make my day" spa treatment at **Dirty Hairy's Pet Wash & Doggie Daycare,** where you can DIY or leave it to the pros, drop off your pup for an hour, half day, full day, or leave overnight for cage-free boarding. Dirty Hairy's also offers in-home care on Upper Rock Loop Road. There are three enclosed areas and hikes to the creek for canines up to it. At the end of the day, your pooch is bathed and brushed. Pickup from hotels and return delivery is available.

HAUTE DOG

Dress up your dog at Classy Critters, which has a small retail section with apparel and products. In addition to carrying fresh baked doggie treats, **Whiskers Barkery** in the Sinagua Plaza in Uptown Sedona has a fantastic selection of merchandise, including handmade collars adorned with Swarovski crystals and beaded collars from Kenya,

Insider Tip

"I take our Siberian Husky, Lacey, to the dog park just off Soldiers Pass Road. The views from the park are breathtaking! Many hotels, shops, and restaurants are dog friendly, and we especially like to go to Ken's Creekside on Ariz. 179. The dog-friendly outside seating offers wonderful views of our red rocks, and the sound of the rushing water in Oak Creek is so tranquil."

— BARBARA MOORE

strollers for summer when the pavement is hot, bandannas, T-shirts, carriers, bowls, supplies, and treats. **Sedona Pet Supply,** in the Bashas Shopping Center, focuses on holistic care and offers a wide variety of high-quality pet foods and other nutritional supplies.

CHOW TIME

There are always pooches on the rear deck at **Ken's Creekside,** where the views are superb, dogs receive filtered ice water, and a doggie menu with steak tartare, wood-fired chicken and Chef Michael's dry mix, and five-star venison stew among the options. You can also dine with your dog al fresco at the elegant **Dahl & DiLuca Ristorante Italiano,** which serves dinner nightly, and its sister restaurant, **Cucina Rustica** in the Village of Oak Creek. In Tlaquepaque Village, **René Restaurant & Wine Bar** and **The Secret Garden Café** have darling pooch-friendly patios. **Troia's Pizza, Pasta, Amoré** in West Sedona, **The Hideaway Restaurant,** and **Wildflower Bread Company** in The Shops at Piñon Pointe are other options.

COME

Take your tyke for a stroll around historic and pet-friendly **Tlaquepaque,** Sedona's popular arts-and-crafts village, named for a picturesque suburb of Guadalajara, Mexico, and offering eclectic shopping and fine dining. The preferred way to explore Sedona is in a jeep. **A Day in the West** allows Fido on its tours, if none of the other guests mind. Lapdogs are free and pooches over 20 pounds pay a child's fare. Or book a private, custom jeep tour for yourself and your pal with **Sedona Hiking Adventures.** El Portal Sedona Hotel, 70 percent of whose guests bring their bowwows, has its own pet-friendly jeep tour company, **Sun Country Adventures,** which offers a variety of red rock and vortex jeep tours. It can also send you and your furry friend to the Grand Canyon with your own personal guide and a gourmet picnic. In the evenings, El Portal Sedona's guests gather around a fire pit in the hotel courtyard with their dogs and a glass of wine for social time. With Arizona wines catching on with more oenophiles, wine tastings have grown in popularity. Wine dogs can hang out at **Javelina Leap Vineyard & Winery,** about 15 minutes from West Sedona in the historic valley of Page Springs, where the tasting room, winery, and vineyard are located on the slopes of a volcanic mountain overlooking the verdant greenbelt of Oak Creek.

Take your tyke for a stroll around historic and pet-friendly Tlaquepaque, Sedona's popular arts-and-crafts village.

If you visit in April, you and your hound can have a howling time at **Pet-A-Walkie,** a pet parade held in the Tlaquepaque village to benefit the Humane Society of Sedona, also featuring contests, psychics, vendor booths, entertainment, a pet blessing, and more. In May, **Paw Prints Thrift Shop** in the Village of Oak Creek puts on an auction to benefit HSS. And HSS puts on a **Bone to be Wild** motorcycle ride annually in May to raise funds. **Red Rose Inspiration for Animals, Inc.** organizes regular art and craft shows for animal rescue.

🐾 UNIQUE ACTIVITY

In the summer, you and man's best friend can dog paddle together in **Oak Creek,** a 14-mile gorge connecting Flagstaff and Sedona. Hounds love to swim in the creek year-round while their humans admire them from nearby. There are pullouts along Oak Creek Canyon's Ariz. 89A. Other swimming holes are **Brewer Road** (residential area), **Beaver Creek, Fossil Creek,** and **Dry Creek Road.**

Emergency Veterinarian
Oak Creek Small Animal Clinic—ocsacdvms.com; 928-282-1195; ▪ After hours: Canyon Pet Hospital (Flagstaff)—canyonpet.com; 928-774-5197

🏠 *Stay* All Pups Welcome

▪ *L'Auberge de Sedona:* Bed, bowls, goodie bag with toy, treats and cleanup bags, plus a map of nearby walking trails, and local pet resources. Petsitting and dog walking bookable in advance. Leashes upon request. Two dogs/no size restriction. Fee. lauberge.com

▪ *Amara Resort & Spa, A Kimpton Hotel:* Bed, bowls, treats. No number/size restrictions. amararesort.com

▪ *El Portal Sedona Hotel:* Dog-themed bath towel, free petsitting, and staff to feed and walk guests' dogs.

Rooms on the bottom floor have fenced yards. No number/size restrictions. elportalsedona.com

▪ *Sedona Rouge Hotel & Spa:* One dog/50 lb max. Fee. sedonarouge.com

Telluride, Colorado

With its dramatic landscapes, ski slopes, and festivals, tony Telluride in southwestern Colorado is delightful in the winter and summer and dandy for your discerning dog anytime. There's no dog park, but on any given summer day you'll find dozens of dogs playing fetch and frolicking at Telluride Town Park. There is a loosely enforced leash law in Telluride and neighboring Mountain Village, but Fido can romp freely on all the trails surrounding Telluride. The **San Miguel River Trail,** adjacent to the river (a swimming paradise for Fido), **Jud Wiebe Trail,** and **Bear Creek Trail** are worth sniffing around. Pickup bags and waste containers are sprinkled throughout the river trail and town. "Puppy parking" stations in both towns let you hitch your pup, although **Mountain Tails** dog boutique welcomes well-mannered dogs. Every third car is dog friendly on the **Telluride Gondola,** which connects Telluride and Mountain Village and lets pups ride free. The **Galloping Goose,** Telluride's complimentary bus service, also welcomes pups. **Dog Day Afternoon,** held in August, is pet-tastic. Dine al fresco with your privileged pooch at several restaurants, including **Cornerhouse Grille** and **Oak.** The **Fairmont Heritage Place Franz Klammer Lodge, Hotel Madeline, Peaks Resort and Spa,** and **Hotel Telluride** welcome discerning dogs.

West & Hawaii

Carmel-by-the-Sea, California

Achic resident joked that if you're not wearing dog hair on your clothes in Carmel-by-the-Sea, then you're not properly dressed. That's because furry family members are in abundance in this European-style village on California's Central Coast, outnumbering children in the city's birthday party and parade held the Saturday before Halloween. Teacups to Great Danes can be found at the idyllic off-leash beach, and in art galleries and wine-tasting rooms. Thirsty pups can lap from the Fountain of Woof, which provides a stream of water to the flowers on Carmel Plaza, and locals bring mats for their pooches to rest on while dining al fresco.

🎾 PLAY

At **Carmel Beach,** dogs graciously share with humans the 1-mile-long stretch of white, sandy beach where panoramic views of Pebble Beach to the north and Point Lobos to the south dazzle. From sunup to sundown, four-legged friends frolic freely, especially at sunset and on Sunday afternoons. They need not wear leashes, but their people are required to be within 25 feet, in control of their pooch, and to carry a leash. Just south of town, **Carmel River State Park** welcomes dogs on leash on its beaches. Coddled canines congregate at **Piccadilly Park,** a small and quaint park where no leash is required and voice command will do. An energetic Brutus can enjoy a hike in the 35-acre **Mission Trail Nature Preserve,** the city's second-largest park. The nature preserve filled with oaks, Monterey pines, and other native vegetation follows the same off-leash rules as the beach. But beware of letting unleashed Lulu wander into poison ivy. Mutt Mitt dispensers are sprinkled throughout the city to make it easier to abide by the law requiring waste pickup.

SIT

There is no shortage of groomers in Carmel-by-the-Sea and neighboring Carmel to shampoo, fluff, and buff four-legged friends. **Grooming-by-the-Sea** caters to senior and special-needs dogs in its downtown Carmel-by-the-Sea location. **The Pet Spa** offers a variety of special spa and grooming treatments. **Hair of the Dog** in the Barnyard Shopping Village does hand stripping, while **Signature Paw Spa** prides itself on having no cages and also offers massage, boarding, and private doggie parties. **Suds 'N Scissors** in the Crossroads shopping center never uses hot dryers and picks up and delivers pooches; it also boasts a small boutique and veterinary technician on staff. Doggie day care playgroups are available in nearby Monterey at **Dawg Gone It,** which also offers day and overnight lodging in a large climate-controlled space. DIYers can utilize the self-service wash facilities at **Pet Express** in Crossroads.

HAUTE DOG

Diggidy Dog, a 2,000-square-foot dog and cat boutique, boasts a vast collection of stylish apparel—everything from formal wear to T-shirts and tank tops—as well as leashes, harnesses, beds, natural and gourmet treats, strollers, and more. Napisa and Jeff Pollock, the proprietors, pride themselves on stocking merchandise to fit every size dog and offer their own clothes line in addition to the fashionable Tanner & Dash. Sarah Adams's store in Carmel, the **Raw Connection,** also offers a sizable selection of supplies in its 7,200-square-foot spot, but the healthy pet store is best known for its enormous offerings of raw food diets, grain-free diets, natural treats, and a knowledgeable staff willing to share its wisdom.

Insider Tip

"**Garland Ranch Regional Park** is a dog's heaven on earth, with more than 4,000 acres, many leash free. Fields, streams, ponds, and back trails abound. The **Carmel Mission Trail Park** gives your dog a chance to get breathing and you a chance to take a deep breath. Five miles of trails weave through willows, redwoods, and buckeyes, leading you up to breathtaking views of Point Lobos and the mission."
— JEFFREY ANDREWS, *pet parent to Lash*

⬤ CHOW TIME

"Bone appétit" is a familiar term, since dogs are welcome at 30 of the city's 53 restaurants, many of which provide water bowls and treats for Fido. Four-legged diners can feast on chicken and beef at the Cypress Inn, where pets are welcome inside **Terry's Lounge** at breakfast, lunch, dinner, and at the Yappy Hours held nightly Monday through Friday. They're also welcome in the garden, at afternoon tea in the **Day Room** and in the **Living Room,** where nightly live entertainment draws a spirited crowd. A dog menu is available at **The Forge in the Forest,** where Fido can feast on the Oak Tree Patio or Upper Garden Patio. Although there is no formal pet dining menu at **PortaBella,** the chef routinely whips up filet mignon, poached vegetables, and other requested treats for pampered pups. Furry family members can dine on PortaBella's front patio, ideal for pooch and people watching along Ocean Avenue, or in the rear garden patio, which is heated, covered, and serene. Locals and their hounds gather around the fire pit at **Village Corner** and on the chic, heated back patio at **Grasing's,** known for its ultrafresh local ingredients. For a romantic lunch or dinner with man's best friend, book a table on the front heated patio at **Casanova,** where whatever is in the kitchen can be ordered for canines and a sign reads "Chien Gentil."

Carmel Bakery & Coffee Co., a popular spot dating back to 1906, sells adorable baked goods like pink or blue dog bones with the words "Good Girl" or "Good Boy"

🏠 *Stay* All Pups Welcome

■ *Cypress Inn:* Historic inn partly owned by Doris Day provides bowls, blankets, and beach towels. Pet-washing station and pickup bags in courtyard. Three pets/no size restriction. Fee. cypress-inn.com

■ *La Playa:* Bowls, plush bed, and goody bag full of pet products are provided. Two dogs/35 lb each max.

(hotel may be flexible about weight). Fee. laplaya hotel.com

■ *Svendsgaard's Inn:* Bowls, blankets, and beds in room; crates, leashes, and other amenities upon request. Treats available. Front desk staff can make petsitting arrangements. Two dogs/ no size restriction.

Fee. svendsgaardsinn.com

■ *Carmel Country Inn:* A photo display of previous pet guests lines the lobby of this inn, which has an outdoor grassy area and provides a Mutt Mitt dispenser and endless supply of dog biscuits in the kitchen. No number/size restrictions. Fee. carmel countryinn.com

drizzled in white icing, as well as dog cookies resembling hot dogs. Take paws at **Pastries and Petals,** tucked away from the main-drag action and offering homemade dog treats and a peaceful, pet-friendly patio that attracts locals for breakfast and lunch.

COME

Well-behaved pups can accompany their humans on **Carmel Walks'** leisurely, off-the-beaten-track two-hour tour to backstreets, secret pathways, and places where famous authors, artists, and movie stars have lived and lounged. Monterey County wines are well respected, and Carmel-by-the-Sea features 15 tasting rooms. Oenophiles who purchase a **Carmel Wine Walk by-the-Sea Passport** can bring their pooch to all but one of the nine tasting rooms to which the passport gives access. Or take a furry friend on a private sailing cruise with pet-friendly **Monterey Bay Sailing.**

"Bone appétit" is a familiar term, since dogs are welcome at 30 of the city's 53 restaurants.

Carmel-by-the-Sea is flooded with art galleries, but pet lovers may particularly enjoy **Mountainsong Galleries,** where more than 100 bronze sculptures of canines delight and Mr. Bo Jangles, an Australian Shepherd, greets customers. At **Rodrigue Studio,** renowned artist George Rodrigue's Blue Dog works are on display, and visiting pooches can expect cookies and treats. Look for Hudson, a gregarious fox-red Lab, to greet visitors at **Avant Garden and Home,** which sells pet-themed art and gifts.

Nearly every dog has its day in Carmel-by-the-Sea, where breed-specific events are held annually, including the **Cavalier King Charles Spaniel Beach Party** in April, **Carmel Retriever Day** in May, the Carmel Dachshund Club's **Wiener Roast** in July, and **Poodle Day** in early October. Any breed of four-legged friend can participate in the 2K walk during the annual **Run in the Name of Love** event every Father's Day.

UNIQUE ACTIVITY

Enjoy an evening bonfire with man's best friend on Carmel River State Beach, where fires are allowed south of Tenth Street until 10 p.m. Remember that dogs must be on leashes on this beach.

Emergency Veterinarian

The Animal Hospital at the Crossroads—carmelvet.com; 831-624-0131 ▪ Monterey Peninsula Veterinary Emergency & Specialty Center—mpvesc.com; 831-373-7374

Del Mar, California

As well known as the Del Mar Thoroughbred Racetrack is, horses don't carry the status of hounds in this laid-back coastal town north of San Diego, where locals say, "Dogs have the right of way." Since incorporating in 1959, Del Mar has considered itself a dog-friendly city. And for most of the year, canines are in control.

PLAY

Del Mar boasts more than 2 miles of unspoiled, sandy beach divided into three sections, **North Beach, Main Beach,** and **South Beach,** and two major parks, **Seagrove Park** and **Powerhouse Park,** all of which allow four-legged friends nine months of the year.

The portion of the beach that matters most to pet lovers is North Beach, commonly called Dog Beach. Beginning at 29th Street and stretching nearly .5 mile north to Solana Beach, Dog Beach is where canines can frolic freely, as long as they are under voice control, from the day after Labor Day through June 14. From June 15 through Labor Day, tail waggers are restricted to a six-foot leash.

The more restrictive Main Beach, from the northern end of Powerhouse Park to 29th Street, also mandates that furry friends be on leashes after Labor Day through June 14, but it does not allow dogs at all from June 15 through Labor Day.

On South Beach, from Powerhouse Park south to the border of Torrey Pines at Sixth Street, dogs must be leashed year-round.

Leashed pooches can kick up their paws at most San Diego County parks, including **San Dieguito County Park** in Del Mar.

SIT

When saltwater wreaks havoc on a pet's coat, head to **The Curry Comb,** an institution in Del Mar, for grooming. **The Boulevard Dog,** a cage-free grooming facility inside Tsavo's Canine Rehabilitation and Fitness Center, is equipped to handle elderly and injured dogs. **Beauty for the Beasts** brings its mobile grooming salon to clients. Just to the north of Del Mar, **Solana Beach Do-It-Yourself Dog Wash** offers just that, as well as doggie day care.

HAUTE DOG

In the winter, **Dexter's Deli** carries fleece apparel and sweaters. Year-round you can find plenty of toys there to keep Fido busy at the beach, as well as collars, leashes, beds, and bowls. Furry fashionistas can head north to **Muttropolis** in Solana Beach, the next town north.

CHOW TIME

Dexter's Deli may sound like a place to grab a sandwich, but it is a health food store for dogs and cats, with a staff willing to share its vast knowledge about the raw-food diet movement. In addition to stocking an eye-popping inventory of raw food, Dexter's Deli also offers dehydrated, freeze-dried, high-quality canned and dry food; supplements; USA-sourced treats; and fresh-baked cookies and cakes for pawties made at a human bakery with human-grade ingredients. Fresh-baked goodies are also available at **Three Dog Bakery,** on the lower level of Flower Hill Promenade.

For pet-friendly restaurants, soak up the sunshine and gaze at the ocean with Fifi at **Pacifica Breeze Café,** a relaxing outdoor restaurant on the second floor of Del Mar Plaza, open for breakfast and lunch. Directly below, **Smashburger** welcomes pups on its patio. Join the locals and their pooches on the shaded patio of **Stratford Court Cafe,** which is open for

Stay
All Pups Welcome

■ *L'Auberge del Mar:* Gourmet treats, "champagne" water dish and "caviar" food bowl provided. French Poodle Sofie is the mascot. One dog/15 lb max. Fee. laubergedelmar.com

■ *Hotel Indigo:* Treats from Dexter's Deli and a coupon to be used at the store. Upon request, bed and bowls. Two dogs/no size restriction. Fee. hotelindigo.com

breakfast and lunch. **En Fuego Cantina** and **Burger Lounge** also welcome pets on their patios.

COME

The Helen Woodward Animal Center puts on a variety of events throughout the year but none bigger than the annual **Surf-a-Thon,** held every September on Dog Beach. The dog surfing competition and human costume surfing contest raise funds for orphaned animals. Pug Rescue of San Diego County throws its **Annual Pug Party** at Del Mar Fairgrounds the first Saturday of every May, drawing between 500 and 600 Pugs. Muttropolis in Solana Beach hosts fun events, such as Cinco de Mayo fiestas and parties for designated breeds, and also partners with local shelters.

Insider Tip

"Go to **Prepkitchen,** which is always happy to cook a meal for your dog."
— OWEN COBB, *pet parent to Maya*

UNIQUE ACTIVITY

Adventurous canines can take surfing lessons taught by members of the **SoCal Surf Dogs Club,** in partnership with the Helen Woodward Animal Center, from June through August. Start with a GromMutt class to introduce pooches to the water, or jump right into a dog surf lesson. animalcenter.org/donate/donate_surf_clinics.aspx

Emergency Veterinarian
All Creatures Hospital, Inc.—allcreatureshospital.com; 858-481-7992

Huntington Beach, California

When Henry Huntington wanted to lure tourists to his namesake city in the early 1900s, he hired the "king of the surfers," George Freeth, to perform wave-riding demonstrations. Today, surfing is not just an activity in Huntington Beach, the city officially nicknamed Surf City USA—it's a way of life. Dogs are nearly on equal par with surfers. Canines have their own beach, dining menus at several restaurants, Walk of Fame, and, of course, annual surfing competition, where they can "hang 20" in this laid-back city in Southern California's Orange County that fills up from May to September.

🐾 PLAY

Pooches can prance down the paved ocean path that runs alongside the 10 miles of continuous beaches, or they can head straight to the 1.5-mile **Dog Beach,** where it's not unusual for a dog wedding to take place. Located on Pacific Coast Highway between 21st and Seapoint Streets, Dog Beach is free, open 5 a.m. to 10 p.m., and provides bio-degradable pickup bags. As HB's only beach that allows canines, Dog Beach is where well-socialized pooches frolic freely in the surf and sand and romp with other playful pups. Although a city ordinance decrees dogs must remain leashed, in recent years only potentially dangerous dogs have been cited or removed if unleashed.

Diva dogs, which may not appreciate sand between their precious toes, can mingle off leash with other princesses at **Dog Park,** located inside the 350-acre **Huntington Beach Central Park** just off Edwards Street on Inlet Drive. Follow the **Dog Walk of Fame,** with more than 850 dog paw prints embedded in the cement path that leads to the fenced-in 1.5-acre Dog Park. Open weekdays from 9 a.m. to 7 p.m. and weekends from 10 a.m. to 7 p.m., there are separate sections for small and large dogs, benches, and tables, with water and snacks available.

Leashed dogs are allowed in the rest of the scenic park, the largest city-owned park in Orange County, where an array of events takes place throughout the year, including auto shows in the summer, cross-country racing events in the fall, and a jumping show at the equestrian center each spring. It's also the perfect place to picnic with a furry friend, stroll along the paved path, or bicycle with a purse-size pooch in a basket. In all, HB offers 70 parks, and all of them welcome leashed hounds.

🐕 SIT

Dogs can clean up well at the **Doggie Spa** in Seacliff Village and **Dirty Dog Wash** downtown. Both offer self-service and full-service grooming.

Doggie day care comes in handy when pet-totin' travelers go horseback riding or want to visit Bolsa Chica Wetlands, a protected nature reserve ideal for bird-watching and hiking, or to check out HB's iconic 1,850-foot pier, where the famous red-roofed Ruby's Diner sits and pooches are prohibited. **Doggietown USA** offers more than 5,000 square feet of indoor playground in a cage-free, leash-free, and supervised environment. **Your Animals Best Friend** also offers cage-free doggie day care in its 3,000-square-foot **Dog House.**

🏠 *Stay* All Pups Welcome

■ *Hyatt Regency Huntington Beach Resort & Spa:* Provides bed, feeding dishes, treats, pickup bags, and a doggie room-service menu that includes "yappitizers." Two dogs/75 lb combined. Fee. hyattregency huntingtonbeach.com

■ *The Waterfront Beach Resort, a Hilton Hotel:*
"Wag It at the Waterfront" amenities include bed, bowls, pickup bags, treats, and a free shuttle to Dog Beach; petsitting and walking services available. No number restriction/25 lb each max. Fee. waterfront resort.com

■ *Shorebreak Hotel, a Joie de Vivre Hotel*
(Downtown): "Something to Bark About" program provides bed, bowls, and list of local dog-friendly locales. Dog-walking services available. "Pet-a-potty" on second floor terrace and treats at the front desk. Zimzala Restaurant + Bar offers gourmet doggie menu. Two dogs/no size restriction. shorebreakhotel.com

HAUTE DOG

While HB offers an abundance of beach fashions at stores for humans, doggies may prefer retail therapy at one of the two **Petco** locations (Warner and Adams Avenues) or **PetSmart** (Edinger Avenue). Also, **Kahoots Pet Store** in 5 Points Plaza on Main Street sells name-brand products, while **Pet Supply** on Yorktown Avenue also has a great selection of quality and low-price dog supplies.

> ### Insider Tip
>
> "I've found early mornings and evenings the best times for Dog Beach because there are few people; it seems we're the only ones out there. Sunrise and sunset can be enjoyed in solitude while holding your four-legged fur baby."
> — GISELA CAMPAGNE

CHOW TIME

After Bruiser works up an appetite cavorting with other canines at Dog Beach or Dog Park, head down Golden West Street to the **Park Bench Café** in Central Park. At this family-owned outdoor café nestled among trees, pooped pups can rest in the grass at their guardians' feet and feast on dishes from the Canine Cuisine menu, featuring the wildly popular Bow Wow Wow (boneless, skinless chicken fillet cut into bite-size pieces) and Rover Easy (two scrambled eggs). On any given weekend, as many as 200 dogs visit the café, a favorite for locals. Sister restaurant **Kokomo's Surfside Grill** on the boardwalk, open March through October, on weekends in spring and every day in summer, also offers a similar dining menu for famished four-legged friends.

Chic canines and their people also have separate menus at Shorebreak Hotel's **Zimzala Restaurant & Bar** in vibrant downtown. Sit on the fashionable patio on the second floor and take in the ocean breeze. Hot dogs can cool off with Skippy Treats (house-made vanilla ice cream and smooth peanut butter), stay healthy with Trail Blazer (granola and yogurt), or go all out with Nibbles and Bits (8 oz. grilled burger patty, fried Yukon gold potatoes, and pan gravy). Paws up to **Shorebreak** for also making it convenient for canines to take care of their business. On the same deck as the restaurant, but out of sight and smell of diners, a large PETaPOTTY is available so tail waggers don't have to go downstairs and outside to relieve themselves.

Just as the name implies, hounds can also lounge at their owners' feet on the patio of **Lazy Dog Café,** an inland restaurant that boasts a doggie menu. A variety of restaurants on Main Street in downtown

HB allow pets on their patios as well. **Fred's Mexican Café** even hosts regular Doggie Date Nights on its patio each Monday. Customers who purchase an entrée receive a complimentary doggie dinner.

COME

As Orange County's largest beach city, with a population of nearly 195,000, HB hosts numerous surf competitions, including the U.S. Open of Surfing, the largest surf competition in the world, traditionally held in late July or early August. But none delights like **Surf City Surf Dog** event, where hounds of all sizes and breeds "hang 20" in their own surfing contest, held at Dog Beach every September. Three days of festivities include a doggie fashion show, Yappy Hour, canine costume and owner look-alike contests, and canine surfing lessons.

Dog lovers also gather annually for a tail-waggin' time at **Wags N Wine,** a wine-tasting fund-raiser that takes place on a day between Father's Day and the Fourth of July at the dog-friendly Waterfront Beach Resort. It benefits Waggin' Trails, a nonprofit that rescues and transports companion animals scheduled for death due to lack of space in California shelters. Premium California wines, fine food, live music, live and silent auctions, and a Pooch Pageant help make this HB's social event of the year for dogs and their people.

HB hosts numerous surf competitions ... But none delights like Surf City Surf Dog event

Leashed pets are welcome at the **International Surfing Museum,** as long as their nails are trimmed, and **Surf City Nights,** a weekly street fair that takes place every Tuesday along Main Street and features a farmers' market, live entertainment, children's activities, and food and merchandise vendors, including **Sawyer's Pet Bakery,** which sells hypoallergenic treats for dogs.

UNIQUE ACTIVITY

Take man's best well-behaved friend along on a romantic gondola ride through Huntington Harbor at sunset, one of the city's best-kept secrets. sunsetgondola.com

Emergency Veterinarian
AAA Animal Hospital—myaaavet.net; 714-536-6537

Las Vegas, Nevada

Sometimes you may wish your four-legged friend could talk. But a trip to Las Vegas with your high-roller hound may not be one of them. The city, whose slogan is "What happens in Vegas stays in Vegas," has long prided itself on its adult offerings. Only in recent years did Sin City begin seducing four-legged customers. Hotels doubled down on opening their accommodations to dogs, betting that doing so would give them a leg up on the competition. The Cosmopolitan of Las Vegas, one of the newer megaresorts on the Strip, featured dogs in more than one of its marketing campaigns. In addition to boasting about its restaurants helmed by celebrity chefs, nightclubs with famed A-list resident deejays, and day clubs that are all the rage, hotels can also brag about drawing top dogs.

🔵 PLAY

Pooches can get their daily exercise just walking down the seemingly never-ending hotel corridors. But fresh air for Fifi is a necessity. Most of the pet-friendly resorts have a designated outdoor area for dogs. The Cosmopolitan even boasts a fenced run near its **Bamboo Pool,** on the 14th floor of the West Tower. Prance your pooch on the Strip at your own risk. Crowds and local laws are a deterrent. In 2012 the county passed an ordinance banning pets on the Strip except between 5 a.m. and noon in an effort to prevent animal bites and discourage panhandlers from using dogs to attract sympathy.

For a different take on wildlife, head to **Red Rock Canyon National Conservation Area,** 17 miles west of the Strip on Charleston Boulevard/Nev. 159. In addition to a 13-mile picturesque drive, there are more than 30 miles of dog-friendly hiking trails and a picnic area for you and your favorite canine companion to spend some quality time.

Las Vegas also has several off-leash dog parks open from 6 a.m. to 11 p.m. The closest two to the Strip are **Molasky Family Park Dog Run** and **Sunset Park.** For downtown visitors the closest is **Justice Myron E. Leavitt Dog Park.**

SIT

When it comes to services, be prepared to venture away from the Strip. Drive 15 minutes to **Shaggy Chic** in Tivoli Village, where your pampered pooch can get a blowout, blueberry facial, and pawdicure while you enjoy this shopping/dining destination. At **Las Vegas Pet Spa,** in Southeast, Fifi can get a dye job and blueberry facial. **LV Dog Resort,** about 7 miles off the Strip in Westside, also offers doggie day care, along with

Stay All Pups Welcome

■ *The Cosmopolitan of Las Vegas:* Bowl, treats, toy, and pee pads. Dog run at entrance of Bamboo Pool. Walking/sitting services available for a charge. Two dogs/25 lb each max. Fee. cosmopolitanlasvegas.com

■ *Trump International Hotel Las Vegas:* Treats, bed, bowls, bottled water, toys. Dog-walking services can be arranged. Gift shop sells doggie treats, collars, and toys. Two dogs/25 lb each max. Fee. trumphotel

collection.com/las-vegas

■ *Four Seasons Las Vegas:* Bed, bowls, and treats made by hotel's pastry team. Can arrange for dog-sitting. No number restriction/25 lb each max. Fee. fourseasons.com/lasvegas

■ *Caesars Entertainment:* Caesars Palace, Planet Hollywood Resort & Casino, Paris Las Vegas, Harrah's, Bally's, Flamingo Las Vegas, The Quad Resort & Casino, and Rio

All-Suite Hotel: PetStay program provides treats, bowls, mat, map of dog-walking routes, and on-property designated relief areas. Two dogs/50 lb each max. Fee. caesars.com

■ *Vdara Hotel & Spa:* Amenity, in-suite dog dining menu, eco-friendly dog bowls, crates available upon request, access to 24-hour dog park with walking path. One dog/70 lb max. or two dogs/70 lb combined. Fee. vdara.com

overnight boarding, grooming, dog training, and a pet photography studio. A bonus is being able to pick up or drop off your dog 24 hours a day.

🦴 HAUTE DOG

For pet boutiques, you'll have to head to the residential neighborhoods. **Bogart's Bone Appetit,** with locations in Southwest, Summerlin, and Southern Highlands, sells apparel, food, toys, and accessories.

🐾 CHOW TIME

Despite all the deserved hoopla surrounding the city's superb culinary scene, the odds aren't great for finding one that is dog friendly on the Strip. Instead, head to **Pasquale's Ristorante** at the Lakes. Also, local pooches and their people hang out at Tivoli Village. **Poppy Den,** a gastropub that allows pooches on its patio, brings a bowl of water to your thirsty tyke. Meaningful Monday takes place weekly, and the

Tivoli Village ... hosts a number of pet-related events to benefit local charities.

restaurant donates a portion of proceeds to help local nonprofits, including pet shelters. In Town Square Park, **Double Helix Wine & Whiskey Lounge** and **Kabuki Japanese Restaurant** welcome pets on their patios. As the name implies, **Bogart's Bone Appetit** sells fresh-baked goods made with all-natural ingredients and will customize a canine birthday cake. All natural, fresh-baked food and treats for dogs can be found at **Three Dog Bakery** in Summerlin.

🐾 COME

Tivoli Village likes to think of itself as a European village and therefore boasts a dog-friendly environment. In addition to providing pet waste bags and containers throughout the mall, it offers luxury brands in one-of-a-kind boutiques and hosts a number of pet-related events to benefit local charities. When visiting, remember to keep your pet on a leash, and note that individual stores have their own pet policies.

Pet-friendly **Rumor Boutique Hotel,** two blocks off the Strip and across from the Hard Rock Hotel & Casino, throws monthly Yappy

Insider Tip

"**SuperZoo** has the most amazing dog-grooming competitions. Some of the freestyle winners I've seen were a Standard Poodle that looked like a giant bumblebee and a Husky that had its fur carved into an ocean scene. I'd love to get a lawn chair on the sidewalk and watch all the contestant dogs on the way back to their cars."
— ADRIENNE BREEN

Hours, complete with a live deejay, yapatizers, and cocktails. Among less frequent events, the Animal Foundation's **Best in Show** takes place every spring, the **Vegas Pet Expo** rolls through town every February, and **Pet-a-Palooza,** a full day of canine competition and entertainment, is held in April. Halloween is always a fun time to be in Vegas, and that means for pets, too. Las Vegas Hot Diggity Dachshund Club and Rescue puts on its biggest fundraiser of the year, the **Hallo-Wiener,** with dachshund races, silent auction, raffle, costume contest, photographer, music, games, food, and vendors.

UNIQUE ACTIVITY

Stay at Trump International Hotel Las Vegas and book the **Paws Massage,** a couple's massage for you and your favorite canine companion, in your hotel suite.

Emergency Veterinarian
Veterinary Emergency and Critical Care Center—vecc24.com; 702-262-7070

Los Angeles County, California

C anines need not possess Uggie's acting talent or be as famous as Lassie or Rin
Tin Tin to receive the star treatment in Los Angeles County. This sprawling
metropolis rolls out the massive red carpet with a bevy of dog-friendly hotels,
cutting-edge pet boutiques, year-round weather ideal for active tykes, and celebrity-
studded pooch events open to the public. Whether it's an urban hound that prefers to
pound the pavement in revitalized downtown L.A., a beach Bowser partial to Santa Monica, a posh pet accustomed to Beverly Hills–style pampering, or a dapper dog that wants
to be a bone's throw from the Hollywood lights, the tail-waggin' offerings are endless.

PLAY

Fifi should have no problem maintaining her figure in this fitness capital that offers an
abundance of exercise venues. Worth braving the crowds for the breathtaking views on
a smog-free day, and possible celeb sighting, is **Runyon Canyon Park** in the Hollywood
Hills, which offers off-leash trails and an off-leash dog park open from dawn to dusk.
Pooches can also romp freely at **Laurel Canyon Park,** in the hills of Studio City, from
7 a.m. to 10 a.m. and 3 p.m. until closing. A little off the beaten path is **Silver Lake Dog
Park,** the part of Silver Lake Recreation Center where pups are welcome.

Canines ready for their close-up should head to **Lake Hollywood Park,** where they can be photographed with the Hollywood sign in the background. Open from 5 a.m. to 10 p.m., this hidden gem up a windy road overlooks Lake Hollywood in the Hollywood Hills and is seldom packed.

Dogs dig the **Boneyard** at Culver City Park. Open from sunrise to 10 p.m., this off-leash recreation area designates separate areas for small/timid and large dogs. Other popular places for pooches to stay in shape and socialize are the 3-acre **Redondo Beach Dog Park,** located at the North end of Dominguez Park and open every day except Wednesdays from dawn to dusk, and the **Sepulveda Basin Off-Leash Dog Park** in Encino, also open dawn to dusk but closed until 11 a.m. on Fridays.

From Malibu in the north to Long Beach in the south, Los Angeles County boasts 33 beaches stretched over more than 70 miles. But only one, **Belmont Shore Dog Beach** (aka Rosie's Dog Beach) in Long Beach, legally allows dogs off leash, one dog per adult from 6 a.m. to 8 p.m. At **Leo Carrillo State Beach** in Malibu, leashed dogs are allowed except at the heavily trafficked areas between lifeguard towers 2 and 3. Otherwise, dogs are not permitted on the beaches.

It may seem that anything goes on the sidewalk circus of **Venice Beach Boardwalk,** but there are rules. Dogs must be on leashes at all times, and from Memorial Day to Labor Day they are prohibited on the boardwalk from 11 a.m. to 8 p.m. on Saturdays, Sundays, and holidays. During daylight hours, **Santa Monica's beachfront pedestrian path** is full of dogs out for a stroll with their guardians, especially at sunset. Hounds are allowed on the **Santa Monica Pier,** but not inside individual businesses.

Canines ready for their close-up should head to Lake Hollywood Park, where they can be photographed with the Hollywood sign in the background.

🐕 SIT

Don't let the pawparazzi catch Mingus unkempt. At **Euphuria Pet Salon** in North Hollywood, pooches can express their free spirit by getting a Mohawk or hair dye. **Healthy Spot,** with locations in Marina del Rey, Santa Monica, and West Hollywood, offers spa grooming, including blueberry facials and pawdicures. Those who prefer do-it-yourself dog washing can head to **Soggy Dog** in Long Beach or **Eco Dog Wash and Daycare** in L.A.'s Mid-City area.

Highland Avenue has turned into the home for hound hotels, with **D Pet Hotel, L.A. Dogworks,** and **Pooch Hotel Hollywood** within a block of each other. All offer doggie day care, which is also available at **Bark Avenue** in downtown L.A. and the **Barkley Pet Hotel & Day Spa,** a giant, 50,000-square-foot pet campus in Westlake Village that will send a stretch limo to pick up pampered pooches in need of day care, overnight boarding, grooming, or training.

⬤ HAUTE DOG

Furry friends can put on the dog at **Fifi & Romeo,** an elegant boutique complete with chandeliers on Beverly Boulevard. Founder/designer Yana Syrkin whips up canine couture sweaters from recycled cashmere and counts Oprah Winfrey, Jessica Simpson, Usher, Al Pacino, and Nicole Richie among her celebrity clientele. **Beverly Hills Mutt Club,** across from the Peninsula Beverly Hills, also outfits dapper dogs.

The **Modern Dog,** housed in a twenties-style bungalow on trendy Abbot Kinney Boulevard in Venice, cleverly lays out everything contemporary canines need: living and entertaining products in the living rooms, bed and sleeping accessories in the

Stay All Pups Welcome

■ *Beverly Hills Hotel and Bungalows:* Canine Connoisseur Program includes bed, bowls, and bone-shaped dog cookie with pet's name on it. One dog/35 lb max. Fee. beverly hillshotel.com

■ *Fairmont Miramar Hotel & Bungalows (Santa Monica):* P.A.W. (Pets Are Welcome) program includes bed, bowls, treats. Three dogs/100 lb each max. fair mont.com/santa-monica

■ *Hotel Bel-Air:* Precious Paws program includes bed, bowl, personalized biscuits, and departure gift. Two dogs/35 lb each max. Fee. hotelbelair.com

■ *Hotel Palomar (West-wood) & Hotel Wilshire (mid-Wilshire):* Amenities at these two Kimpton hotels include beds, bowls,

and treats. No number/size restrictions. hotelpalomar-lawestwood.com; hotel wilshire.com

■ *Hyatt Regency Century Plaza:* Hyatt Gold Passport members receive a Hyatt Gold Pawsport for their pooch, loyalty program points, and canine welcome amenities. Two dogs/35 lb each max. Fee. centuryplaza.hyatt.com

■ *Loews Hollywood Hotel and Loews Santa Monica Beach Hotel:* Loews Loves Pets program includes room-service menu and dishes. Two pets/25 lb each max. Fee. loews hotels .com/Hollywood-Hotel; loewshotels.com/Santa-Monica-Beach-Hotel

■ *Peninsula Beverly Hills:* Pampered Puppy menu and doggie amenities. Hotel

can coordinate services. No number/size restrictions. Fee. peninsula.com/ Beverly_Hills

■ *Westin Bonaventure (Downtown):* Signature Westin Heavenly beds for four-legged guests. No number restriction/40 lb each max. thebonaventure.com

■ *W Hollywood & W Los Angeles (Westwood):* P.A.W. program includes custom W bed and feeding dishes. No number restriction/40 lb each max. Fee. whollywoodhotel.com; wlosangeles.com

■ *Sheraton Universal Hotel (Universal City):* Two dogs/80 lb each max. sheratonuniversal.com

bedroom, and gourmet foods and treats in the kitchen. Equally cool is **Pussy & Pooch,** with an outpost in downtown L.A. and two in Long Beach. Billed as an urban oasis for pets and their people, Pussy & Pooch combines retail, dining, and grooming to make it the ultimate destination for posh pets.

CHOW TIME

All three Pussy & Pooch locations feature an in-store pet café, **Pawbar,** where four-legged customers can feast on gourmet meals and drink dog beer. The Pawbar is the rare place where canines can dine indoors. Pets are prohibited inside human restaurants, but an abundance of eateries welcome well-behaved pooches on their patios. At the W Hotel in Westwood, near UCLA, coddled canines also have their own menu and can dine with their guardians in the hotel's outdoor restaurant, **The Backyard.**

Fittingly, there's also a menu for hungry hounds at all **Lazy Dog Café** restaurants, with locations in Torrance, Cerritos, Valencia, and West Covina. **Coupa Café** on North Canon Drive not only provides some of the best people watching in Beverly Hills but can prepare a side of chicken or bacon for four-legged diners. **The Pub at Golden Road Brewing** near Glendale features a Doggy Deck, where Golden Rod dog treats made from the spent grains used in brewing beer are for sale. Pet parents and their furry friends can soak up nature together at the rustic **Trail's Café,** off the beaten path yet near one of **Griffith Park**'s most popular trails. Offering outdoor dining only from 8 a.m. to 5 p.m. (closed Mondays), it's the perfect place to refuel after hiking with a leashed Rover.

A few other popular pet-friendly restaurants include **3 Square Café** on hip Abbot Kinney Boulevard in Venice, weekend brunch at the über-romantic **Cliff's Edge** in Silver Lake, and the **Fat Dog,** a gastropub that serves canine-themed cocktails (think Best in Show Tini, Top Dog, and Pick of the Litter) at its restaurants. One is in West Hollywood, conveniently located next door to **Tailwaggers** pet supply store. Or treat man's best friend to healthy baked goods at **Three Dog Bakery,** which has locations in Old Pasadena and at the Farmers' Market.

COME

Visit the stars and paw prints of famous canines on the pet-friendly **Hollywood Walk of Fame.** Lassie's star is at 6368 Hollywood Boulevard, between N. Cahuenga Boulevard and Ivar Avenue. Rin Tin Tin's star is at 1627 Vine Street, just south of Hollywood Boulevard. Uggie's paw prints are at the legendary TCL (formerly Grauman's) Chinese Theatre. Even A-list dogs can't get inside **Universal Studios Hollywood,** but park guests can leave their furry friend at the park's complimentary kennel, indoors and climate controlled.

Fido can soak up views of Los Angeles from the iconic **Griffith Observatory,** located on the south-facing slope of Mount Hollywood in Griffith Park. Also at Griffith Park, visitors and their pups can explore dozens of old-time railroad locomotives and cars and learn about rail history.

Pet events take place regularly and are known to draw Hollywood stars. The Humane Society of the United States puts on its annual **Genesis Awards Benefits Gala** every March and honors boldface names. The Amanda Foundation, a rescue organization, throws tail-waggin' fund-raisers, including **Bow Wow Beverly Hills,** an annual Halloween costume party. Haute Dog, a community of dog lovers based out of Long Beach, holds numerous events, including beauty contests and a **Howl'oween** parade. Pussy & Pooch welcomes visitors to monthly **Mutt Mingle** mixers at its three locations.

For the most dog-friendly shopping experience, head to the open-air **Westfield Century City Mall** where doggie treat dispensers, bowls with filtered water, and a dog park with Mutt Mitts and a doggie obstacle course await. **The Grove,** a retail and entertainment complex adjacent to the landmark Farmers Market, is also dandy for dogs. Many shops welcome four-legged customers, and the Grove prohibits guardians from leaving unattended pets tied up outside stores. Enjoy the dancing fountains or take a ride on the free trolley with Fido. The **Beverly Center** also allows pooches small enough to be carried.

UNIQUE ACTIVITY

Fledgling pawsengers can experience travel by airplane at Air Hollywood's **K9 Flight School,** which provides fundamental training for canines and their companions in the hope of making flying as stress free and easy as possible. At this aviation-themed studio, dogs learn how to handle airport sights and sounds, TSA checkpoints, crowded jetways, sitting in an airplane, as well as takeoff, landing, and turbulence. airhollywood.com/K9

Emergency Veterinarian
VCA West Los Angeles Animal Hospital—vcahospitals.com/west-los-angeles; 310-473-2951

Insider Tip

"Every week my dogs, Harvard, an Australian Shepherd, and Konga, a Yorkiepoo, get a full day of freedom to meet and greet other pooches and their parents off leash at **Rosie's Dog Beach** in Long Beach. Afterward, we walk to **La Palapa del Mar** restaurant, where they welcome you and your fur family to enjoy outdoor patio seating with a clear view of the shore and ocean. The staff promptly serves your exhausted babes fresh bowls of cold water and a dog menu with tasty options. The wonderful thing about this restaurant is that they do not mind misbehaving pooches. There's no grumbling or frowns. That was important for me, because my dogs don't always have the best manners."
— FRANCYNE ELLISON

Maui, Hawaii

Maui's first official dog park, **Keopuolani Park,** opened in Wailuku in 2013, giving Rover one more place to romp on the second-largest of the Hawaiian islands, and some would argue the best. Its dreamy beaches, led by breathtaking **Ka'anapali,** and picturesque setting earned it the moniker "the magic isle." All of its eighty-plus beaches are dog friendly but require your favorite canine companion to remain on leash, unless in the water. Leashed dogs are also welcome on all trails on Maui except in Haleakala Crater. **The Pet Shop** in the Maui Mall in Kahului sells essentials and offers services like grooming and petsitting. From formal restaurants such as **5 Palms** in Kihei, where you can catch a furbulous sunset, to the homey atmosphere at **Grandma's Coffee House** in Kula, many restaurants with outdoor seating welcome your little pal to join you. Four-legged guests are fawned over at the **Four Seasons Resort Maui** (Wailea), **Fairmont Kea Lani** (Wailea), and **Westin Maui Resort & Spa** (Ka'anapali).

See the Introduction (pages 12–13) for information on how to avoid Hawaii's 120-day animal quarantine.

Napa/Sonoma, California

Whether in Italy, France, or California, dogs and vineyards go together like wine and cheese. Remember the huge presence of canines in Jonathan Nossiter's 2004 wine documentary *Mondovino*? No wonder Napa and Sonoma counties, which make up the majority of California's famed wine country, welcome four-legged travelers nearly as eagerly as they do oenophiles. In Healdsburg, Mutt Lynch Winery sells bottles of Unleashed Chardonnay, Merlot Over and Play Dead, and Chateau d'Og Cabernet Sauvignon. In St. Helena, Frenchie Winery (at Raymond Vineyards) is named after a French Bulldog and is just one of the more than 90 dog-friendly wineries in Napa Valley. Whether visiting from September to November, or while one of the many off-season festivals is under way, there is plenty to keep Fido busy in both Napa and Sonoma, where food, wellness, and arts are crowd magnets too.

🎾 PLAY

If your pup loves parks, **Alston Park** on Dry Creek Road in Napa is a must. Canine Commons, on the lower level, is a fenced, off-leash area, open dawn to dusk, with plastic wading pools for hot dogs to cool off during summer's dog days, separate areas for small and big dogs, and chairs for you. Dogs are also allowed off leash, under voice control, at

Alston Park's upper area above the Canine Commons, offering terrific views of vineyards and magical sunsets. Be aware of foxtails in the spring. Dog parks at **Shurtleff Park** and **Kennedy Park** also allow hounds off leash under voice control. As long as your best friend is on a leash of six feet or less, they are allowed at any park or on any trail in Napa Valley except for Skyline Park. If you want to keep it super simple, trot Trixie along downtown Napa's brand-new riverfront path.

In Sonoma County, there is an off-leash dog park inside **Ernie Smith Community Park** on Gillman Drive in El Verano. The **Elizabeth Perrone Dog Park** inside Sonoma Valley Regional Park on Calif. 12 in Glen Ellen has a doggie fountain and gazebo for shade. And Rover can romp freely at Sebastopol's **Animal Care Center of Sonoma County Dog Park,** inside Ragle Ranch Regional Park on Ragle Road, home of the Gravenstein Apple Fair and Peace Garden. For a little

A dog whisperer is as much a necessity as a groomer in these parts.

serenity, head to **Armstrong Redwoods State Natural Reserve,** where dogs must remain on leashes on paved roads, but you can have a lovely picnic in a developed area. Finding a place for Fido to frolic on beaches in Sonoma County isn't easy, due to the state's efforts to protect seals and the western snowy plover. However, leashed dogs are allowed at **Doran Regional Park** in Bodega Bay, where there are 2 miles of sandy beach; **Blind Beach,** south of Goat Rock Beach (where dogs are prohibited); and **Monte Rio Beach.**

SIT

A dog whisperer is as much a necessity as a groomer in these parts. In Santa Rosa, dog behaviorist Sapir Weis, who has worked with pups for more than 35 years, owns **Olivet Kennel & Dog Training Resort,** which offers doggie day care, boarding, and training. **Ruff Dog Day Care & Hotel** in Napa is also ready for those times when you and your little friend must be apart. Grooming comes to you with **Taryn's Traveling Pet Spa** in Napa Valley. Or, do-it-yourselfers can stop by **Pet Food Express** in Napa's Bel Aire Plaza.

HAUTE DOG

When Fido needs a designer dog bed or Swarovski crystal collar, head to **Fideaux,** one of the first pet boutiques in St. Helena, now with an equally alluring store in Healdsburg. Upscale apparel, collars, gourmet treats, carriers, and totes are among the items displayed at **Healdsburg Dog House,** owned by Healdsburg native Natalee Tappin. Your pampered pooch may have no interest in the bottles of wine you ship home, but the dog bed made from local wine barrels at **Vineyard Dog Boutique and Bakery** in Yountville is a different story. Vineyard Dog also sells bowls, carriers, clothes from cotton to cashmere, collars from rhinestone to studded leather, leads, toys, premium and raw food, and pet-themed home decor. Napa also has a **Pet Food Express,** a Bay Area chain that carries raw food like Primal, and **Petco.** Apparel, leashes, toys, and accessories can be found at Sonoma's **Three Dog Bakery.**

🐾 CHOW TIME

Man does not live on wine alone, even in Napa and Sonoma. The region is a haven for foodies, whose four-legged friends receive bowls of water, treats, and their own pooch menu at **Lucy Restaurant & Bar** at the dog-friendly Bardessono hotel in Yountville. Also in Yountville, where it's easy to get around on foot, Thomas Keller's **Bouchon, Redd, Bistro Jeanty,** and **Hurley's** welcome pets on their patios. Guests staying at the **Vintage Inn** can enjoy breakfast al fresco with Fifi at their feet. But keep an eye out for the two large, lurking cats, Maya and Louie.

In Napa, **Angèle, Bistro Don Giovanni, Ca'Momi Winery & Enoteca, Kitchen Door,** and **Q Restaurant and Bar** welcome pooches. Dog-friendly restaurants in Calistoga include the Michelin-starred **Solbar at Solage Calistoga** and the casual **Buster's**

🏠 *Stay* All Pups Welcome

■ *Harvest Inn (St. Helena):* Bed, custom pet bowls, doggie bags, treats, list of pet-friendly restaurants and wineries in the area, and a discount coupon for pet store Fideaux. Two dogs/35 lb combined. Fee. harvestinn.com

■ *Calistoga Ranch, an Auberge Resort (Calistoga):* Pet bed with velvet Italian sheets, organic treats, bowls, spring water, pet room-service menu; "Happy Tails" doggie newsletter with information on pet-friendly wineries, restaurants, and hiking and walking trails. G. Two dogs/ no size restriction. Fee. calistogaranch.com

■ *Bardessono (Yountville):* Bardessono water bowl, pet bed, dog waste bags, welcome pet amenity. Pets welcome throughout the property, including Lucy Restaurant. Two dogs/no size restriction. Fee. bardessono.com

■ *Vintage Inn (Yountville):* Water and food bowls, bed with cushions, doggie turndown service, treats at check-in, and a dog amenity package with treats and other dog essentials. Pet-friendly breakfast patio. No number/size restrictions. Fee. vintageinn.com

■ *Napa River Inn (Napa):* Very Important Pet (VIP) program provides custom-designed pet blanket; logo place mat; bowls; Napa Valley–based Cab-Bone-Nay or Char-Dog-Nay dog biscuits (made with real wine); plastic doggie walk bag; welcome letter with a list of pet support services, including dog walkers, on-call veterinarian, and souvenirs. Two dogs/30 lb each max. Fee. napariverinn.com

■ *Fairmont Sonoma Mission Inn and Spa (Sonoma):* Bed, bowls, gourmet treats, and biodegradable pet waste bags. No number restriction/60 lb each max. Fee. fairmont .com/sonoma

Southern BBQ. St. Helena has **Cindy's Backstreet Kitchen** (Cindy Pawlcyn is the owner and exec chef of fave Mustards Grill, which unfortunately does not have outdoor seating), **Tra Vigne,** where pooches can expect to receive water, and **Gott's Roadside. Rutherford Grill** in Rutherford is dog friendly.

In Sonoma, **Sunflower Caffé Espresso & Wine Bar**'s rear garden is a wonderful place for pets to relax and enjoy the aroma of the famous smoked duck breast sandwich all around them. **El Dorado Kitchen** and **LaSalette** also welcome coddled canines in their outdoor dining areas. Sonoma's fantastic cheese offerings get lost in the food, but the patio at the **Sonoma Cheese Factory,** on Sonoma's picturesque and historic Plaza, is an ideal place to enjoy cheese and wine with your furry friend.

> ## Insider Tip
>
> "A favorite morning long walk with Fletcher starts with breakfast on the patio at the **Community Café** in Sonoma, where Fletch is treated to biscuits, and if owner Margie is there, some bites of bacon. Then we head up the highway to **Spring Lake Regional Park** for a 3-mile stroll around the lake, along the paved loop, and some wading in the water for Fletch, or a more ambitious 6-mile walk on the trails connecting to nearby **Howarth Park.** Our best reward is lunch on the patio at the **Rutherford Grill,** splitting a grilled chicken salad and their giant burger, medium rare, of course."
> — CECE HUGO

Healdsburg, the most en vogue spot in California's wine country, boasts several pet-friendly restaurants, including **Charlie Palmer's Dry Creek Kitchen, Willi's Seafood & Raw Bar,** and **Barndiva.** There are doggie menus in Glen Ellen at the **Garden Court Café and Bakery,** which also provides cookies and water bowls, and in Occidental at **Howard's Station Café,** great for breakfast. In Santa Rosa, **Rosso Pizzeria + Wine Bar** in the Creekside Center and **Five Guys Burgers and Fries**

For good boys and good girls: **Bouchon Bakery** in Yountville, nearly impossible to walk by without being seduced by aromas, makes doggie biscuits. The baked goods at Yountville's Vineyard Dog Pet Boutique & Bakery, ensconced in an 1886 building, are so healthy you could eat them too. Three Dog Bakery in Sonoma also sells healthy items for pooches.

🐾 COME

The problem in Napa Valley and Sonoma County isn't finding a dog-friendly winery but deciding on which ones to visit. A few that offer something extra in Napa Valley: Your posh pet can have its own shady dog suite and wine-barrel bed at **Frenchie Winery** (at Raymond Vineyards) in St. Helena. A "Frenchie Cam" lets you spy on—er, watch your best friend while you wine-taste indoors. At **V. Sattui Winery** in St. Helena, pick up lunch at the winery's Italian marketplace and deli and adjourn to the 2.5-acre picnic grounds with your favorite canine companion. **V Wine Cellar,** located on the 23-acre Vintage Estate in Yountville, offers Sip and Swirl with Spud, a wine boutique, and tasting lounge. While you enjoy a private wine tasting at the shop, your pooch is treated on the outdoor patio to water bowls made from recycled wine boxes and gourmet dog treats.

In Sonoma County, the North Canon Drive in Kenwood offers a canine-friendly, 4-hour vineyard hike led by fourth-generation winegrower Jeff Kunde and his dog, Riley, that concludes with a wine tasting and wine country lunch. **St. Francis Winery & Vineyards** in Santa Rosa offers its furry visitors water and dog biscuits. Plus, it has a nice selection of pet-related merchandise in the gift shop. The tasting room at **Mutt Lynch Winery,** in Healdsburg, is open only by appointment but loves canine visitors, which receive doggie treats. It's a pawsome place to throw a pawty or Bark Mitzvah.

Bark your calendar for these charitable annual events: in late March, Napa Humane's **Pawsport Napa Valley,** a four-day event with exclusive wine tastings at select Napa Valley wineries, also featuring food pairings, dog treats, souvenirs, drawings, discounts on wine purchases, and meet-and-greets with winery dogs. In August, **Walk for Animals,** a fun Napa Humane event and leisurely walk through downtown Napa in support of pets throughout Napa Valley. In Sonoma County, St. Francis Winery & Vineyards in Santa Rosa hosts a **Blessing of the Animals** event in October that draws more than 200 animals and includes a "Winery Dog of the Year" contest, wine, nibbles, and raffle prizes to benefit Sonoma Humane Society.

Worth a stop either coming or going is **Cornerstone Sonoma** at the Southern Gateway to Napa and Sonoma. Dogs are welcome at this eclectic collection of art galleries, shops, wineries, and a gourmet café and market, nestled in 9 acres of garden installations created by the world's leading landscape architects.

UNIQUE ACTIVITY

If your pooch is people and dog friendly, take him or her on **Vineyard Walks,** which gives you inside access to private vineyard lands and people you would otherwise never see or meet. Some wineries won't allow dogs and others might require a leash, so inform the company in advance. sonoma vineyardwalks.com

Emergency Veterinarian
Napa Valley Veterinary Hospital—napavalleyvets.com; 707-224-8604 ▪ VCA Animal Care Center of Sonoma County—vcaspecialtyvets.com/sonoma-county; 707-584-4343

Oahu, Hawaii

Oahu translates to "the Gathering Place." And, as the most popular Hawaiian island, Oahu is where coddled canines can congregate as well, while they enjoy a pawsome vacation with their humans. If Hawaii's infamous 120-day quarantine has kept you from taking your pampered pet to a Pacific paradise that offers urban excitement in Honolulu and a country experience on the North Shore and Windward Oahu, know there is a five-day-or-less direct-release program, which allows your furry friend to be released to you after arriving at Honolulu Airport if certain requirements are met. Utilizing this program entails advance planning of at least four months, paperwork, and cash (see pages 12–13), but your posh pet will thank you for allowing him or her to experience the beauty of the 50th state.

🐾 PLAY

A bevy of beaches allow bowwows to kick up their paws, but restrictions vary by the strength of the tide. All mandate that dogs must be on leashes at all times except when in the water. A whopping 38 of Oahu's beaches allow leashed pups in all beach areas. For calm waters, head to any of these: **Kahala Beach** is a favorite because of its proximity to Waikiki, view of Koko Head (one of the most popular landmarks on Oahu's south shore), and the friendly dogs and pet parents. **Kailua Beach** offers a beautiful view, nearby showers, and ample parking. **Niu Beach** (Niu Valley area) is for those who want a little seclusion. And **Ala Moana Beach** boasts a long stretch of beach with a sidewalk alongside it, plenty of parking, and multiple showers. Ala Moana, along with **Waikiki Beach,** is an ideal spot for Brutus to try his paw at surfing. The paddle isn't too far out, but also take into account the size of the waves, which could be one to two feet.

Oahu boasts five off-leash dog parks, with plans in the works for a sixth. **Bark Park,** at Diamond Head Road and 18th Avenue, offers lots of parking and is open daily during daylight hours. **Hawaii Kai Dog Park,** at the makai (ocean) end of the Hawaii Kai Park & Ride, is open daily from dawn to dusk except Tuesday mornings, and provides pickup bags and water fountains for pets and their people. **Moanalua Dog Park,** at Moanalua Community Park off Pu'uloa Road, is open during daylight hours every day except Tuesday morning. **Mililani Dog Park,** at Mililani Mauka District Park at Park & Ride, is open during daylight hours every day except Wednesday morning. **Humane Society Dog Park,** .33 acre of grass, trees, and tropical foliage at the Hawaiian Humane Society, is open Monday through Friday from 11 a.m. to 7 p.m. and weekends and most holidays from 10 a.m. to 4 p.m. **Ala Wai K-9 Playground** at Ala Wai Community Park, is not open yet, pending approval.

A bevy of beaches allow bowwows to kick up their paws, but restrictions vary by the strength of the tide.

Fifi doesn't need to wear a lei to strut at a regular park, just a leash. She can also go around the perimeter of Kapiolani Park, Hawaii's largest and oldest public park, but not enter it. The leash is also a necessity when pooches prance down county sidewalks in Waikiki. Note that store and mall-front areas are often private property. Stay off the oceanfront walkway from Queen's Beach to the Waikiki Aquarium because it is a county park; remain on the Kalakaua Avenue roadside sidewalk.

The Hawaiian Humane Society's **Paws on the Path** hiking club has monthly outings and welcomes visitors.

SIT

If all that outdoor fun takes its toll on Fifi's skin and fur, head to **Cocojor Emporium & Spaw** (Kaka'ako), billed as Hawaii's first Eco Zen spa, where Micro Bubble technique removes dirt, odors, and excess oil without drying. Afterward, soak up the rays with your little pal in Cocojor's natural herb garden. Doga (yoga for dogs) and massages are available to those pups boarded at Cocojor or at the facility for day care. **Waikiki Dog Grooming** (Waikiki), **Wan Wan Paradise** (Kaka'ako), and the **Naked Poodle Salon & Boutique** also offer grooming, while **Aloha Dog** (Kaka'ako), **Pets in the City,** and **Ohana Doggie Day Care & Spa** (Kakaʻako) offers doggie day care, boarding, and grooming. You can even throw your pooch a pawty at Pets in the City that would satisfy Carrie Bradshaw.

HAUTE DOG

After your pampering session at Cocojor, pick up "made in Hawaii" apparel for your tyke at the spa and boutique, which can dress dogs from two to 200 pounds. **Calvin & Susie,** in Kilohana Square on Kapahulu Avenue, also sells apparel, collars, leads, wholesome natural foods, beds, and treats.

CHOW TIME

If you haven't spoiled Sadie enough at Cocojor, stop by the **Barkery,** which sells fresh-baked dog treats that are all natural and organic. **Hawaii Doggie Bakery,** around since 1998, travels to different farmers' markets, so check its website to find out where it will be next. **Naturally Pet** (Kakaʻako) offers food that is just what the name implies, and **City Feed** (Moʻiliʻili) stocks super-premium food.

When it comes to pet-friendly restaurants, most of the eateries with outdoor seating welcome your traveling companion to sit with you. Hot spots include **Greek Marina** (Hawaii Kai), **Nico's at Pier 38, The Fat Greek** (Ala Moana), and **Wahoo's Fish Tacos** (Kakaʻako).

COME

An array of annual festivals and events welcomes four-legged attendees: the **Pan-Pacific Festival** and the **King Kamehameha Floral Parade** in June; the **Aloha Festivals** in September; **Vans Triple Crown of Surfing** on the North Shore in November and December; and the **Quiksilver Big Wave Invitational in Memory of Eddie Aikau** from December to February. These annual pet events are something to bark about: **Pet Expo,** Hawaii's biggest pet event of the year, held at the Neal Blaisdell Center Exhibition Hall in May; the Hawaiian Humane Society's **PetWalk** at Ala Moana Beach Park every October; the **Hawaii Kai Dog Walk,** a 2.3-mile walk

Stay
All Pups Welcome

■ *Trump International Waikiki:* Plush bed, water bowl, water, treats, in-room dining menu, toys, map of the city highlighting dog-friendly parks. Two dogs/20 lb each max. Fee. trumphotel collection.com/waikiki

■ *The Modern Honolulu (Waikiki):* Pet basket with treats, chew toy, water bowl. Two dogs/25 lb each max. Fee. themodernhonolulu.com

■ *Hyatt Regency Waikiki Beach Resort:* Welcome letter, dog-on-vacation door hanger, pet ID tag, dog bed, bowls, mat, rubber chew toys, biscuits. No number restriction/50 lb each max. Fee. waikiki.hyatt.com

through beautiful Hawaii Kai, which offers a mini-route for smaller and older dogs; and the **Hawaii Wiener Derby,** which draws a large turnout every year.

UNIQUE ACTIVITY

Enjoy a special bonding experience when you book a side-by-side spa treatment with your buddy at Cocojor Emporium & Spaw. Your best friend can have the Minicle Microbubble service, the signature treatment that promises to leave pooches clean, detoxed, and anxiety free, while your Massage Scrub Therapy rejuvenates and detoxifies you. For an added bonus, schedule a healing self-awareness session to strengthen the relationship between you and your pal. cocojor.com

Insider Tip

"While many tourists visit **Kailua Beach** and **Lanikai Beach** on the windward side of Oahu, they might not know that both beaches are pet friendly. This slice of doggy heaven includes pristine blue water, fluffy white sand, and long beaches for walks. It also has paddleboards and kayaks for rent, so you can enjoy the water and exercise with your fur *keiki,* or bring your own. You can finish off the day by sitting back and enjoying the picnic area, which includes BBQ pits for grilling a delicious meal in the shade!"

— LIBBI ROED, *Makaha, Oahu*

Emergency Veterinarian
Veterinary Emergency + Referral Center of Hawaii—verchawaii.com; 808-735-7735

San Diego, California

F or years much has been written about San Diego's inferiority complex, but never as it relates to dogs. Considering the abundance of beaches where Fido can frolic freely and the many other outdoor activities for your furry companion, the place dubbed "America's finest city" does more than hold its own against the more popular southern California metropolises.

PLAY

When it comes to where to dog paddle, Fido has a few choices. He'll have plenty of company at **Dog Beach,** a 24-hour off-leash beach at the west end of Voltaire Street in Ocean Beach, between the San Diego River and the hills of Point Loma. At **Mission Bay Park,** on Fiesta Island, the water is calmer than the ocean, and there are sand dunes to run on. Open daily from 6 a.m. to 10 p.m., no leash required. **North Beach Dog Run** on Coronado Island, just across San Diego Bay from the city, is a 24-hour off-leash beach as well. There's also Dog Beach in Del Mar, so furbulous that it warrants its own chapter. For other beaches, dogs on leashes are allowed after 6 p.m. from April 1 to October 31 and after 4 p.m. from November 1 to March 31. Legally licensed, leashed dogs are allowed on the beach, and on sidewalks and park areas near the beach, at night and during early morning hours until 9 a.m.

Spend a day with your favorite canine companion at **Balboa Park,** the nation's largest urban culture park. Inside you'll find two 24-hour off-leash dog parks: **Nate's Point** (at Balboa Drive at El Prado, south side of Cabrillo Bridge), one of the most popular in the region, with a drinking fountain, picnic tables, and a double-entry gate, and **Morley Field** (southwest of the tennis courts). The 5-acre **Grape Street Dog Park** (South Park), the largest of the three dog parks inside Balboa, is off leash 7:30 a.m. to 9 p.m., Monday through Friday, and 9 a.m. to 9 p.m. on weekends. When you're in the rest of the Balboa Park, a leash is always required, including on trails and in canyons.

Take your hound hiking in **Mission Trails Regional Park,** where dogs on leashes less than eight feet long are welcome, and you and your furry friend can enjoy the more than 40 miles of hiking and biking trails that wind along the San Diego River. Rover isn't allowed inside **Cabrillo National Monument** except in the coastal and tide pool areas, where dogs must be on a leashes no longer than six feet.

Stay All Pups Welcome

■ *Loews Coronado Bay Resort:* Loews Loves Pets amenities include a tag, bowls, door hanger sign, pickup bags, gourmet treats, in-room dining menu, brochure on San Diego pet services. Dog-friendly restaurant. Pet walking and petsitting services available. No number/size restrictions. Fee. loewshotels.com

■ *Hotel Palomar, A Kimpton Hotel (Gaslamp):* Bed, bowls, mat, cleanup bags. No number/size restrictions. hotelpalomar-sandiego.com

■ *U. S. Grant Hotel (Gaslamp):* Bowls, bed, mat, and a pet welcome kit. Dog-friendly Grant Grill provides a pet bed and food/water dish. One dog/40 lb max. Fee. usgrant.net

■ *The Keating Hotel by Pininfarina (Gaslamp):* Dishes, bed, walking services, canine turndown. Two dogs/40 lb each max. Fee. thekeating.com

■ *Westin Gaslamp Quarter San Diego:* Westin Heavenly dog bed, bowls, welcome amenity. Designated dog area less than a block away. Two dogs/25 lb each max. Fee. westingaslamp.com

■ *Hotel Solamar, A Kimpton Hotel (Gaslamp/ East Village):* Bed, bowls, dining mat, cleanup bags. Petsitting, grooming, and walking referrals through concierge. Unique pet massages and local pet dining can be arranged through guest services. No number/size restrictions. No fee. hotelsolamar.com

■ *Hotel Indigo (East Village):* Amenities in the VIP (Very Important Pet) program include bowls, bed, and treats. No number/size restrictions. hotelinsd.com

Or stay in the mix in **Little Italy,** considered one of the city's most walkable and dog-friendly neighborhoods, with ample pickup bags and trash cans throughout. It's easy to strike up a conversation with other pet parents, and the community's decorations, especially during fall, Christmas, and spring, are notable. Take paws in one of Little Italy's piazzas with your *cane.* **Piazza Basilone** boasts a fountain and view of the San Diego Bay.

🐾 SIT

Just two blocks from Dog Beach, you'll find **Dog Beach Dog Wash** for do-it-yourselfers. **City Dog,** downtown, not only offers full grooming services and DIY facilities but delivery and/or drive-by pickup. At **Embarkadero Dog Spa and Resort** downtown and **Holiday Pet Hotel** in Encinitas, there's grooming, doggie day care, and boarding. Hounds can run amok at **Camp Run-a-Mutt,** a cage-free facility with outposts in Mission Hills, Point Loma, and Kearny Mesa that offers doggie day care and overnight boarding. On Coronado, head to **Wag'n Tails,** which offers a do-it-yourself dog wash.

🍔 HAUTE DOG

Dapper dogs will enjoy the selection of upscale apparel at **Muttropolis,** with locations in La Jolla and Solana Beach. City Dog also has apparel, carriers, premium food, and essentials.

🦴 CHOW TIME

Guests staying at Loews Coronado Bay Resort can order in-room dining for their four-legged traveler, which can accompany their humans to breakfast, lunch, or dinner at the outdoor sections of **Market Café.** At the **Grant Grill** at the U. S. Grant Hotel, pups can relax on a bed and receive a food/water dish. The **Manchester Grand Hyatt** also allows dogs on the patios of all its restaurants, including **Sally's Seafood on the Water. Lazy Dog Restaurant,** in the Mission Valley Mall, also has a canine-cuisine menu. In Little Italy, pet-friendly restaurants include **Davanti Enoteca, Zia's Bistro, Cafe**

Insider Tip

"I love to take my Great Dane, Izzy, to one of the many 'dog beaches' in San Diego County. Our favorite is **Ocean Beach's Dog Beach.** It's big and there are so many dogs running off leash and having a blast. There are also dog beaches in Coronado and Del Mar. Each beach has its own personality. If you go to Ocean Beach, go early because the parking is better. Bring a poop bag and bottle of water for your pooch—it's thirsty work chasing all those other dogs!"
— CHRIS BERNET

Italia, and **Burger Lounge,** which also has pet-friendly patios at its locations in La Jolla, Kensington, Gaslamp, Hillcrest, Del Mar, and Coronado. Ditto for **Miguelito's,** a popular spot on the island. **Fred's Mexican Café,** with outposts in the Gaslamp, Old Town, and Pacific Beach, is known for hosting regular events for pooches. In the East Village, check out **Asti Ristorante, Café Chloe, Bare Back Grill,** and **Café 222** with your furry friend.

Costumed pets come out in force for the annual Gaslamp Holiday Pet Parade, held every December.

For a special treat, pick up healthy, fresh-baked goods at the **Original Paw Pleasers** in North Park, San Diego's first dog and cat bakery, or **Wag'n Tails** on Coronado.

🐾 COME

Stop by the **William Heath Davis House,** the oldest wooden structure in the Gaslamp District at Fourth and Island Avenues, to see a bronze statue of the 19th century "town dog," Bum. **Seaport Village** welcomes leashed pets to stroll around the waterfront collection of shops, eateries, and outdoor entertainment. **SeaWorld** visitors can take advantage of the kennels located at the park's main entrance, available on a first-come, first-served basis. Although dogs aren't technically allowed at the **Little Italy Mercato,** the largest farmers' market in San Diego, held every Saturday, specialty pet vendors who sell everything from organic dog food to artisan dog collars peddle their wares among the 150 booths.

Watch dogs hang 20 in the **Loews Surf Dog Competition** that takes place every June and attracts the maximum number of pup participants. Furry fashionistas won't want to miss the **Fur Ball,** the city's only black-tie dog-friendly event, hosted by the San Diego Humane Society every August. The organization also puts on **Walk for Animals,** which draws approximately 5,000 two-legged and countless four-legged walkers each May; and **Doggie Café,** which takes place twice a month and teaches pooches how to be calm around exciting distractions like people, other dogs, and food. Costumed pets come out in force for the annual **Gaslamp Holiday Pet Parade,** held every December.

🅵🅸🅳🅾 UNIQUE ACTIVITY

Enjoy **Dog Paddle on San Diego Bay,** a two-hour guided kayak tour that begins with a quick session to make your canine comfortable in the kayak and a paddling lesson for you. You'll kayak to the beach for a romp and playtime, then back to the launch site. familykayak.com

Emergency Veterinarian
VCA Emergency Animal Hospital & Referral Center—vcaspecialtyvets.com/emergency; 619-299-2400

San Francisco, California

Breathtaking scenery, hills that make drivers' hearts stop, one of the world's most recognizable bridges, and romantic fog aren't enough for San Francisco, arguably one of the most beautiful and beloved cities on earth. There are also the diverse neighborhoods like Fisherman's Wharf, Pacific Heights, Haight-Ashbury, Nob Hill, the Castro, and the Marina, which, distinct as they are, have a common thread running through them—their acceptance of man's best friend. San Franciscans take their dogs as seriously as their liberal views. The City by the Bay (please don't call it Frisco) claims more registered canines per capita than children and, perhaps coincidentally, is headquarters for pet-friendly Kimpton Hotels, which has nine properties here, all waiting to fuss over Fifi. There's even *Bay Woof,* a monthly newspaper that keeps dog lovers up to date on all the pet-tastic news. Keep in mind what Mark Twain did or did not say ("The coldest winter I ever spent was a summer in San Francisco") and pack a sweater for Fido in the summer.

🐾 PLAY

Finding a place for pups to romp freely is rarely a problem in San Francisco, which has an enviable amount of open space for a big city. Part of it falls within the **Golden Gate National Recreation Area,** which, together with areas in Marin and San Mateo

Counties, makes up one of the world's largest urban parks and, with 14.5 million visitors a year, one of the most visited National Park units. When under voice control, furry friends can frolic freely in **Baker Beach,** north of Lobos Creek; **Crissy Field** (excluding the Wildlife Protection Area at the west end of Crissy Field Beach, where leashes are required all year except from May 15 to July 1); **Fort Funston** (excluding the 12-acre enclosure in northwest Fort Funston and the northern end of the Coastal Trail, closed due to erosion); **Fort Miley; Lands End;** and **Ocean Beach** (excluding the Plover Protection Area from Sloat Boulevard north to Stairwell 21, where leashes are required all year except from May 15 to July 1).

With its scenic views of sky, land, and ocean, **Fort Funston Doggie Beach** is a pawsome place to picnic with your well-socialized pal, who will have oodles of playmates from Terriers to Great Danes at this premiere location off Calif. 35. Hang gliders, horseback riders, and bird-watchers gather here, so bring a leash, just in case. An abundance of trails makes for terrific hiking. Get an up-close view of the Golden Gate Bridge and the bay from beloved Crissy Field, a trail between Marina Green and Fort Point that offers picnic tables and an off-leash beach for Brutus to show off his dog-paddle skills. If you have a leash, you can walk or run with your canine companion along the street to the famous **Hopper's Hands plaque** beneath the bridge next to Fort Point, the farthest west joggers can go along the bay. For years, runners and walkers have placed their hands on the plaque to mark their arrival. Dogs can do the same with the pawprints plaque at their level.

In addition to the National Park areas, unleashed pooches can play in a slew of dog parks throughout the city. With 39 leash-free acres and spectacular panoramic views from the top of Bernal Hill, **Bernal Heights Dog Park** is worth the drive. Also popular: **Dolores Park** in the Mission, where the city skyline dazzles but parking can be difficult; **Golden Gate Park,** San Francisco's largest and best-known park, which has three off-leash dog runs and one dog-training area but requires dogs to be on leashes throughout the rest of the park; **Alamo Square Park** (Fulton Street at Scott Street), where canines can cavort with restraints in half the park, which offers a memorable view of the colorful Victorian houses known as the Painted Ladies; and **Buena Vista Park,** the oldest park in San Francisco.

 SIT

After pooches kick up their paws outdoors, a grooming session is

> *Insider Tip*
>
> "While there are no dog-specific parks in the Financial District, there are parks every 10 blocks that give my Papillons, Mikey and Katey, a piece of grass to romp on. Our favorite is **St. Mary's Square,** where we can enjoy watching nearby residents practicing tai chi and walk the meditation circle."
> — DENISE L. PAULSON

in order. **Russian Hill Dog Grooming,** which has locations in Russian Hill and Pacific Heights, uses nationally certified master groomers, hypoallergenic, natural shampoo and conditioner, and hand drying. **The Dog Spa,** in West Portal, boasts certified pet groomers who are also Pet Tech First Aid and CPR certified. **Mudpuppys,** on Castro Street, is not only where your pooch can get a bath and pawdicure, but you and your pal can relax before and after his wash in a 120-year-old renovated carriage house in the garden. **Wags Pet Wash and Boutique** on Polk Street specializes in sustainable and earth-friendly grooming products. Do-it-yourselfers can head to one of three **Pet Food Express** locations (California Street, Market Street, and Stonestown).

Canines will be content after a session with **Happy Hounds Massage'**s Shelah Barr, a certified small-animal massage therapist who will come to hotels and businesses in the SF city limits. Doggie day care is available at **Wag Hotels** (Mission District), open 24 hours a day for check-in and checkout; **Pet Camp** (Bayview/Hunters Point), where Rover can swim indoors in a heated pool and roam in the Savannah, a 13,000-square-foot dog park complete with trees, native grasses, and a dried-out riverbed; **Fog City Dogs** (Marina/Cow Hollow), where a play group webcam allows you to peek at your pup; and **Moulin Pooch** (Marina/Cow Hollow), formerly known as Bella & Daisy's, featuring jungle gyms and mentally stimulating games.

🐾 HAUTE DOG

Moulin Pooch is also the place for chic canines, offering fashionable apparel and accessories, leads, harnesses, specialty foods, including raw and organic options, carriers, and beds. Furry fashionistas will appreciate the selection at **YAP** in Ghirardelli Square, where the Italian Greyhound mascot Pronto proudly dons the eponymous apparel, which places just as much emphasis on style as safety. In the Castro district, check out **Best in Show,** where you can pick up an "I Have 2 Daddies" bandanna, toys, upscale apparel, leashes, harnesses, and doggie birthday cakes.

On any given sunny day in this foodie town, patios at ... restaurants are full of tail waggers chilling at their humans' feet.

🐾 CHOW TIME

On any given sunny day in this foodie town, patios at San Francisco restaurants are full of tail waggers chilling at their humans' feet. Popular spots include **Chow Food and Drink** (Castro); **Park Chow** (Sunset); **The Butler & the Chef** (SoMA), great for pooch watching; **SoMA Inn Café** for breakfast; and the **Liberty Café** (Bernal Heights). The addition of dog-friendly restaurants like **Choquet's,** which brings cold water for pooches, and **SPQR** give tourists another reason to visit Pacific Heights, where the grand mansions along Billionaire's Row draw lookie-loos and history buffs. In Cow Hollow, **Betelnut,**

Balboa Café, **Nettie's Crab Shack, Capannina,** and **Rose's Café** draw local pet parents and their four-legged friends. **Dolores Park Café** (Mission) and **Duboce Park Café** (Duboce Triangle), across the street from dog-friendly **Duboce Park** (on and off leash), welcome canines as well.

With a name like **Bloodhound,** it's apropos that this SoMA bar allows hounds. Other dog-friendly bars include **Doc's Clock** (Mission) and **El Rio** in Bernal Heights/Mission.

When your dog deserves a special treat, head to **Le Marcel Dog Bakery** (Marina/ Cow Hollow), where a display of cookies, cakes, and pastries made with all-natural, human-grade ingredients will make your mouth water. There's also a paw-tio with synthetic turf, where you can sit and watch your posh pet play and munch on goodies. Humans are encouraged to bring their own food and drinks. The boutiques Best in Show and Moulin Pooch also have doggie bakeries.

😸 COME

A dog's trip to San Francisco is incomplete without a **cable car** ride. For an adult fee, pooches can ride weekdays, except from 5 a.m. to 9 a.m. and 3 p.m. to 7 p.m. One muzzled and leashed dog per vehicle is allowed. Other pets and nonservice animals must be carried in small, closed containers. Head to the popular **Pier 39,** a waterfront complex with dining, entertainment, and shopping, where leashed pets can frolic outdoors in the common area while human visitors take in superb views and watch sea lions. **Le Beastro** boutique carries a variety of dog-themed gifts and pooch apparel. Board a **Blue & Gold Fleet** ferry for a 60-minute bay cruise with your leashed pet.

Stroll around **Union Square,** a 2.6-acre shopping mecca in the heart of downtown, and take paws in the grassy quad. During the summer, cultured canines, or those aspiring to be, can attend **Free Shakespeare in the Park,** professional productions held in Bay Area public parks since 1983.

Fillmore Street, in tony Pacific Heights, has gone from blocks of secondhand shops to a world-class shopping street lined with trendy designer boutiques and salons, many of which leave water dishes at their entrances and stock doggie treats at their counters.

Annual events for top dogs include **Haute Dog San Francisco,** a doggie runway show held every February at the SF Design Center to benefit Canine Companions for Independence; **Bark & Whine Ball,** held in March to benefit the Cinderella Fund at the San Francisco SCPA; San Francisco Animal Care & Control's **Pet Pride Day** at Golden Gate Park in October; **DogFest** in April in Duboce Park; and the San Francisco Giants' **Dog Days of Summer** at AT&T Park.

Moulin Pooch hosts Yappy Hour the first Friday of every month and has a canine cab service (advanced arrangements suggested). Doc's Clock, a bar in the heart of the Mission, throws a Yappy Hour the first Saturday of every month to benefit animal charities and hosts regular fund-raisers and adoption events for local animal rescue/shelter groups. Wag Hotels also hosts regular social gatherings for pets and their people.

FIDO UNIQUE ACTIVITY

Enjoy a two-hour Hornblower yacht cruise of the scenic City by the Bay with a favorite canine companion during the San Francisco SPCA's annual **Dog Day on the Bay,** usually held in June. Gourmet champagne brunch buffet for humans and bowwow buffet and water bar for dogs, live entertainment, raffle prizes, and doggie relief area on the "poop deck." dogdayonthebay.com

Emergency Veterinarian
Pets Unlimited—petsunlimited.org; 415-563-6700

Stay All Pups Welcome

■ *Kimpton Hotels:* **Hotel Monaco** (Tenderloin/ Union Square), **Hotel Palomar** (Financial District/Union Square), **Sir Francis Drake** (Union Square), **Harbor Court** (Embarcadero/Financial District), **The Argonaut** (Fisherman's Wharf/ Russian Hill), **Tuscan Inn** (Fisherman's Wharf/North Beach), **Triton** (Union Square), **Prescott** (Union Square), **Serrano** (Theater District): All provide bed and bowls. Concierge can arrange grooming, dogsitting, walking, and a massage at most. No size/ number restrictions. kimptonhotels.com

■ *Fairmont San Francisco (Nob Hill):* Bed, feeding dishes, and in-room pet dining menu. No number/ size restrictions. Fee. fairmont.com/san-francisco

■ *Mandarin Oriental* (Financial District): Bed, dishes, and in-room pet menu. Two dogs/20 lb each max. Fee. mandarinoriental.com/sanfrancisco

■ *W Hotel (SoMA):* P.A.W. (Pets Are Welcome) program provides bed, food, and water bowl with floor mat, turndown gift, and in-room pet menu. Two dogs/ no size restriction. Fee. wsanfrancisco.com

■ *Galleria Park Hotel (Financial District):* This green-certified Joie de Vivre hotel provides green welcome amenities to pups, including eco-friendly dog bowls made from recycled materials, organic biscuits, and bed. Yappy Hour Thursday–Sunday. Fee. jdvhotels.com

■ *The Westin San Francisco Market Street (Union Square):* Westin Heavenly dog bed, bowls, mat, dog-in-room sign, pickup bags, latex gloves, Dog ID tag. No number restriction/40 lb each max. westinsf.com

Yosemite, California

With mule deer, black bears, and bobcats roaming around, it may seem that California's Yosemite National Park is no place for a dog. But the majestic park known for its waterfalls and giant sequoias welcomes pets in developed areas (with leashes six feet or less), on paved roadways and trails (except where noted), and in the camping areas (except for Tamarack Flat and hike-in sites). Pets are not allowed off the floor of Yosemite Valley, including the trail to Vernal Fall. So where exactly can you take Rover? For starters, on the 3.5-mile **Wawona Meadow Loop.** Pets are also allowed on **Four Mile Fire Road** in Wawona, on the **Carlon Road,** and on the **Old Big Oak Flat Road** between Hodgdon Meadow and Hazel Green Creek. If you decide to tackle Mirror Lake/Meadow Trail on your own, an option for Rover is the dog kennels at **Yosemite Valley Stable,** available for day and overnight use from Memorial Day through Labor Day. Pets are also not allowed in park lodging or on shuttle buses. **Tenaya Lodge at Yosemite,** right outside the park's south gate, makes for a great base camp and offers dogsitting and dog walking, plus all the trails around the lodge are in the Sierra National Forest and dog friendly.

Canada

Banff National Park, Alberta

Staring is impolite, but not when you're gawking at the beauty of Banff National Park, Canada's first national park and a UNESCO World Heritage site. Here, you'll find the town of Banff and Lake Louise, the crown jewel whose emerald waters radiate most in the summer when hordes flock here to gaze, go whitewater rafting and canoeing, and hike the park's 930 miles of trails, more than any other mountain park. Trails range from Banff's easy (**Fenland Trail** and **Bow River Loop Trail**) to challenging climbs that reward with amazing vistas. Unlike in the U.S. parks, hounds are allowed almost everywhere here. Leashes are required. Off limits to pooches is the shuttle to Sunshine Meadows ski area. But you and your athletic ally can trek up to the lodge and pick up the trails from there. In the winter, snowshoe or cross-country ski with your pal, or enjoy a horse-drawn sleigh ride along Lake Louise with **Brewster Tours.** For a spectacular view any time of year, the dog-friendly **Banff Gondola** whisks you and Fifi up Sulphur Mountain to the Summit Upper Terminal (7,486 feet). Or book a sightseeing helicopter tour on dog-friendly **Icefield Heli Tours** or **Kananaskis Heli Tours.** For a royal experience, check into the majestic **Fairmont Banff Springs.** The **Mount Royal Hotel** in Banff also welcomes four-legged guests, while the **Fairmont Chateau Lake Louise** pampers pooches too.

Calgary, Alberta

Calgary calls itself Cowtown, but Caninetown is equally apropos for this bustling metropolis, located on the Bow River in the province of Alberta. Famous for hosting the annual Calgary Stampede, Canada's largest rodeo, Calgary also boasts a whopping 150 public, off-leash areas in its multi-use parks that add up to more than 3,000 acres, perhaps the most in North America. Devastating floods in 2013 affected off-leash areas, especially those that border a river like the popular 153-acre **Sue Higgins Park** (formerly Southland) and **Sandy Beach** along Elbow River in the southwest. But there are still plenty of wonderful off-leash opportunities for Rover to romp, such as at **River Park,** which sits above Sandy Beach; **Nose Hill Park,** in the northwest quadrant; and, in the southeast, **Jim Davidson Bark and Play,** an off-leash area where an agility run and a doggie drinking fountain are available. Calgary's position in the foothills of the Alberta Rocky Mountains also affords pet-tastic hiking trails for hounds on leashes up to 6.6 feet long at **Natural Environment Parks (NEP),** including **Nose Hill** and **Fish Creek. Blink** and **Milestones Grill + Bar** are just two of the eateries on happening Stephen Avenue downtown where your buddy is allowed on the outside of the railing. **Ranchman's Cookhouse,** Calgary's iconic western bar, regularly hosts Yappy Hour. The **Fairmont Palliser Hotel, Westin Hotel,** and **Hotel Arts** are among the dog-friendly hotels.

Montreal, Quebec

T he French are famous for treating their *chiens* well, and in Montreal, where English and French mix beautifully, look for Pepé to receive similar affection. MTL, located in southwestern Quebec and the province's largest city, impresses with its lavish dog-friendly hotels, resorts exclusive to pets, gastronomy offerings, numerous summer and winter festivals, and a joie de vivre intrinsic to the French. This UNESCO City of Design is particularly striking in the fall, when the foliage atop pet-friendly Mount Royal, for which the city is named, beckons people and their pets for a saunter.

PLAY

There is no shortage of off-leash dog parks and runs in Montreal. The renovated **Percy Walters Park** downtown, on the northern slope of Mount Royal, offers your pooch plenty of playmates in a grassy area and opportunities to explore on the hill. Rover can also romp off leash at **Summit Parc,** a forested walking trail on the top of Westmount, except during the April 15–June 15 bird-nesting period, when a leash is required.

Leashes are required at other parks. The jewel is **Mount Royal,** originally designed by Frederick Law Olmsted and opened in 1876. This nature oasis in the heart of the city, is as much a part of Montreal as the Eiffel Tower is of Paris. It's where Montrealers go for a breath of fresh air in the summer and to cross-country ski in the winter.

Not to be missed is the beautiful 9-mile multipurpose trail along the **Lachine Canal,** where pups on leashes are permitted. Hounds aren't allowed in the canal, but people let them swim anyway at the risk of being fined. Leashed dogs can take a dip at the **Verdun Waterfront** and **Sandy Beach** in Hudson, where there are also trails at the **Sandy Beach Nature Park.**

SIT

When Fifi needs grooming, head to **Pet Spa** on Rue Sherbrooke in Westmount or **Pampered Pets de Westmount. Muzo,** a pet resort located alongside the Lachine Canal, offers stimulating doggie day care with exercise programs in such a fabulous setting that your pooch may beg to stay the night in the Presidential Suite. In addition to Club Muzo, as the day care is called, there's also a grooming salon, training, boutique, and MUZOLimo, a van to whisk your pampered pooch to and from. In addition to providing upscale boarding in suites with four-poster beds, **Hotel Balto** offers doggie day care and grooming, and has a boutique and gourmet kitchen to whip up palate-pleasing dishes for pooches.

HAUTE DOG

Diva dogs will dig **Döghaus,** in the heart of Westmount on Sherbrook, offering everything from gear and apparel to accessories and grooming. The popular boutique **Little Bear Animalerie,** also in the Westmount neighborhood, sells premium pet products, including trench coats and boots. **Bailey Blu Animalerie,** located in

Stay All Pups Welcome

■ *Hotel Le St-James (Old Montreal):* Bed and dishes. Dog walking and dogsitting (outsourced) can be arranged. Two dogs/40 lb each max., though flexible. Fee. hotellestjames.com/

■ *Hotel W (Old Montreal):* Bed, bowls with floor mat, pet-in-room door sign, toy, turndown treat, doggie room-service menu, birthday cake, dog walking, grooming. No number/size restrictions. Fee. wmontrealhotel.com

■ *Hôtel Le Germain (Downtown):* Bed, bowls, place mat. Pet items in the Germain signature collection. Two dogs/no size restriction. Fee. germain montreal.com

■ *Loews Hôtel Vogue Montreal (Downtown):* Loews Loves Pets program offers room-service menu, local pet services info, bed, bowls, placement leashes, collars, rawhide bones, pooper scoopers. Pet walking and petsitting available. Two dogs/no size restriction. Fee. loewshotels .com/montreal-hotel

Notre-Dame-de-Grâce (NDG) and a champion of raw-food diets, prides itself on being a 100 percent grain-free store.

🐾 CHOW TIME

During the summer, many restaurants accept well-mannered pets on their terraces. **La Brioche Lyonnaise** offers a delightful outdoor space, and **Jardin Asean** in NDG also allows dogs outside. **Byla Byla Restaurant** in Lasalle is perfect for breakfast or brunch, or grab a burger at **Five Guys** in the Village. After a stroll along the Lachine Canal, take paws with your leashed dog at the scenic St-Ambroise Terrace at the **McAuslan Brewery.** At **Brandy's Holistic Centre and Canine Café** you can enjoy a beverage and read while your little pal plays off leash.

> *In the summer, the main drag in the Village . . . is closed to vehicles, allowing for a lively stroll with your pooch.*

🐾 COME

You'll see signs prohibiting dogs throughout **Atwater Market,** but small dogs appear to get a pass as their humans shop for cheese, bread, produce, and more at this farmers' market located in the Saint-Henri area. In the summer, the main drag in the Village, Saint Catherine Street, is closed to vehicles, allowing for a lively stroll with your pooch past boutiques and restaurants. **Animatch,** a nonprofit canine adoption center, frequently hosts events and annual fund-raisers including **Bark n Brunch,** a Valentine's Day brunch with your best friend.

🐾 UNIQUE ACTIVITY

For a one-off experience, check into **Domaine Summum,** a unique, 230-acre resort with a private lake in Mont-Tremblant, where you and your pal can enjoy hiking, swimming, canoeing, paddleboats, and more. About 80 miles northwest of Montreal. domainesummum.com/

Emergency Veterinarian
Centre Veterinaire DMV—centredmv.com; 514-633-8888 ▪ Hôpital Vétérinaire Rive-Sud—hvrs.com; 450-656-3660 ▪ University of Montreal Animal Hospital—medvet .umontreal.ca; 450-773-8521

Insider Tip

"The island of Montreal has quite a few green spaces and more and more dog-friendly cafés, but one of the most popular and beautiful spots is the **Summit Park Nature Reserve** in Westmount. With 57 acres of meandering nature trails, beautiful foliage, and panoramic views, I never get bored exploring with my Chihuahuas, Chachi and Flea. Dogs are always welcome, but may only roam off leash from December to March, as the reserve does double duty as a protected bird sanctuary during nesting season."
— NAT LAUZON, *montrealdogblog.com*

Ottawa, Ontario

As the capital of Canada, Ottawa may appear formal with its Supreme Court, Parliament Hill, embassies, and high commissions, but your pup can have a tail-waggin' time. It is located on the south bank of the Ottawa River in the eastern portion of southern Ontario. You'll find loads of green space and recreational opportunities in the heart of the city and the surrounding area, a slew of festivals, and national museums. Rideau Canal, a UNESCO World Heritage site, in winter is the world's longest naturally frozen skating rink (4.8 miles), and draws visitors to the city that until 1855 was called Bytown.

PLAY

Ottawa is awash in off-leash dog parks. Your pooch will find plenty of social opportunities while romping at **Bruce Pit** in the city's west end, the region's largest and most pup-ular dog park. Acres of forested land and numerous trails and water features assure a good time. Also well-trafficked is the **Rockeries**, offering spectacular views and trails through Rockliffe Park, part of the Capital Pathway network for cycling, biking, and walking.

Take your tyke on a hike at **Gatineau Park,** where 94 miles of hiking trails are open to leashed dogs from spring to fall. Year-round walking is available on three trails: **Sugarbush Trail** (Chelsea), **Lauriault Trail** (Mackenzie King Estate), and **Pioneers Trail**

(Hull sector of Gatineau). Ottawa's Greenbelt, which includes Bruce Pit, permits pooches on and off leashes; from December 1 to April 14, however, Greenbelt trails are reserved for cross-country skiing and snowshoeing and not open to dogs. Most city parks designate whether dogs can be off leash, so be sure to check. Locals take their dogs swimming at **Lemieux Island,** a small island in the middle of the Ottawa River. As long as your pal is on leash, he or she can stroll through **Rideau Falls Park,** with its spectacular twin waterfalls where the Ottawa River meets the Rideau River. You can also visit **Hog's Back Park,** overlooking the stunning Hog's Back Falls on the Rideau River.

Insider Tip

"**Stanley Park,** in the neighborhood of New Edinburgh, is where Maddux, our Golden Retriever, meets friends. This beautiful park has a great off-leash area with ample space for dogs to play and a trail that winds along the Rideau River. Not only is Stanley Park a great park for your dogs, it also has one of the best views of Ottawa, and the sunsets are spectacular. Another spot worth mentioning is **Pine Hill,** alongside the residence of the governor general of Canada and within walking distance of Stanley Park."
— JAN GOTH

SIT

After Fido kicks up his paws with his new furry friends, freshen him up at a doggie spa or groomer. Options include **The Groomer** and **Dawn of a New Day** in Central Ottawa; **Masters 'n Dogs** in dog-fanatical Westboro Village; and **The Pampered Pet,** which has outposts in Ottawa South and Orleans. DIYers can go to **Pet Valu,** with a slew of locations. Doggie day care is available through **Dawg Gone It,** which comes to you, and **My Little White Dog** in Centretown.

HAUTE DOG

Shop for your active ally at **Bark & Fitz,** where dog gear and clothing ranging from protective slippers and boots to T-shirts and sweaters are stocked at the suburban locations in Barrhaven and Kanata; doggie ice-cream cones and baked goods are also sold. **Masters 'n Dogs** also sells products, high-quality foods, and baked goods, while the **Pampered Pet** has leashes, collars, and a full line of raw diets. **Natural Pet Foods** in Westboro and at Carleton Place also has healthy food and treats.

CHOW TIME

During the warm months, you'll find that many casual restaurants with patios permit pups, especially Westboro, the Glebe, and New Edinburgh, where hounds are in abundance.

City laws do require your pal to remain tied up on the outside of the patio. In the Glebe, take paws at the **Doggin' It Café,** where you can enjoy a beverage and your pooch can nibble on doggie treats while *inside* **Wag,** a "posh shop for spoiled pets." **Bridgehead,** a coffee shop and bakery with locations throughout Ottawa, brings water to Fido.

COME

Furry friends on leashes are welcome at **ByWard Market,** one of Ottawa's top tourist attractions, and at all three **Ottawa Farmers' Market** locations (Brewer Park, Byron Park/Westboro, and Centrum Plaza/Orléans), generally open early May through mid-November. **Paul's Boat Lines** welcomes friendly, leashed canines on its Historic Rideau Canal and Ottawa River tours. Masters 'n Dogs throws regular **doggie socials,** and the Ottawa Humane Society hosts an array of events, including the **IAMS Wiggle Waggle Walkathon** in September and the **FurBall** in March.

UNIQUE ACTIVITY

In the winter, you and man's best friend can learn how to skijor, where humans on cross-country skis are pulled by their pets of a certain weight. **Best Friends Dog Training** offers skijoring lessons for dogs weighing as little as 35 pounds. Guardians should know how to ski. bfdogtraining.ca

Emergency Veterinarian
Animal Emergency Ottawa (Vanier, slightly east of downtown)—animalemergencyottawa.com; 613-745-0123 ■ Ottawa Veterinary Hospital (near Westboro; slightly west of downtown)—ottawavet .com; 613-729-6139 ■ Alta Vista Animal Hospital (Ottawa South)—avah.on.ca; 613-731-6851

Stay All Pups Welcome

■ *Westin Ottawa (Downtown):* Welcome kit includes list of services available through the concierge. Also available, waste bags, gloves, an ID tag, bowls, mat, and Westin Heavenly dog bed. Two dogs/80 lb each max. westin.com/ottawa

■ *Brookstreet (West End):* Toys. Dog walking can be arranged. Two dogs/no size restriction. Fee. brookstreet.com

■ *Lord Elgin (Downtown):* Two dogs/ no size restriction. lordelginhotel.ca

■ *Fairmont Chateau Laurier (Downtown):* One dog/20 lb max. Fee. fairmont.com/ottawa

■ *Quality Hotel (Downtown):* Doggie treat bag upon check-in and pickup bags. Staffers take pets for walks. Three dogs/any size. qualityhotelottawa.com

■ *Hotel Indigo (Downtown):* Two dogs/contact hotel for pets weighing more than 50 lb Fee. ottawadowntownhotel.com

Quebec City, Quebec

As the only fortified city in North America north of Mexico, Quebec City oozes history. But along the **Plains of Abraham,** where the British defeated the French in 1759, the doggie waste bag dispensers are a sign that the capital of the province of Quebec keeps up with the times. Fifi can saunter on leash down the paths and trails of the Plains, located within the Battlefields Park, and also stroll through **Parc Bois-de-Coulonge,** one of the most spectacular parks in the city, with an enviable location overlooking the St. Lawrence River. Of course pooches can frolic freely in their own dog parks, including **Belvedere, Ste.-Foy Park,** and **Parc Canin de la Pointe-aux-Lièvres** on the St. Charles River. Easy and beautiful year-round is a hike along **Parc Linéaire de la Rivière Saint-Charles,** a 19-mile trail that runs along the St. Charles River. Pets can join their people on the patios of eateries **Le Lapin Sauté, Bistrot Pape Georges,** and **Buffet de l'Antiquaire.** Although Quebec City can boast North America's only ice hotel, **Hôtel de Glace,** you and your pal, unless your pal is a Husky, may be more comfortable at Fairmont's grand **Le Château Frontenac,** where Santol, the canine ambassador, is famous, or **Hôtel Loews Le Concorde,** which offers a gourmet room-service menu for pooches.

Toronto, Ontario

As ethnically diverse as Toronto is, with approximately half of its population foreign born, many people speak dog. Dog parks open just about 24/7, pooch-friendly beaches, off-leash hiking trails, doggie bakeries and spas, and a shopping center so pet friendly it offers complimentary dogsitting are among the perks for pets in Canada's most populous city, capital of Ontario province.

🐾 PLAY

Most of the popular 50 designated off-leash dog parks, such as **High Park** (the fave), **Trinity Bellwoods Park,** and **Sunnybrook Park,** are open much of the day. It's not unusual to see well-behaved and unrestrained pups in the non-off-leash area inside High Park, with its 400 acres of beautiful gardens, hiking trails, and a 35-acre pond.

Your buddy will find plenty of playmates at **Cherry Beach** (a.k.a. Clarke Beach), a 10.9-acre off-leash spread on Lake Ontario, open Monday through Friday with no restrictions, and Saturday and Sunday from 8 p.m. to 10 a.m. from July 1 to September 15. Fido can enjoy a game of fetch at **Kew Balmy Beach** as well. Explore the wilderness at the **Eldred King Woodlands,** where Daisy can take a dip in the pond before you two settle down for a picnic lunch. Although **Humber Bay Park East** isn't off leash, in the winter freely frolicking dogs are tolerated at this location close to downtown. Out a ways in Oshawa, hiking hounds will enjoy the 25-acre, off-leash dog park inside **Harmony Valley Conservation Area.** Worth the short jaunt, **Presqu'île** (French for "almost an island") **Provincial Park** is about 1.5 hour from Toronto, on the north shore of Lake Ontario, five minutes south of the town of Brighton. There are five walking trails, ranging from less than a mile to nearly 3, and insect repellent is a must.

🐕 SIT

Doggie day care comes in handy when bipeds with busy schedules want to explore the CN Tower, the tallest structure in North America; St. Lawrence Market, one of the world's best food markets; or other Toronto attractions that don't permit pups. Your pooch can get a workout at **Unleashed in the City,** which offers active day care at its Ossington facility, as well as **Unleashed B&B** for overnight boarding and canine massages. **UrbanDog Fitness + Spa** downtown also offers an activity center, grooming, bakery, and retail. **My Dog's Daycare,** in Roncesvalles Village near High Park, provides day care, grooming, and retail. Grooming is also available at **Pawfect Spa**'s uptown and downtown salons.

> *Dog-friendly dining means having your pal tied up on the other side of the railing where food is served.*

🦴 HAUTE DOG

Stylish apparel, products, and accessories are well stocked at **Bark & Fitz,** with outposts in North and South Oakville. Also, snap up a new outfit for your pooch at **Cosmopawlitan Pet Boutique & Spa** or either of **Timmie Doggie Outfitters'** two locations, in Queen West or Leslieville. Both businesses also do grooming. At **The Bone House,** you'll find a thorough selection of organic, human-grade food, supplements, treats, and products such as stylish handcrafted collars and leashes.

🦴 CHOW TIME

As is common practice throughout Canada, dog-friendly dining means having your pal tied up on the other side of the railing

Stay
All Pups Welcome

■ *The Ritz-Carlton, Toronto (Downtown):* Bed, food and water bowls, and treats. Dog walking upon request. Two dogs/40 lb max. ritzcarlton.com/en/ Properties/Toronto/Default.html

■ *Hazelton Hotel (Yorkville):* Bowls, treats, bed. Two dogs/no size restriction. thehazeltonhotel.com

■ *Westin Harbour Castle (Downtown):* Westin Heavenly dog bed upon request. Doggie Welcome Kit at check-in. One dog/40 lb max. westinharbour castletoronto.com

where food is served. Your options include **Café Novo,** where dog treats are also sold, **Lion on the Beach,** the **Black Bull Tavern, Le Sélect Bistro, Mildred's Temple Kitchen, Victory Café,** the **Charlotte Room,** and **Rooster Coffee House,** which doles out dog treats. At **PawsWay,** a Pet Discovery Centre located on Toronto's harborfront, **Williams Fresh Café** has a dog-friendly eating area inside the restaurant.

COME

When you visit **Shops at Hazelton Lanes** in Yorkville, in downtown Toronto, you can leave your favorite canine companion for up to 45 minutes with its complimentary dogsitting service. You'll find doggie waste bag stations at the **Shops at Don Mills,** where most of the

> ## Insider Tip
>
> "My city-dwelling Wheaten Terrier, Otis, has it all. He loves exploring the outdoors and enjoys sniffing around at pet-centric events. Toronto is home to Woofstock, the largest outdoor dog festival in North America, which draws more than 300,000 people and their canine companions annually. **PawsWay** is a unique pet-centric community center, with learning programs and events. Besides several off-leash parks within the city, you can get the full nature experience at a stunning walking ravine like the off-leash **Etobicoke Valley Park** and at **Rouge Park** and **Todmorden Mills Heritage site.** And there are also several Lake Ontario beaches. It's a dog's life for sure, eh?"
> — BIANCA KAPTEYN, *canineculture.ca*

boutiques have an open-paw policy. Look for a dog bowl outside the door. Your pal is also welcome inside **Holt Renfrew**'s flagship department store downtown. From June through September, Dog Paddling Adventures offers several **Summer Paws and Paddles** trips that make for terrific bonding experiences with your best friend. Bark your calendar for **Woofstock,** a two-day festival that takes place every June in the St. Lawrence Market neighborhood.

UNIQUE ACTIVITY

Take a side trip with your sidekick to **Toronto Islands,** a series of islands just off the coast of downtown Toronto and reachable via a dog-friendly ferry. Leashes are required as you check out the trails, ponds, gardens, and beaches. Fifi can even go to the amusement park, although she can't enjoy a ride, and can also join you at the outdoor seating areas of restaurants. torontoislands.org/

Emergency Veterinarian
Toronto Veterinary Emergency Hospital—tveh.ca; 416-247-VETS (8387)

Vancouver, British Columbia

With so much natural beauty in this bustling British Columbia metropolis, it is almost unfair that Vancouver gets called everything from Hollywood North, because of all the films and television shows made here, to Vansterdam, for its cannabis culture. Loads of dog-friendly green spaces, ranging from small neighborhood parks to destination parks, access to the Pacific Ocean and Frazer River, beaches, mountains, trails, and forests help create an ideal canine culture year-round.

🐾 PLAY

The toughest decision to make during your petcation in Vancouver is where to go with your active ally. Of the 36 designated off-leash areas sprinkled in the city, **Stanley Park,** Vancouver's ginormous, nearly 1,000-acre park, is a must. The fenced-in dog park is open from 7 a.m. to 9 p.m. and located in the shuffleboard court area. A waterfall pond makes **Charleson Park** an attractive choice. Your pooch can be off leash in the grass bowl from 6 a.m. to 10 a.m. year-round, but in the pond area use a leash June to September from 10 a.m. to 5 p.m. No leash is needed from October through May all day, and from June through September before 10 a.m. and after 5 p.m.

Vancouverites never let a little water dampen their spirits, so take your tyke for a hike where trees provide cover. A favorite is **Lynn Canyon Park,** where 617 forested acres, waterfalls, swimming holes, and the popular **Baden-Powell Trail** delight. On the west side, **Pacific Spirit Regional Park** offers leash-required and leash-optional trails. Rules for dogs vary at beaches. Some ban bowwows altogether, though most allow four-legged beach-goers in the winter. But you can't go wrong at **Spanish Bank Beach Park** in West Point Grey or **Sunset Beach,** both offering off-leash access year-round from 6 a.m. to 10 p.m. Salty dogs lap up **Vanier Park,** at the edge of English Bay in Kitsilano, flaunting fab views of downtown Vancouver and Stanley Park. Fido can frolic off leash here from 6 a.m. to 10 a.m. and 5 p.m. to 10 p.m. from May 1 to September 30, and from 6 a.m. to 10 p.m. the rest of the year.

🐕 SIT

After fun in the sun or romping in the rain, your posh pooch can clean up well at **Pawsh Dog Spa & Boutique** in Yaletown. In addition to being groomed at **Barking Babies,** the leggiest member in your party can have a therapeutic massage or Reiki healing session. A nursery-themed day care is also available for dogs up to ten pounds. At **Rex Dog Hotel + Spa,** private suites for overnight boarding and a custom water park are on offer; "day care for the urban dog" can also be found at **The Doghouse,** with locations on West Eighth Avenue and Granville Island (small dogs only). **Woof Wash** brings its mobile dog-grooming business to you.

🏠 *Stay* All Pups Welcome

■ *The Loden:* Provides doggie bed, dishes, and signature dog biscuits plus a complimentary copy of *Modern Dog* magazine. Two small dogs or one large dog. Fee. theloden.com

■ *Fairmont Pacific Rim:* Welcome package includes bedding, treats, and walking map. Petsitting available through concierge. One dog/no size restriction. Fee. fairmont .com/pacific-rim-vancouver

■ *Fairmont Waterfront:* Dog bed, water bowls, and treats provided. Two dogs/50 lb each max. Fee. fairmont.com/ waterfront-vancouver/

■ *Fairmont Hotel Vancouver:* Treats, bed, welcome mat, toys, info sheet on pet activities, and water bowl provided. Golden Retrievers Mavis and Beau are the hotel's canine ambassadors. No number/size

restrictions. Fee. fairmont .com/hotel-vancouver

■ *The Sutton Place Hotel:* VIP pet program includes in-room dining. Petsitting available through concierge. Two dogs/45 lb each max. Fee. vancouver.suttonplace.com

■ *Rosewood Hotel Georgia:* Offers dog bed, water bowl, and treats. Two dogs/25 lb each max. Fee. rosewoodhotels.com

🐾 HAUTE DOG

Hip hounds will yelp over the selection at **Barking Babies,** a lifestyle boutique in downtown Vancouver, where designer duds, cool canine collars, and gourmet dog treats are sold. **Bark & Fitz** in Coal Harbour sells stylish apparel and more for dapper dogs, plus has a bakery for pups. For doggie raincoats and handmade organic treats, head to **Woofles and Meowz,** a boutique and bakery on Granville Island.

Insider Tip

"The hike from **Pacific Spirit Park** to Spanish Banks Beach is convenient if you don't have all day and gives you a little slice of all that is great about Vancouver. Hiking through the dense forest surrounded by huge trees feels like something from *Lord of the Rings.* After about a mile it dumps you out in front of a huge meadow that runs along Spanish Banks Beach."
— SYLVIA SCOTT

🦴 CHOW TIME

As is the case in other parts of Canada, pets aren't allowed to sit with their people on restaurant patios. However, you may see dogs tied on the outside of a patio railing. With that in mind, some of the dog-tolerant eateries include **Francesco's Ristorante Italia** in downtown Vancouver, **Le Gavroche** in the West End, **Little Nest, Trixi's Crepe and Coffeehaus, Viva Fine Foods & Bakery, Juliet's Café, Bon Crepe, Blue Parrot Organic Coffee House, BG Urban Cafe, Aphrodite's,** and **Bread Garden Bakery & Cafe.**

🐾 COME

Stroll the 5.5-mile paved route of the **Seawall,** the famous Stanley Park feature, with your little pal on leash. Have a picnic with your pooch on **Granville Island,** an ideal walking place. Although canines aren't allowed inside the Granville Island Public Market, you can pick up food and take it to one of the parks or the market's courtyard. Afterward, enjoy a beverage on the patio at **AGRO Café,** in Railspur Alley.

🐾 UNIQUE ACTIVITY

With a name like **Dog Mountain,** this trail is a must with a pup. This easy path starts at the top of Mount Seymour in North Vancouver; pack a picnic lunch in the summer, or go snowshoeing in the winter. Dogs are required to be on leashes. vancouvertrails.com/trails/dog-mountain/

Emergency Veterinarian
Vancouver Animal Emergency Clinic—animaler.com; 604-734-5104

Vancouver Island, British Columbia

Whether you choose only to visit Victoria or branch out to some of the other equally fascinating places on Vancouver Island (please don't call it Victoria Island), your paw-footed pal can have quite an adventure sniffing around the largest Pacific island east of New Zealand, on Canada's far west coast. Stretching 285 miles from the Juan de Fuca Strait in the south near Victoria, British Columbia's capital, all the way to Queen Charlotte Sound off Cape Scott at its northern tip, this haven for outdoor enthusiasts draws many of its visitors to Victoria, Nanaimo, and Tofino. Your pup will have plenty of canine company, as dogs accompany their humans almost everywhere on the island.

PLAY

Victoria flaunts its Paws in Parks program, which provides 12 off-leash parks, including the puppy paradise known as **Dallas Road Pathway,** close to downtown and boasting a paved footpath and beach set against a spectacular view of ocean and mountains. Fido can frolic here year-round. However, your pooch needs to be under good voice control because of the road nearby and no fence. Other faves are the picturesque **Clover Point Park,** located off Dallas Road, and **Songhees Hilltop,** where you can watch the floatplanes take off and land from scenic Inner Harbour.

Popular hiking trails in Victoria include the **Galloping Goose Trail,** which connects to the Trans-Canada Trail and allows hounds off leash if under control, and the **Thetis Lake Trail,** where your little pal needs to be leashed from June 1 to September 15 when passing through the beach and picnic areas. Sorry, but pups can't stay.

Nanaimo boasts several off-leash areas, including the oft-used **Beban Dog Park,** which has a separate area for small dogs and a perimeter trail, and is connected to a wooded on-leash trail. Popular off-leash hiking trails are **Cable Bay Trail,** which winds through a forest to a rocky beach where wildlife can occasionally be spotted, **Colliery Dam,** and **Westwood Lake.** Tofino's proximity to the **Pacific Rim National Park Reserve,** boasting sundry trails and some of the country's best beaches, makes this area popular with nature-loving pet parents. It's one of Canada's few protected areas that still allows canines beach access, but leashes are required. Pups love to explore the Pacific Rim's **Tofino Lighthouse Trail** and **Nuu-chah-nulth Trail.**

SIT

When it's time to clean up Rover, in Victoria head to **Bark, Bath & Beyond Pet Boutique** on Oak Bay Avenue or **Top Dog Daycare and Spa,** in Esquimalt, on the edge of downtown, which also offers day care. The **Mucky Mutt Pet Salon,** on Burnside inside Bosleys, offers full-service grooming and a U-Bath facility for the DIYers. **Whiskers Urban Ranch, Diamond Dogs,** and **Nirvana Pet Resort** all offer day care and grooming.

Stay All Pups Welcome

■ *Fairmont Empress (Victoria):* Bed, basket or kennel, bowls, food, bottled water, treats, and waste-disposal bags upon request. Two dogs/ 25 lb each max. Fee. fairmont.com/empress

■ *Hotel Grand Pacific (Victoria):* Pampered Pooch package provides bed, bowls, treats, pickup bags, doggie do-not-disturb sign, doggie

room-service menu. One dog/40 lb max. Fee. hotel grandpacific.com

■ *The Oswego Hotel (Victoria):* Custom-made dog beds, designer bowls, and organic treats. Two dogs/ size at hotel's discretion. Fee. oswegovictoria.com

■ *Long Beach Lodge (Tofino):* Bed, dishes, towels, treats. Fee. long beachlodgeresort.com

■ *Wickaninnish Inn (Tofino):* Bedding, blanket, bowls, treats, *Modern Dog* magazine, toy. Petsitting and pet shower station. Two dogs/no size restriction. Fee. wickinn.com

■ *Inn on Long Lake (Nanaimo):* Treats and bowls. Large front and back garden. Dogs allowed to go down to lake. Two dogs/no size restriction. Fee. innonlonglake.com

U Dog offers mobile doggie day care and will pick up your pooch for a mountain hike. In Nanaimo, grooming and doggie day care are available at **Dog n' Suds Pet Services** and **Happy Hound Dog Care Company.**

HAUTE DOG

Shop for your environmentally conscious and healthy diva dog at **Paws on Cook,** in Victoria's Cook Street Village, near the Dallas Road off-leash area, and **Bark, Bath & Beyond Pet Boutique.** Both stores pride themselves on selling quality pet food, stylish apparel, and eco-friendly pet accessories, gear, and toys. **Paws on Cook** also stocks travel carriers from Sleepypod and Sturdi Products. Pick up wheat-free, all-natural homemade goodies at **Dogs in the Bakery,** in Victoria's Chinatown. In Nanaimo, **Woofles Barking Boutique** carries everything from snazzy apparel and rain gear to carriers and fresh-baked doggie goods, while **Bark & Fitz** also tends to glamour dogs and has a bakery.

The Galloping Goose Trail . . . connects to the Trans-Canada Trail and allows hounds off leash.

CHOW TIME

As is the case throughout much of Canada, health regulations in Victoria don't allow dog-friendly dining, so you may have to tie your pooch on the other side of the railing. Sometimes the rule is ignored. You'll find that some of the places with outdoor seating in Cook Street Village, a trendy area with coffee shops and gift shops, permit pups on their patios. **Adrienne's Restaurant and Tea Garden, Buon Amici's Coffee, Red Fish Blue Fish** on Victoria's Inner Harbour, and **Sol Fine Foods,** open for breakfast and lunch, are among the Victoria eateries that don't mind if you bring your little pal. In Nanaimo, **Delicado's** has a pet-friendly deck, dog biscuits, and water

for dogs. **Javawocky Coffee House, Baby Salsa,** and **Ohana's Café** also bring water. **Bocca Café,** next to Woofles Barking Boutique, is popular with pets and their people.

COME

Throughout Vancouver Island, you'll find a wide array of activities and attractions to enjoy with your pup. Most of the outdoor farmers' markets in Victoria allow your ally on leash. Pets are allowed on the **"pickle boats"** from Nanaimo to Newcastle Island for a stroll around the provincial marine park. Also in Nanaimo, go wine tasting and relax on the patio at **Millstone Estate Winery,** where Daisy, a yellow Lab, welcomes playmates. Also, **Silva Bay Kayak Adventures,** about 3 miles east of Nanaimo on Gabriola Island, lets pets join their humans on kayaking and stand-up paddleboard tours. Tail-wagging events include **Bark & Fitz Nanaimo's Wednesday social gatherings** and **Pet-A-Palooza,** a two-day festival that takes place every August in Victoria.

Insider Tip

"My eight-year-old Border Collie/Lab, Donia, and two-year-old Retriever mix, Henry, love to romp off leash in the **Mount Tzouhalem** trail system in the Cowichan Valley, between Victoria and Tofino. But remember you are sharing the areas with other outdoor recreationalists, so be courteous. And be prepared—keep a water bottle handy for your dog, as sometimes water may not be immediately available. If your dog loves balls, bring a spare to the **Dallas Road** off-leash area in Victoria, in case yours gets taken by one of the many other dogs that loves balls too."
— LANA KINGSTON

UNIQUE ACTIVITY

The **Butchart Gardens,** a designated National Historic Site of Canada, near Victoria and open year-round, welcomes four-legged visitors on short leashes. It loans leashes and provides pickup bags and five pet water fountains throughout its grounds. However, it discourages pets from attending the firework shows on Saturday evenings in summer. butchartgardens.com

Emergency Veterinarian
Central Island Veterinary Emergency Hospital—civeh.com; 250-933-0913 or 877-773-7079

Whistler, British Columbia

Whistler is known as a winter wonderland, but this Canadian resort town in the Coast Mountain Range of British Columbia packs plenty of punch year-round, not just when skiers flock here to attack the slopes. Your dog can have a dandy time swimming, hiking, cross-country skiing (not on his own skis, of course), and being pampered by one of the 20-plus dog-friendly hotels.

PLAY

Fido can frolic off leash at a variety of areas, but you'll need to keep a leash visible. A haven for hounds is **Canine Cove,** to the right of the public beach at Lost Lake Park. Your little pal can romp on the sandy beach, go for a swim, and take advantage of the floating dock that provides pooches ramp access 24/7, during the season. Furry friends will find their pot of gold at the south end of Rainbow Park, where **Barking Bay,** a gated off-leash beach area, is also available 24/7. Play a game of fetch with your favorite companion at **Arf'a Lake Dog Area,** on the east side of Alpha Lake Park. **Rainbow, Alpha,** and **Meadow Parks** also allow dogs off leash throughout before 10 a.m. and after 8 p.m. Leashed dogs are allowed in other parks, except Garibaldi Provincial Park. When the baseball diamond outfields empty at Meadow Park and **Spruce Grove,** Rover can run unrestrained.

More than 20 miles of trails on Lost Lake make it a popular hiking spot, although it's not available to bowwows in the winter. **A River Runs Through It,** on the other side of the valley, is an exceptional trail, and the **Emerald Forest** is available year round. When the black bears hibernate, you and your tail wagger can go cross-country skiing and snowshoeing on the groomed **Valley Trail,** from Meadow Park to Rainbow Park, and on the multi-use trail at **Green Lake.**

SIT

After Fido is finished kicking up his paws, take him for a hydro-massage bath at **Bubbles Dog Spa,** in Function Junction, where he can take paws in the sun in the fetching, fenced-in backyard. Or let **Shampooch Mobile Dog Grooming** come to you. When your agenda differs from your dog's, call on **Spoil Your Pet Services,** a member of Pet Sitters International; **Alpine Dogs,** which offers adventurous hikes and pet-sitting; **Whistler Dog Sitting;** or **Whistler Trail Dogs,** which offer pickup and drop-off.

Many Whistler businesses don't just have an open-paw policy, they also dole out complimentary dog treats.

HAUTE DOG

If you forgot any pet products, chances are you'll find them at **Whistler Happy Pets,** Whistler's lone pet store, located in the southern end of Function Junction. It also

Stay All Pups Welcome

■ *Four Seasons Whistler:* As part of the Very Important Pet Program, dogs receive welcome mat, dog bowl, house-made biscuits, bottled Whistler water, and a doggie bed. No number/size restrictions. Fee. fourseasons.com/whistler

■ *Fairmont Chateau Whistler:* Offering room service menu, kibble, treats, welcome letter, dish, personal chew toy. No number/size restrictions. Fee. fairmont.com/whistler

■ *The Westin Resort and Spa, Whistler:* Westin Heavenly dog bed, food bowl, and mat. No number/size restrictions. westinwhistler.com

■ *Pan Pacific Whistler Village Centre:* Unique registration card and welcome treats. No number/size restrictions. Fee. panpacific.com/en/WhistlerVillageCentre/Overview.html

■ *Summit Lodge & Spa:* Rooms stocked with food bowl and treats, pet's name on welcome board. Possible to arrange pet-sitting and dog walking. No size/number restrictions. summitlodge.com sells foods high in protein with no fillers added and locally produced organic treats.

CHOW TIME

Whistler restaurants don't allow pups on their patios, so expect to leash your loved one close by. The eateries on the Village Stroll with al fresco dining are your best options. Popular restaurants are **Citta', Amsterdam Pub, Tapley's Neighbourhood Pub,** and **Garibaldi Lift Co. Bar and Grill,** known by locals as "the GLC." **Fix Café,** at the exclusive, pet-friendly Nita Lake Lodge, makes and sells homemade dog treats.

> ### Insider Tip
>
> "Whistler is a fantastic year-round paradise for dogs. We enjoy exploring all the dog-friendly trails, parks, and beaches in summer. Come winter, when there are 2 feet of snow on the ground, my favorite way to exercise Kody (my five-year-old blue Heeler) is to take him cross-country skiing. Three miles of the Valley Trail are groomed, so I can skate along with him by my side. He gets excited on powder days just like the humans!"
> — DEBBIE COOK

COME

Many Whistler businesses don't just have an open-paw policy, they also dole out complimentary dog treats. Leashed dogs are welcome at the outdoor farmers' market as well. Every April, the big event is **Whistler Dogfest,** which takes place during the World Ski and Snowboard Festival and benefits Whistler Animals Galore (WAG), a no-kill shelter. The shelter's big annual fund-raiser, in September, is the **K9 Wine & Dine,** which includes a three-course dinner for dogs and a large buffet spread for their humans.

UNIQUE ACTIVITY

Fido can feel like a gold medalist with a trip to **Whistler Olympic Park,** host site of the Nordic events for the 2010 Olympic & Paralympic Winter Games. In the winter, dogs are allowed in parking lots on leash and off leash on designated pet-friendly trails. In the summer, leashed pooches can be in the park and on trails. Purchase a pet pass at the front gate upon entrance. www.whistler olympicpark.com

Emergency Veterinarian
The Animal Health Clinic of Whistler— whistlervetservices.ca; 604-905-5088 ▪ Coast Mountain Veterinary Services—coastvet .com; 604-932-5391 ▪ After hours: Vancouver Animal Emergency Clinic —animaler .com; 604-734-5104

Resources

Top Hotel Chains for Dogs in North America and Canada

Fairmont Hotels: All accept pets, but policy and amenities vary by property. Fee varies. fairmont
.com; 800-257-7544

Four Seasons Hotels: Small to medium pets are generally accepted and receive amenities. Policy
varies by location. fourseasons.com; 800-819-5053

Mandarin Oriental: Small to medium-size pets generally welcome for a fee; amenities and policies
vary. mandarinoriental.com; 800-526-6566

Peninsula Hotels: Small pets receive luxe amenities and services. Fee varies. peninsula
.com; 866-382-8388

Ritz-Carlton: Many, but not all, properties accept pets. Expect amenities at those that do. Policies
vary by location. ritzcarlton.com; 800-542-8680

Trump Hotel Collection: Trump Pets program available at most U.S. properties, providing amenities and services. Fee varies. trumphotelcollection.com; 855-TRUMP-00 (855-878-6700)

Delta Hotels and Resorts: Delta hotels and resorts welcome dogs under 50 pounds for a fee, with a
maximum of two pets per room. deltahotels.com; 888-890-3222

DoubleTree by Hilton: More than 120 properties welcome dogs for a fee. doubletree3
.hilton.com/en/index.html; 800-445-8667

Hotel Indigo: Policies vary by property. ihg.com/hotelindigo/hotels/us/en/reservation;
877-660-8550

Hyatt Hotels: Most full-service and select-service hotels in the Hyatt brand (Park Hyatt, Andaz,
Hyatt Regency, Hyatt, and Grand Hyatt) accept pets and provide amenities. Policies vary by
location. hyatthotels.com; 800-233-1234

Kimpton Hotels: All pets welcome, regardless of size, weight, or breed, with no fees or deposits, at
every Kimpton Hotel. www.kimptonhotels.com; 800-KIMPTON (800-546-7866)

Loews Hotels: Loews offers the Loews Loves Pets program, with specialized services and amenities
at each property. Fee. loewshotels.com; 800-235-6397

Sheraton Hotels and Resorts: Many Sheraton hotels and resorts welcome dogs—many of which
are provided a Sheraton Sweet Sleeper dog bed upon request, along with a welcome kit. sheraton
.com; 800-325-3535

W Hotels: P.A.W. (Pets Are Welcome) provides lots of amenities, including a custom W bed, and
services. Standard policy is one pet, 40 pounds maximum, but each property is free to go above
and beyond to assist guests as needed. Fee. whotels.com; 877-946-8357

Westin Hotels & Resorts: Dogs welcome at all properties and receive a Westin Heavenly dog bed among the amenities. Policies vary. westinhotels.com; 800-325-3535

🦴🦴🦴-🦴🦴

Aloft: ARF (Animals Are Family) program welcomes pets up to 40 pounds at each property. Fee varies by location. alofthotels.com; 877-GO-ALOFT (800-462-5638)

Best Western: Pet-friendly properties allow up to two domestic dogs in room, with a maximum size of 80 pounds per animal. bestwestern.com; 800-780-7234

Candlewood Suites: Pets weighing less than 80 pounds are welcome at all properties for a fee. ihg.com; 877-660-8550

Element by Westin: Love That Dog program welcomes dogs up to 40 pounds, though may vary by hotel. Fee varies by location. elementhotels.com; 877-ELEMENT (877-353-6368)

Extended Stay America: A maximum of two pets are allowed in each guest room. Fee. extended stayamerica.com; 800-804-3724

Four Points by Sheraton: All locations are pet friendly, but policies vary. fourpoints bysheraton.com; 800-368-7764

La Quinta Inns & Suites: Pets are welcome at most locations nationwide. lq.com; 800-SLEEPLQ (800-753-3757)

Red Roof Inn: One well-behaved family pet is permitted unless prohibited by state law or ordinance. redroof.com; 800-RED-ROOF (800-733-7663)

Pet-Friendly Airlines

Air Canada: In cabin, baggage, and cargo: aircanada.com; 888-247-2262

AirTran: In cabin; airtran.com: 800-AIR-TRAN (800-247-8726)

Alaska Airlines: In cabin, baggage, and cargo: alaskaair.com; 800-ALASKAAIR (800-252-7522)

American Airlines: In cabin, baggage, and cargo: aa.com; 800-433-7300

Delta Air Lines: In cabin, baggage, and cargo: delta.com; 800-221-1212

Frontier Airlines: In cabin: flyfrontier.com; 800-432-1359

Hawaiian Airlines: In cabin, baggage, and cargo: hawaiianairlines.com; 800-367-5320

JetBlue Airways: In cabin: jetblue.com; 800-JETBLUE (800-538-2583)

Southwest Airlines: In cabin: southwest.com; 800-I-FLY-SWA (800-435-9792)

Spirit: In cabin: spirit.com; 801-401-2222

Sun Country Airlines: In cabin and baggage on select routes: suncountry.com; 800-359-6786

United: In cabin and cargo through PetSafe program: united.com; 800-UNITED-1 (800-864-8331)

US Airways: In cabin: usairways.com; 800-428-4322

Virgin America: In cabin: virginamerica.com; 877-FLY-VIRGIN (877-359-8474)

WestJet: In cabin, baggage, and cargo: westjet.com; 888-WESTJET (888-937-8538)

About the Author

Kelly E. Carter and her lovable longhair Chihuahua, Lucy, have been practically inseparable since first meeting at an airport in 2001. The two have traveled together throughout the United States, Canada, Mexico, the Caribbean, and Europe, stopping in Italy for two years. Inspired by her pooch and her desire to help others travel with their furry friends, Kelly founded The Jet Set Pets, where she gives the inside scoop for pets on the go. A popular speaker at travel conferences, Kelly is also the pet travel expert on AOL's pet site PawNation and a contributing editor at *Elite Traveler*. Formerly a celebrity reporter at *People* and *USA Today*, where she previously covered sports, the Los Angeles native has written for numerous publications. She teamed up with tennis phenom Venus Williams to co-author the *New York Times* best-selling book *Come to Win: Business Leaders, Artists, Doctors, and Other Visionaries on How Sports Can Help You Top Your Profession*. Kelly and Lucy reside in San Francisco.

thejetsetpets.com

Acknowledgments

uthors are sometimes criticized for thanking their pets in this space. In my case, I'm not barking up the wrong tree by saying that my faithful four-legged traveling companion, Lucy, is my ultimutt source of inspiration. But there are many others who warrant thanks for helping me with this book, which was a joy to research and write, and which I hope will serve as both an inspiration for fellow pet parents to take their little pals on the road and a resource for those who already do. I'll always be grateful to *National Geographic Traveler* associate editor Susan O'Keefe for introducing me to the National Geographic Society. Thanks also go to National Geographic Books' senior editor Barbara Noe and project manager Caroline Hickey for their patience; to designer Elisa Gibson, whose talents are apparent throughout these pages; to photo editor Nancy Marion for selecting images that will motivate people to do more than take Buster for a walk around the block; and to Keith Bellows, editor in chief of National Geographic Travel Media, for coming up with the pawsome idea for National Geographic to publish its first dog-friendly travel guidebook. Fellow travel writer and friend Kimberley Dumm Lovato, agent Katherine Cowles, Maren Rudolph of Travel Classics, and researcher Damelvy Rodriguez merit recognition for their contributions. Special thanks to my beau, William Smith, whose love and support is immeasurable, and to Ginger Campos and Charles Federico, who, after a chance meeting in dog-fanatical Carmel-by-the-Sea, California, generously allowed me to be their "writer-in-residence." The encouragement from my family and friends, including my brother Kevin Carter, Shindana Neal, Renata Elmore, Teri Washington, Maureen Jenkins, Stacie Henderson, and Regina DiMartino, kept me going through the writing process. But more than anything, I'm especially appreciative to all of those who help elevate the status of our furry friends to family members.

Index

Illustrations Credits

Published by the National Geographic Society
1145 17th Street N.W., Washington, D.C. 20036

Library of Congress Cataloging-in-Publication Data
Carter, Kelly E.
  The dog lover's guide to travel : best destinations, hotels, events, and advice to please your pet-and you / Kelly E. Carter.
     p. cm.
  Includes index.
   ISBN 978-1-4262-1276-5 (pbk.)
  1. Travel with dogs--North America--Guidebooks. 2. North America--Guidebooks. I. Title.
SF427.4574.N75C37 2014
636.7'0887--dc23

                    2013036635

The National Geographic Society is one of the world's largest nonprofit scientific and educational organizations. Its mission is to inspire people to care about the planet. Founded in 1888, the Society is member supported and offers a community for members to get closer to explorers, connect with other members, and help make a difference. The Society reaches more than 450 million people worldwide each month through *National Geographic* and other magazines; National Geographic Channel; television documentaries; music; radio; films; books; DVDs; maps; exhibitions; live events; school publishing programs; interactive media; and merchandise. National Geographic has funded more than 10,000 scientific research, conservation, and exploration projects and supports an education program promoting geographic literacy. For more information, visit www.nationalgeographic.com.

National Geographic Society
1145 17th Street N.W.
Washington, D.C. 20036-4688 U.S.A.

For information about special discounts for bulk purchases, please contact National Geographic Books Special Sales: ngspecsales@ngs.org

For rights or permissions inquiries, please contact National Geographic Books Subsidiary Rights: ngbookrights@ngs.org

Interior design: Elisa Gibson

Printed in China

13/RRDS/1

FETCH. SIT. READ.

More books for dog lovers to devour (and dog-ear).

▲ From the v̶... becca Ascher-
celebrated ...sents 38 heart-
and New ...tories with
best-selli ...mazingly
practical, ...ogs who
guide wil ...eterans, learn
a happier ...tect cancer,
relations ...he day.
canine c

Sure to d ...n Facebook.com:
and wag ...Books
this play ...onTwitter.com:
photo-dr ...Books
your fam
language

...TIONAL
...OGRAPHIC